Stand and Deliver

A Manual for Deliverance

*To Becca — my prize student
and anointed counselor!*

Mark 16:17-18

*Love & blessings,
Beth*

TIM AND BETH SCOTT

xulon PRESS

Table of Contents

Dedication

W e dedicate this labor of love to those who are yet to be set free from the captivity in which Satan and his demons have enslaved them. It is our heartfelt desire—and purpose in writing this book—to see their souls escape like a bird, out of the snare of the fowler. Those that the Son sets free are free indeed. There is liberty where the Spirit of the Lord is. You are entitled to deliverance just as you are entitled to salvation and healing—by the blood shed at Calvary's cross by the sacrifice lamb, *Jesus.*

Acknowledgements

T he production and printing of this book has been a selfless demonstration of Christian love and support by many individuals. Without such, its publication could never have been accomplished. Only by the encouragement, intercession, spiritual warfare, and financial support of a community of exhorters who believed in us, could the task have been completed. Therefore, it is with deep gratitude and warmest appreciation that we extend our special thanks to you: Peggy, Les, Amy, Sonya, Christy, Lynn, Marthalyn, Susan, and the members of Safe Harbor Fellowship. To all others (too numerous to name) who believed in this project and contributed in word or deed—God bless you!

Foreword

When it became apparent to us that we were called into the deliverance ministry, we set out to learn all we could about this oft misunderstood and sorely neglected subject. We discovered an abundance of material on the origin of demons, how they enter and how they oppress Christians (as well as unbelievers). What we found precious little of in our search was practical instruction in conducting deliverance sessions. To say that one is to simply command the demons to leave in Jesus' name was like sending a soldier into battle with a BB gun. Deliverance is simple, yet complex too. We conduct deliverance only through the authority given us by the shed blood of Jesus our Savior. But just as most of us haven't raised the dead, neither can we assume in each case that we simply command demons to leave, as Jesus did, and the person will be instantly delivered. God's word promises in John 14:12 that believers will do greater works than Jesus. We believe that scripture and stand on it, but until such time as it is manifest in our lives, we must all use Holy Ghost led "procedures."

This book is written, therefore, so that others might be spared our years of trial and error in deliverance. While it is exciting to be taught by the Holy Ghost, we find that He is quite willing to allow others to benefit from our own experiences in the "school of hard knocks" (and thus be spared the bumps and bruises we endured). Our desire to see the captives set free has kept us motivated despite setbacks, roadblocks and just plain ignorance. There is no pat formula for successful deliverance. Each case is unique (although there are some common denominators). We learn something new with every deliverance session in which we're involved. It is humbling, exciting and sometimes frustrating. The frustrating times have in essence produced the keys we have presented in this book. We don't pretend to know it all. In fact, we're quite sure we've only scratched the surface. But if our "scratch" is deeper than yours we are blessed to be able to share our findings with you.

Beth Scott
2003

Introduction

Compare a working blueprint to an architect's design of the building. Compare a road map to a landscape painting. Compare the assembly directions for a new bicycle to the sales promotion for the product. This gives you some idea of the difference between this book and some others written on the topic of deliverance. This book is a blueprint, a road map, and the assembly directions for deliverance. It deals with the "nuts and bolts" of deliverance ministry. At the core, this book is a "how to" for deliverance. Our goal in writing is to offer a guidebook to those whom the Lord has called and equipped to operate in a ministry of deliverance. We have sought to place within this book the lessons taught us by the Holy Spirit throughout a number of years in deliverance ministry. Our desire is to produce a "manual of war" for those engaged in this vital, front-line, in-the-trenches ministry to the body of Christ. As a book, it is beneficial to those receiving deliverance. However, it would be of greatest benefit to those who minister deliverance.

Therefore, we will not seek to prove/debate issues such as "can a Christian have a demon?" or "can demons enter a Christian following salvation?" We believe these issues in the past have received adequate examination with an affirmative conclusion. Classic books have been written by anointed authors such as Frank Hammond's <u>Pigs in the Parlor</u> and Don Basham's <u>Can a Christian Have a Demon?</u>. These have been followed by more recent works such as Derek Prince's <u>They shall expel Demons</u> and Francis MacNutt's <u>Deliverance from Evil Spirits.</u> These have proven the case for Christians needing deliverance. It is not our intent in this book to belabor what we feel are proven concepts.

Our desire is to place within the hands of those engaged in deliverance ministry a specific "step-by-step" manual for deliverance. It is our hope that with the application of these principles you will call the demonic to account. We believe that with these tools, in each respective ministry case, you will cause demons present to "stand and deliver"; (thereby opening the way for recovery of all that has been stolen from the believer).

Following an overview of deliverance, the content of this book is devoted to the <u>practice</u> of deliverance ministry. We would agree that these are the end times and the return of our Lord is imminent. Yet, we must work until the day ends and the night comes. We must do the works of our Lord Jesus until His return. Part of that work is the ministry of deliverance that "sets the captive free." We must declare freedom to those held prisoner and enforce defeat upon the enemy. Satan is very aware that He has been defeated, yet still he "goes about as a roaring lion seeking whom he may devour" (I Peter 5:8). Revelation 12:12 states: " Woe to the inhabitants of the earth and the sea! For the devil has come down to you, having great wrath, because he knows that he has a short time." Even so, let us remember Revelation 12:10 which states, "Now salvation, and strength, and the kingdom of our God, and the power of His Christ have come, for the accuser of our brethren, who accused them before our God day and night, has been cast down."

The victory has been won. The foundation for deliverance has been accomplished in Christ. This book is intended to help point the way toward the realization of the complete fruit of deliverance in the life of every believer. Due to the wrathful nature of our adversary, Satan, we will not accomplish this without opposition. But through the forceful application of these deliverance principles, every deliverance minister may assist believers to lay hold of the kingdom of God. Thus may we all experience God's righteousness, peace and joy in the Holy Ghost.

Tim Scott
2003

Chapter 1

Overview
and Foundations

for

Deliverance

Overview of Deliverance - Foundations for Deliverance

As stated, this book is to be a practical manual intended for application. It is not intended to be a theological treatise on whether or not Christians need deliverance. Keeping that in mind, this section is offered as a broad statement of background information. It presupposes the validity of certain fundamental spiritual concepts essential to effective deliverance ministry. As a spiritual declaration for freedom "we hold these truths to be self evident"— One: Christians *can* " have" demons and *do* need deliverance. Two: Christians *can* be entered by demons *after* they have been born again. Three: Spirit filled Christians *can* be demonized and subsequently need deliverance. Four: Deliverance and healing *are* co-related and *are* part of the New Testament pattern for the church (which included salvation, healing, deliverance, and Holy Spirit Baptism).

Consider this passage from Peter Horrobin's book <u>Healing Through Deliverance</u>:

"Each of us is walking towards wholeness in our Christian pilgrimage, and as the Holy Spirit exposes darkness, then it is our responsibility to see that the light of Jesus Christ is brought to bear on the demonic and the powers of darkness are cast out. It is as unrealistic to say that once a person is a Christian he will never need any more physical or inner healing as it is to say that he cannot ever need deliverance ministry…I believe this was the normal practice of the early church and that one of the major reasons why deliverance amongst Christians is often so hard is that the church has not been ministering the New Testament pattern for salvation, healing and deliverance."

In his book <u>Demons and Deliverance</u>, Maxwell Whyte states that "Deliverance is not an extra to the preaching of the Gospel— Deliverance is the very center of the Gospel. Jesus came that He might destroy the works of the Devil and set captives free. If people remain sound (static) in our churches, then we are not fulfilling the Great Commission."

With all of this in mind, let's examine several issues related to deliverance.

First, what is deliverance?

Simply put, deliverance is the process of expelling, or "casting out" demonic beings (demons) from people, animals, buildings, or locales. Usually, our focus in deliverance ministry is upon human beings.

A number of scriptures are presented which deal with deliverance in the ministry of Jesus, His disciples, and the early apostles of the church. It is God's desire that present day Christians continue this vital ministry in the manner in which it is described in Mark 16:15-17:

"And He said unto them, Go into all the world and preach the Gospel to every creature. He who believes and is baptized will be saved; but he who does not believe will be condemned. And these signs will follow those who believe: In My name they will cast out demons; they will speak with new tongues; they will take up serpents; and if they drink any deadly thing, it will by no means hurt them; they will lay hands on the sick and they will recover."[1]

These following additional scriptures illustrate the normative practice of deliverance for the New Testament church.

Matthew 8:16-17 – **"And when evening had come, they brought to Him many who were demon-possessed; and He cast out the spirits with a word, and healed all who were ill in order that what was spoken through Isaiah the prophet might be fulfilled, saying, 'He Himself took our infirmities, and carried away our diseases'."**

Matthew 9:32-34 – **"And as they were going out, behold, a dumb man, demon-possessed, was brought to Him. And after the demon was cast out, the dumb man spoke; and the multitudes** marveled, saying, 'Nothing like this was ever seen in Israel'."

Matthew 10:8 – "Heal the sick raise the dead, cleanse the lepers, cast out demons; freely you received, freely give."

Luke 4:33-36 – "And there was a man in the synagogue possessed by the spirit of an unclean demon, and he cried out with a loud voice,' Ha! What do we have to do with You, Jesus of Nazareth? Have You come to destroy us? I know who You are—the Holy One of God!' And Jesus rebuked him, saying, 'Be quiet and come out of him!' And when the demon had thrown him down in their midst, he went out of him without doing him any harm. And amazement came upon them all, and they began discussing with one another, and saying, 'What is this message? For with authority and power He commands the unclean spirits, and they come out'."

Matthew 12:28 – "But if I cast out demons by the Spirit of God, surely the kingdom of God has come upon you."

Luke 9:1 – "And He called the twelve together, and gave them power and authority over all the demons, and to heal diseases."

Luke 10:17-20 – "And the seventy returned with joy, saying, 'Lord, even the demons are subject to us in Your name'. And He said to them, 'I saw Satan fall from heaven like lightning. Behold, I have given you authority to tread upon serpents and scorpions, and over all the power of the enemy and nothing shall injure you. Nevertheless do not rejoice in this, that the spirits are subject to you, but rejoice that your names are recorded in heaven'."

Acts 8:6-7 – "And the multitudes with one accord were giving attention to what was said by Philip, as they heard and saw the signs which he was performing. For in the case of many who had unclean spirits, they were coming out of them shouting with a loud voice; and many who had been paralyzed and lame were healed."

Acts 16:16-18 – "And it happened that as we were going to the place of prayer, a certain slave-girl having a spirit of divination (Python) met us, who was bringing her masters much profit by fortune-telling. Following after Paul and us, she kept crying out, saying, 'These men are bond-servants of the Most High God, who are proclaiming to you the way of salvation'. And she continued doing this for many days. But Paul was greatly annoyed, and turned and said to the spirit, 'I command you in the name of Jesus Christ to come out of her!' And it came out at that very moment."

Acts 19:11-16 – "And God was performing extraordinary miracles by the hands of Paul, so that handkerchiefs or aprons were even carried from his body to the sick, and the diseases left them and the evil spirits went out. But also some of the Jewish exorcists, who went from place to place, attempted to name over those who had evil spirits the name of the Lord Jesus, saying, 'I adjure you by Jesus who Paul preaches.' And seven sons of one Sceva, a Jewish chief priest, were doing this. And the evil spirit answered and said to them, 'I recognize Jesus, and I know about Paul, but who are you?' And the man, in whom was the evil spirit, leaped on them and subdued both of them and overpowered them, so that they fled out of that house naked and wounded."

DELIVERANCE AND CHRISTIANS

Upon such foundation of scriptural precedent we base our ministry of deliverance; and, from the same foundation we derive our mandate to perform this vital ministry. We feel that the scriptures themselves, combined with the experiential results of not only our deliverance ministry, but those of numerous other deliverance ministers, provides an obvious case for its needfulness **among** the Body of Christ. Frank Hammond, author of Pigs in the Parlor, maintains that deliverance is "the children's bread" (based upon Matthew 15:26). As such, he contends that deliverance ministry is primarily intended for those who profess Jesus as Lord and Savior. Thus deliverance, being provided as part of the atoning act of Jesus Christ, should also be a part of the process of sanctification for each Christian. Within the scope of sanctification, deliverance is related to transformation and in connection with healing. We believe that it is a blessing of God intended for the maturation of each believer within the church, Christ's Bride. This would be in keeping with Ephesians 4:13-15 which states: "...till we all come to the unity of the faith and of the knowledge of the Son of God, to a perfect man, to the measure of the stature of the fullness of Christ; that we should no longer be children, tossed to and fro and carried about with every wind of doctrine, by the trickery of men, in the cunning craftiness of deceitful plotting, but, speaking the truth in love may grow up in all things into Him who is the Head – Christ..."

Deliverance is an essential element in the process of "growing up in all things" into Christ. If deliverance is life-giving spiritual "bread" for believers (God's children) then it is in union with the other types of spiritual bread provided by God for His people. Just as the priests of the tabernacle were restored as they ate the show bread infused with God's presence, we as the priesthood of believers today, can be transformed and sanctified through eating the bread of deliverance. Just as Jesus was the Bread of God, the Bread of Life, and the Bread from Heaven (John 6:48), then healing and deliverance (through His crucifixion and resurrection) may also become part of our spiritual "bread." Like manna and showbread before it, the bread of deliverance is part of God's plan (through Christ) for the growth and feeding of His people.

Derek Prince, in his book, They Shall Expel Demons, states that "Deliverance is only the first step in a process leading to the recovery of holiness and the restoration of the church to her original simplicity and purity." Prince cites Obadiah 17 in reference to God's ultimate purpose for His people – "the House of Jacob shall possess their possessions." Prince states that there are two conditions in order to achieve our inheritance. First is the need for deliverance; second is the need for holiness. He says, "Any process that bypasses either of these conditions will not bring God's people into their inheritance. There is a logical and practical reason why deliverance from demons must precede holiness. Demons...have one thing in common: all, without exception, are the enemies of true holiness. Until demons have been driven out, neither the church nor Israel can attain to scriptural standards of holiness."

Finally, concerning Christians and deliverance we direct you to Matthew 12:28 which says, "But if I cast out demons by the Spirit of God, surely the kingdom of God has come upon you." The ministry of deliverance—casting out demons—is a unique demonstration that the kingdom of God has manifest among the people of God. Again citing Derek Prince's writings, "this ministry demonstrates a New Testament revelation of Jesus Christ who went beyond the precedents of God's Old Testament prophets and priests to demonstrate the reality of God's kingdom."

Deliverance ministry clearly demonstrates, in a unique way, that God's kingdom authority is available to us in New Testament power over Satan and his kingdom of darkness. Through the victory of Jesus Christ we now have power over the demonic as it seeks to hinder God's people in their progression toward holiness. We are commanded to exercise that power. As Derek Prince boldly says, (and we heartily agree), "Evangelism that does not include the casting out of demons is not New Testament Evangelism." And regarding the relation of deliverance to prayer for healing Prince states, "It is unscriptural to pray for the sick if one is not prepared also to cast out demons." That is the scriptural example demonstrated by Jesus Christ; and, that is the New Testament example we adhere to in our ministry of deliverance **for Christians**.

HOW DEMONS ENTER

Given the fact that Christians can need deliverance, then "How do demons enter a person/Christian?" Our method of deliverance ministry is based on the following entry points, or "doors," through which demons enter a person's body and/or soul (i.e.; the mind, the will, the emotions). We do not believe demons can enter a Christian's spirit. That would constitute possession. Christians may be inhabited by demons but not possessed by them. For in depth teaching on this subject read the books of Peter Horrobin, Frank Hammond, Derek Prince, and Francis MacNutt (listed in the appendix under "Recommended Reading").

1. Iniquity or Generational Curses

   We have devoted an entire chapter to this issue. However, simply put, it is the "sins of the Fathers visited upon subsequent generations." God holds those in authority accountable (even if they are not saved). Their willful sin can cause the transferring of a desire to sin to subsequent generations that then draws them toward committing the same sins. Strong's Concordance and Vine's Expository Dictionary each define iniquity as a "bent" toward evil and a "predisposition" toward a particular sin. It has been said that iniquity is like spiritual DNA.

2. Shock and Trauma

   Physical as well as emotional injury can open a "door" for demonic entry. Severe accidents, injuries to the head, near-death experiences, and traumatic, life-threatening illnesses can subject one to demonic influence by means of fear, infirmities, worry etc. Victimization and abuse (physical, sexual and verbal) can give demons access to a person. Emotional damage can cause years of torment and agony resulting in a need for deliverance and inner healing.

3. Sexual Sin

   Any sexual practice outside the parameters intended by God is sinful and displeasing to God. Therefore, things such as fornication, adultery, homosexuality and incest are open doors to demonic habitation. Through sexual sin destructive soul ties are usually established that provide a means of transference of spirits from one person to another. For further information see our section on "Soul Ties."

4. Addictions

 Drug and alcohol use open doors to addictive spirits that can be extremely difficult from which to deliver a person. Often they are rooted in issues such as escape, rejection, insecurity, etc. These issues, until dealt with, perpetuate the addiction. This is the case with various forms of emotion-based addiction such as eating disorders, sexual addictions, compulsive relationships, etc.

5. Occult Involvement

 Obviously, this is in direct opposition to the principles of God. The more willful the involvement, the more intense the resulting demonization for the individual. Even innocent or curious participation (dabbling) in the occult may open doors of demonic entry to an individual. Conscious practice of witchcraft and Satanism will result in more severe demonic habitation.

6. Curses

 Curses take many forms and whether spoken against another, spoken toward one's self or spoken by another toward you, they can provide entry to demonic activity in the life of an individual. They may take obvious forms such as: hexes, spells, vows, incantations, etc. Or, they may be less obvious such as idle words, gossip lies, judgments, etc. We have devoted a chapter to this subject.

DETERMINING THE NEED

To determine initially the need for deliverance we must first address the issue of "compulsion" versus "flesh." That is to say, we all face temptation by Satan to lead us into sin. We must as Paul says, "crucify the flesh daily." However, when determining an individual's need for deliverance due to demonic habitation there will be present a "compulsion" to sin. The individual usually is aware of the sin and desires to cease the repetition of it. Yet, they are somehow compelled over and over to practice specific sin or destructive behavior. This may indicate demonic activity and indwelling. Charles Kraft further attributes this repetition of sin to: 1. not yet having the will to stop, 2. lack of strength (willpower) due to emotional damage. He adds these as contributors to a compulsion to repeat sinful practices. Demons then take advantage of and perpetuate that compulsion.

There are, additionally, certain symptoms of demonic harassment and activity that may indicate a need for deliverance counseling. Some of these are:

1. Disturbed Sleep
   Insomnia, fretful sleep, nightmares, physically exhausting dreams
2. Inner Voices
   Continual demonic communication in the mind
3. Recurring Accidents
   Accident-proneness, unexplainable accidents. These may be the result of curses against a person.
4. Physical Illness
   Often with no known cause medically. The symptoms exist without cause. This usually indicates a need for inner healing and deliverance.
5. Lapses of Memory
   Forgetfulness, blocked thought patterns, misplaced objects, losing train of thought. Confusion. Befuddled. Disorientation.
6. Family Turmoil and Tragedy
7. Financial Drain

Peter Horrobin, in his book, Healing through Deliverance lists these additional "observable symptoms of demonization." We have summarized them for clarity and emphasis. In some categories we have added amplification based upon our own deliverance ministry experience.

1. **Addictions**

One of the hallmarks of demonic activity is behavior that is out of control. This is especially true with regard to the intake of addictive substances. Once a person is unable to modify their behavior through free will choice, it is clear that control is no longer in their own hands. They often, thereby, turn to artificial "aids" of behavior modification.

For many who have become addicted, the root cause lies much deeper than the superficial addiction. Their addictive behavior can be a form of compensation for underlying problems that also need attention. This is often termed "self medication." It is an attempt, in some form,(drugs, alcohol, food, sex etc.) to relieve the soul's hurt and pain. Freedom from addiction requires repentance over mistreating the body, exercising the will in wanting to be healed, deliverance from any demons that have gained access through the addiction, and a disciplined lifestyle from then on.

2. **Appetites out of balance**

Failure to look after the body that God has given us is essentially rebellion against the Holy Spirit. More extreme forms of this result in what is defined as "eating disorders." The most common eating disorders are anorexia and bulimia. Anorexics eat a bare minimum of food and gradually waste away. Bulimics binge on excessive amounts of food then purge themselves of it by vomiting or using laxatives.

Additionally, people may be very overweight because they eat for comfort. They eat to hide the pain they are feeling on the inside. Females who have been abused sexually may overeat in order to be overweight and unattractive to men. They may associate an attractive body with vulnerability to abuse.

Some eating disorders are due to allergic reactions to specific substances. The body is unable to absorb certain food products without unpleasant or even life-threatening reactions. Many allergic conditions are present at birth, therefore a generational curse should be investigated. Often there has been witchcraft in the generational line, especially with regard to the use of potions and remedies.

3. Behavior Extremes

There are behavior patterns that tend to alienate people from friends and neighbors. In many cases, there is a demonic dimension to this behavior. Where demons are either responsible or partly responsible in this way, they will usually have "ridden in" on either a relationship that has gone wrong, or be a consequence of generational sin. It is not surprising that one of Satan's tactics is to try to push people to extremes so that their behavior is unacceptable to others, and then they become isolated from and rejected by society. This then increases the impact upon their soul along with a continued pattern of rejection.

4. Bitterness and Unforgiveness

When someone understands the necessity to forgive but then finds it impossible to make the choice, one has to ask whether or not there is a spirit of unforgiveness or bitterness that is holding the person in bondage. Without an understanding of inner healing and deliverance, it is very difficult to release such a person into the healing that begins with forgiving those who have hurt us.

5. Compulsive Behavior Patterns

By "compulsive behavior patterns," we are referring to the compulsive repetition of otherwise normal activities. Compulsive hand washing or repetitive checking that doors are locked are typical examples. Usually people who practice such compulsions fully realize that their behavior is neither normal nor tolerable. Wherever there are compulsive behavior patterns there are usually activities of demons in operation. Compulsion is a hallmark of the demonic. It marks the delineation between demonically driven behavior and fleshly habits.

6. Deceitful Personality and Behavior

When people learn that, by telling lies or being deceitful in their behavior, they can get away with sin and/or get their own way, they may then make a conscious choice to use deception as a routine matter of course. At that point, in effect, they invite a spirit of deception to help them. Such is the depth of this deception that the person may not even know whether or not they are telling the truth. They lose the ability to distinguish truth from lie. This leads to the practice of compulsive or pathological lying.

7. **Depression**

It would be wrong to propose that depression always has a demonic origin. It doesn't. More often than not, the root is in the emotions or in damaged relationships. But a person who suffers regularly from depression is usually affected by the demonic. Once the damage has been done to the emotions the person is very vulnerable to demonization; and, then to being controlled by demons that will, unknown to them, perpetuate the symptoms. Usually there is a network of different spirits affecting the mind as well as the emotions. There even seems to be some evidence that a demonic "link" can be passed down the generational line through ancestral worship of the sun, or some other aspect of the season; the depression is thereby a curse that has been given rights through the idolatry involved.

8. **Emotional Disturbance**

Emotions can get out of balance and damaged through the relationship experiences and circumstances of life. There are some people whose emotional responses never seem to be right. Their responses may be either excessively expressed, inappropriate for the situation, or appear to be completely absent. While demonic activity is not usually the primary cause of the emotional condition, it would be unusual for there not to be some powerful demonic hold over the emotions which entered through the distress that caused the original situation.

9. Escapism

Many times in meetings where there has been a powerful presence of the Holy Spirit, some individuals are not able to stay in the meeting. Escaping in this way is usually not the will of the person, but the will of the demons inside the person (who are struggling to stay in control when the person is exposed to such a heavy anointing of God).

Additionally, individuals may escape into themselves, into a hobby, into watching television, soap operas, novels, even sleep—to name a few! Once absorbed in their chosen escape, they become almost immune to the presence of other people. Such behavior is frequently evidence of a serious relationship breakdown, which has not been acknowledged. The participants cope by so absorbing themselves in their escapist activity that the need to face up to the pain of the relationship is kept well buried. This is a classic way of coping with marriage problems. It is also an underlying drive beneath addictive behavior patterns.

10. Fears and Phobias

When we have a frightening experience, Satan will seek to hold us in the trauma of that experience by using it as an entrance gate for the demonic. When someone is controlled by irrational fear, there is almost always a demonic stronghold behind the manifesting behavior. Irrational fear works closely with spirits of panic and escape. Irrational fear and phobias (fear of spiders, heights, water, germs, etc.) are closely linked.

11. Guilt and Self-Condemnation

When sin has been confessed and forgiven, there is no need for the sinner to continue to feel guilty. If a person continues to feel guilty after the sin has been rightfully dealt with, then it is likely that he has been vulnerable to a spirit which is perpetuating feelings of guilt and condemnation. If someone refuses to forgive "self" for what they have done, then they open the door to the demonic in such a way that continual feelings of guilt and self-condemnation are inevitable consequences.

12. Hearing Voices

What we are speaking of is the ongoing experience of having a voice speaking things into one's mind. For some people, the voice never seems to stop. In some cases, it may be that there is a strong soul-tie to someone who, knowingly or unknowingly, impresses their thoughts and words on the person who hears the voice. Even when this happens, it is only possible through the involvement of demonic power.

13. Hereditary Illnesses (Iniquity of Infirmity)

When a sickness appears to have been passed down the generational line, what is actually being passed down may be the spirit that has induced the symptoms in each generation. We have seen very significant deliverance and healing take place as we have confronted these powers and as the people involved have forgiven their ancestors for whatever it was they did which gave rights to the demonic. This breaks the "cord" of iniquity linking the person to generational sickness and disease. Generational curses resulting from involvement in "secret societies" (free masonry, etc.) often manifest as generational illnesses.

14. Heretical Beliefs

Once people have accepted unscriptural beliefs, as truth, they are then susceptible to receiving a demonic spirit which will ensnare them in entire patterns of false belief and blind their eyes to the truth—just as Satan blinds the minds of unbelievers so they cannot see the light of the Gospel (Cor. 4:4) These are called ungodly beliefs and facilitate the establishing of a demonic stronghold in the person's life. Once a person has accepted deceptive beliefs, especially about the foundational tenets of faith, the authority of the work of God and the work of the Holy Spirit, they are then vulnerable to further demonization, which will control their mind and their understanding.

15. **Involvement in False Religions**

Satan has worked a major deception on the whole of mankind by initiating a plethora of religions, each with its own belief system and behavioral code. Behind every false religion, there is a demonic power seeking to enmesh the worshipers in its hold. When people have been involved in deception, even in a passing way, then they have made themselves susceptible to receiving a demon that imprisons them in the deception they have embraced.

16. **Irrational Behavior**

When a person behaves quite normally most of the time, but every now and again exhibits irrational and unacceptable behavior, there has to be a reason for the conduct. Outbursts of irrational behavior are usually empowered by the demonic. But they will also have a root, often long buried, in the hurts and pains of the past, or even in the ancestral line. This causes an irrational "overreaction" in specific (often similar) situations and conditions.

17. **Lack of Mature Relationships**

Some people find it very hard to maintain mature adult relationships. Frequently, they behave in very childish ways. This type person never seems to be real. You never quite know whom you are talking to, or whether or not you have ever known the real person! They can even have a different voice for different occasions. Usually, where these different aspects of personality are well developed, there is a complex demonic stronghold behind each deceptive behavior pattern. At the root of the person's problem will usually be some major reason to enter into deception in order either to cover something up, or to behave according to the expectations of others. When rooted in trauma differing "personalities" may fragment into multiple personality disorder with each "alter" needing deliverance.

Frequently these individuals operate in an "adult child syndrome" in their behavior patterns. This is rooted in childhood trauma and is perpetuated, often, by the demonic.

18. **Legalism and Spiritual Bondage**

Satan loves division, and if he can turn Christians against each other through the influence of a legalistic spirit, he will have succeeded in insulating the church from the dynamic of Holy Spirit- filled life. The curse of tradition ensures that the spark of real spiritual life, through which God is always doing new things, never gets fanned into a flame. When dealing with demons, we have to remember that they can operate over a group of people just as easily as in and through one person. A legalistic spirit will work closely with a religious spirit to produce "Pharaiseeism." God is a God of growth and change. But change involves risk and legalism is often a way of compensation for fear of risk.

19. **Nightmares**

When there is a regular pattern of nightmares, the scenes are being generated by demons who, when the defenses are down during sleep, push into the subconscious and cause distress to the person. The source of the nightmares could be trauma, abuse, or some frightening experiences of early childhood. The actual incident is often not accessible to the conscious mind, but the demons which gained access through the incident never forget how they got in and, whenever they are able, will try to distress the person. Sometimes demons gained access to the mother or father and have passed down nightmares to the children generationally. These nightmares indicate a need for first, inner healing and, second, deliverance.

20. **Occultic Involvement**

Satan is the one being worshipped through all occultic activities. Satan has power and he uses it to draw people into his control.

That is why spiritual results occur when people practice the occult. The fact that something spiritual happens does not mean that it is of God. Scripture warns us that the days will come when even some of the very "elect" might be deceived. In practice, the demons use the people. Occultists believe they are controlling and using occult power when in fact it is they who are serving as "pawns" of powerful demons.

21. **Out of Control Tongue**

If a demon wants to influence someone, it can only do so through speech or the behavior of the person in which it resides. We have often heard in Christian meetings, especially church council meetings, a voice that has spoken out with what seems to be wisdom. It is in fact the wisdom of this world trying to divert the people of God away from the plans and purposes of God. The tongue is capable of speaking out the wonderful truths of God's word, capable of blessing and encouraging people; but, it is also "...a fire, a world of evil among the parts of the body. It corrupts the whole person, sets the whole course of his life on fire..." (James 3:6). No wonder demons like to control the tongue: they can do much harm through its uncontrolled use. Note: An out of control tongue and a stormy, "tempestuous" pattern of behavior often indicate the presence of an "Ahab" spirit and the operation at large of a "Jezebel" spirit.

22. **Recurring or Long-term Sicknesses**

Where people are vulnerable to one sickness after another, there is often a spirit that is "inviting" spirits of infirmity in at regular intervals. These spirits are very happy for anyone to come and spend time praying for the afflicted person. They know that routine prayer is no threat to the demonic. A spirit of infirmity of this kind has often been given rights to rule strongly through some experience in the past, when sickness was welcomed and used by the person for his own ends, either to gain attention or to get his own way. Whatever the motive, a "revolving door" has been set in place through which a demon has gained control over one's physical condition. Recurring sickness often indicates a concurrent need for deep emotional/inner healing that is manifesting physically.

23. Self-Centeredness

Pride in the form of self-idolatry was the foundational sin for which Satan was thrown out of heaven. Where someone is always putting himself forward and expresses interest in other people only to turn the conversation back to himself, one has to suspect that there is a demonic stronghold operating in their personality. It would not be unusual with such people to find that there is a generational line of similar individuals. The real battle will be with a familiar spirit that has held the whole family in bondage for generations. If the depth of pride demonstrated is compelling enough, it may even be driven by a spirit of Leviathan. Leviathan is a powerful ruling spirit whose chief characteristic is pride. "He is king over all the children of pride" (Job 41:34).

24. Sexual Aberrations

All sexual expression is a form of covenant demonstration, whether participants are aware of this fact or not! God desires to bless the sexual union of a man and a woman in holy matrimony. Their sexual relationship therefore bespeaks of their covenant to one another and to God. Wherever ungodly sex is taking place, Satan will be there—not to bless, but to curse the participants. That is why there is so much sexual activity in the rituals of Satanism and witchcraft. It is also why the sexual activity performed is deeply perverse. Satan rejoices over the satanic covenant that this establishes and traps the participants in the demonic bondage that ensues. Soul-ties established through ungodly sexual activity are a prime entry point for the demonic.

25. **Suicidal Tendencies**

Taking one's own life is the ultimate sin against one's own body—the ultimate rebellion against the Holy Spirit, whose temple the body is. However, we have no doubt that there will be many people who have committed suicide who, when they stand before the Lord, will be amazed at God's love and mercy as they realize they have been more sinned against than they have sinned themselves.

There is always a demonic dimension to suicide attempts or desires. In most cases, the person has been so hurt by the way they have been abused or treated that the future seems utterly hopeless. Be alert for the activity of spirits of hopelessness, depression and death.

Sometimes the person may have received a spirit of death through the generational line, or from someone else close to them who died. This will continue to drive and motivate them, even though they have no personal reason for wanting to die.

Another possible source of feelings of death could be an attempted abortion or thoughts or desires to abort by the person's mother, leaving the inutero baby with feelings that they are not wanted and shouldn't be there.

26. **Undiagnosable Symptoms**

It is not unusual for people to have aches and pains that, upon medical investigation, do not appear to have any known cause. We have found that such persistent symptoms can be demonic and are caused by a spirit of infirmity that has either come down the generational line, or has entered through shock, trauma, or even sexual sin. The trauma of accidents makes people vulnerable to the demonic, and following such incidents, people often need deliverance as well as physical healing. Again, such symptoms most often indicate a related need for inner healing along with or prior to deliverance.

27. **Violent Tendencies**

Violence against another person is also a form of rebellion. Violence removes free will choice from the victim, and is contrary to God's created order. The person who perpetuates violence opens himself up to being used by the demonic; and, the trauma associated with being a recipient of violence leaves the victim vulnerable to the demonic at the time of the attack.

We have seen that violence in one area of life can be an uncontrolled outworking of demons that have been given rights through the controlled violence of activities such as martial arts. Churches that allow martial arts classes to take place in church halls (along with yoga and other occult based activities) are opening their whole ministry up to the influence of demonic power.

28. **Withdrawn Anti-social Behaviors**

Man is a social being. God intended people to enjoy relationships with each other, and to grow and benefit from the experience. He did not intend people to be forced to withdraw into themselves so that they live out most of their days in the isolation of loneliness. To bring healing, inner healing and deliverance is necessary. It is also essential to explore the reasons why, in the first place, the person may have made a choice to want to be alone. Invariably, the root will have its origins in a relationship that has caused hurt and pain (usually in childhood). It could even be that the enemy has taken advantage of experiences in babyhood, or, before birth, in the womb. In that case, rejection has been established at the earliest possible moment, and the demonic will feed on the emotional damage that has already been done to the child.

Count the Cost

We close this chapter with a directive for those who feel called to the ministry of deliverance. Luke 14:27-33 reminds us that there is a price in being a disciple of Christ. Before "building the tower" or "waging war" we must first "count the cost." So, too with deliverance ministry. It is not something entered into lightly. There **is** a price to pay.

There is great personal satisfaction in providing cutting edge ministry that sets captives free. But the cost is equally great. In the words of Jesus, very applicable to the deliverance minister, "So likewise, whoever of you does not forsake all that he has cannot be my disciple" (Luke 14:33).

We urge you now to consider the cost. It is demanding on you (and those closest to you) physically and emotionally, mentally and financially. Though deliverance is more accepted now than 20 years ago, it is still a highly controversial arena of ministry. And many who believe in deliverance would argue that a "ministry of deliverance" is not scriptural. You may be surprised to find that your greatest critics will be fellow believers and ministers rather than those outside the church or those needing ministry. Sad, but true. And you will, for certain, be a demonic target for spiritual warfare. Satan seems to have a particular hatred for those engaged in deliverance ministry.

As to the reality of "no turning back" consider this. In the military, in the conduct of Amphibious Assault Warfare, there is established in each campaign what is called a "line of departure." It is a point on the map located offshore from the beach, and, once landing craft (boats) have passed it, there is <u>no turning back</u>. Strategies and plans can be adjusted and orders reversed <u>prior</u> to the "line of departure" but not past it.

For the deliverance minister, prior to accepting the call, there exists a "Line of Departure" also. Once having said "yes" to the Holy Spirit's call to enter deliverance ministry, you have passed the "Line of Departure." You cannot turn back, as the enemy will never again allow you to operate at a less intense ministry level <u>without consequence</u>. For one thing, you will have gained spiritual knowledge that will forever be a potential threat to Satan in spiritual warfare. As the scripture says, (Luke 9:62) "once having set your hand to the plow, don't look back." For the deliverance minister you <u>cannot</u> look back without consequence.

Just as a former President must have protection by the secret service for life (because of what he knows), a minister of deliverance can never again step away from what he knows without consequence. He or she will have made demonic adversaries that will forever desire retribution. The form of ministry may possibly shift from active practice to teaching and writing but never to inactivity.

Too much spiritual insight will have been gained to discount it consequence free!

With increased knowledge come responsibility, accountability and commitment along with great ministry satisfaction. Luke 12:48 states, "For everyone to whom much is given, from him will much be required; and to whom much has been committed, of him they will ask the more." We urge you again, as a deliverance minister, <u>count the cost!</u>

---

[1] Please make note with this scripture that we are not advocating snake handling and the drinking of poison as practiced by some religious sects. We understand this passage to declare God's protection over those engaged in His ministry along with His command to do deliverance and heal the sick. Nor is the inclusion of casting out demons in this passage an indicator (as some would say) that is should be relegated to the practices of such errant groups.

Chapter 11

Iniquity and Travail

Iniquity Defined

The word "iniquity" is found 300 times in the Bible. Vines Expository Dictionary of Biblical words defines iniquity as "to bend" or "to deviate from the way." Psalm 106:6 helps us to differentiate between sin and iniquity. It says, "we have sinned with our fathers, we have committed iniquity, we have done wickedly." Iniquity is a "bent" or a pull toward the same sin our ancestors battled. If we act on this predisposition we have sinned. If we repeatedly sin in this area of an iniquity a demonic spirit will likely attach to it.

Isaiah 53:5 states that Jesus was "wounded for our transgressions, He was bruised for our iniquities;." Various translations of the Bible use the words "sin," "transgression," and "iniquity" interchangeably. By definition and by effect these are three distinctly individual spiritual conditions. As such each carries its own unique characteristics.

The following scripture references and definitions present a description of each (and explain the differences between them).

Sin: John 1:29 – **Hamartia**, Strong's #266.
Missing the mark, failure, offense, taking the wrong course, wrongdoing.

John 8:34,46; II Cor. 11:7, James 1:15
Demonstrate sin as concrete wrongdoing.

Romans 5:12; 11:3, 20; and Hebrews 3:13
Show sin as a quality of action.

Matthew 12:31; Acts 7:60
Show sin as a wrongful deed.

The focus throughout is wrongdoing and choice for wrongfulness – disobedience to God's law. This general state of sinfulness seems to depict failure to comply with God's law but not so much a willful, rebellious mindset or behavior against God. Such sin might be committed out of ignorance.

Transgression: Represented by two words. The first is contained in Ezekiel 18:31. It is **Pesha**, Strong's #6588. Rebellion, trespass, revolt, rebel. From the root word **Pasha**. Revolting against God's law or government. Going beyond established limits. Breaking out against. The second word is contained in Acts 1:25. It is **Parabaimo**, Strong's #3845, Abandoning a trust. Departing. Stepping aside. Overstep. Violation. Rebellion, aberration, apostasy. Deviation from an original and true direction. Going one's own way.

Transgression seems to carry a tone of more forceful disobedience and willfulness to the extent even of apostasy. It depicts the intentional breaking of covenant relationship whereas "Hamartia" may include unintentional "sins of omission."

Iniquity: The focus of this chapter is represented in Exodus 34:7; Exodus 20:5; Numbers 14:18 and Psalm 130:3. It is from the word **Avon**, Strong's #5771.

Derived from **Avah**: To bend or distort. Crookedness. Iniquity is the evil bent within human beings. It is a predisposition to sin. It is not itself sin but is the evil inner pull toward sin or transgressing. It leads us to commit "warped" deeds or go in a crooked direction.

Cord of Iniquity and the Reins

Iniquity appears to flow through us and affect us by means of "cords of iniquity" and our "reins."

We use the term "cords of iniquity" as defined in teachings by Rev. James Wesley Smith on iniquity and travail. In his research he has determined that the spiritual "seat" of iniquity in us would be in the physical area of the kidneys.

In a fetus, the kidneys are formed early and the ancient Hebrews believed the kidneys were the "heart" of our being. They believed the area of the kidneys was significant spiritually as well as physically. Hence, if a generational curse is flowing to/through us it is connected by a supernatural "cord" to the heart of us (kidney area), by means of the "reins." Reins is another term used in scripture that is unfamiliar to much of the church.

The scriptures state in Jeremiah 17:10, "I the Lord searcheth the heart, I try the reins, even to give to every man according to his ways." In Revelation 2:23, it says "And all the churches shall know that I am He which searcheth the reins and the hearts."

James Wesley Smith observes, "(the reins are) figurative for inner man and located in the area of the kidneys, described as not the comprehensive mind but that which controls it." He points us to Webster's English dictionary which states "reins – the kidney or region of the kidneys; the area of the loins, thought of as the seat of the emotions and affections."

Thus iniquity, like a spiritual DNA, flows in cordlike form through our reins and thereby influences our comprehensive mind and actions. In Strong's Concordance in the Greek, #3510, "reins" are: **nephros**: a kidney, i.e. (fig.) the innermost mind, the reins.

And in Strong's concordance in the Hebrew, #3629, "reins" are "Kilyah: a kidney, (fig.) the mind, the interior self, the reins.

Therefore, as we minister deliverance, where we encounter a need to "break" the effects of iniquity over an individual we often lay hands on the area of their kidneys. This is not a mandatory action but we often find it more effective to do so in breaking the power of iniquity. As we do this we declare out loud that "We are severing the cord of iniquity in the area of (whatever area of deliverance we are addressing)." For an in-depth teaching on this topic we recommend: The Mystery of Iniquity Revealed by Rev. James Wesley Smith.

Note that in order to sever cords of iniquity it requires agreement and consent from the recipient. One cannot sever another's cords of iniquity without their willingness. And keep in mind that just as every problem isn't a demon, every negative behavior isn't caused by iniquity. The root of the ministry need must be determined as to flesh, inner healing need, deliverance issues and/or iniquity. If the flesh is causing the negative thoughts, feelings or behavior, neither deliverance nor breaking iniquity curses will bring relief. Only ceasing fleshly, sinful habits, making Godly choices, and renewing the mind will affect change.

Transferring of iniquity

If you have never thought of the possibility of Generational iniquity or Generational Curses you may argue that each generation is responsible for it's own sin. Our answer is that people die but demons don't! They are spirit beings in search of a home of their own (in which to carry out their job descriptions). The most likely recipient is the next generation. Many times we can trace the onset of a serious sin pattern or infirmity to the exact time that a person lost a parent to death. Iniquities multiply (increase in force) from generation to generation. If we plant an apple seed, we reap a whole tree. If we plant trees, we reap an orchard! If a deed is a seed, it continues. We see this clearly in the generational consequences of abortion. We killed babies in the previous generation and now our children are killing other children in their own schools. Thus, as one generation passes, its iniquities are transferred to the next and related demons then attach to them. Please note that an iniquity itself is not the demon. It is a "predisposition" resident within a person that demons use to gain their own access.

In addition to the death of a family member, the most common way iniquity can be transferred is during conception. It is important to note that iniquity is passed through the maternal as well as paternal family lines. In Lev. 26:40 we read that the iniquity of our "fathers" must be confessed. This word is "Pater" in the original Hebrew, which means "parents." The same word is found in Heb. 11:23 in the Greek. It is a plural word meaning both Father and Mother. The word "forefather" (Progonos) is the same as the word "parents" in I Tim 5:4. The meaning, according to Vines Expository Dictionary and Strong's Concordance is "born before; ancestor or grandparent."

As Peter Horrobin states in his book Healing through Deliverance, "the sin of one generation 'uncovers' the next generation, leaving the children unprotected in the area of that particular sin." Lev. 23:2 tells us that those of illegitimate birth shall not enter into the house of the Lord for 10 generations. We have often seen how difficult it is for those born out of wedlock to receive and keep their salvation. Because of their deep sense of shame and lack of belonging and acceptance, it is hard for them to believe in Christ's acceptance, forgiveness and redemption.

Generational curses can actually change forms. For instance, several generations of curses of obesity can change into several generations of anorexia. This iniquity affects eating and appetite. The course that it takes varies, in this case, from generation to generation.

Sometimes an inner vow can aid and abet iniquity. For instance, a daughter who vows never to get fat like Mom may go the other extreme and starve herself to remain thin. If a child is continually told, "you are just like your father," he can expect to inherit his father's weaknesses. These words spoken over him, along with the expectation, make him particularly vulnerable to generational curses.

Psalm 106:6 explains that "we have sinned, as did also our fathers; we have committed iniquity, we have done wickedly (Amp.). We can cross-reference that scripture with Lev. 26:40-42 which says, "but if they confess their own and their fathers' iniquity in their treachery which they committed against Me—and also that because they walked contrary to Me...and they then accept the punishment for their iniquity, then I will earnestly remember My covenant with Jacob, Isaac and Abraham."

According to Vine's Expository dictionary, the term "iniquities" and "guilt" are often interchangeable. It implies that we experience guilt for our forefather's sins. Let us be clear. We do not change the fact of our ancestor's sins. That was between them and God and cannot be changed after the fact. God's consequences imposed resulting from their sin are established and repeat to subsequent generations guilty of the same sin. What God requires of us is to forgive our ancestors *for their iniquity*. Following that we may then sever cords of iniquity that link us to their sin. Having said that, however, it should be noted that a race or group of people may stand in for their ancestors when effecting repentance/forgiveness for past wrongs committed to another race or group.

As an aside, in our research for this book we found numerous opinions as to what constitutes a "generation" ("unto the third and fourth generation" Ex. 20). The clearest definition we found was in the Vines Expository dictionary and the Strong's concordance. These define a generation as a "coming full circle of life." It is a time period occupied by each successive generation. Because life spans were much longer in Biblical times, there could be numerous generations alive at the same time. Iniquity would be more obvious and easier to spot. In contrast, few of us today have any idea what sins our grandparents committed. We can only know by means of a word of knowledge from the Holy Spirit.

Iniquity and Idolatry

The classic scripture from which we draw the teaching on iniquity is found in the Ten Commandments. Exodus 20:5-6 says "For I the Lord your God, am a jealous God, visiting the iniquity of the fathers upon the children to the third and fourth generations of those who hate Me." We see from this scripture that the generational "visiting of iniquity" is directly linked to idolatry. Lest we dismiss this concept as not valid, we must look at the true meaning of idolatry. The Hebrew word for idol is "terapim" which means "spirit" or "demon." Hurrian law of this period (i.e. when the events recorded in Exodus took place) recognized household idols as deeds to the family's succession and goods. IChronicles 16:26 (Amp.) reads, "for all the gods of the people are lifeless idols, but the Lord made the heavens." In summation then, to worship or idolize anything more than God, "deeds" to our family for generations the demonic inheritance (through iniquity) of that idol.

An idol is that which has your heart. Human beings like to worship things they can see and touch. We idolize people, money, fame, success, appearance, possessions, etc. Idolatry is worshipping something or someone other than the true and living God. We worship by serving, honoring and doing homage (giving it time and attention). Webster's dictionary expounds on this definition by saying that to worship is "to have intense love or admiration for; to adore or idolize." Any object, relationship or activity can be idolatrous. Looking at idolatry in that light, we find that we are all guilty. Most sin is ultimately a form of idolatry. In Ezekiel, God likens idols to "dung pellets!" Through willful idolatry we commit sins which unleash on our households the effects of iniquity. These, in comparison to the riches and blessings of God that we could have, are as dung.

Truth about Iniquity

Some naysayers use Jeremiah 31:29-30 to try to refute the concept of iniquity "visiting" future generations. It states that "the fathers have eaten the grapes and the children's teeth are set on edge. But every one shall die for his own iniquity; every man who eats the sour grapes, his teeth shall be set on edge." The Spirit-filled Bible footnote on this passage clears it up for us. It says, "Individual responsibility is stressed by this quotation..apparently, people had misinterpreted the intent of some Scriptures (Ex. 20:5, Num. 14:18) so that they excused their own sinful behavior and blamed God for his judgment on their predecessors. Corporate or collective responsibility is an important theme in the Old Testament (Josh. 7:24-25), but Jeremiah and Ezekiel both stress that the calamity about to befall Jerusalem is due to the sin of those then living, not on their ancestors." As always, we must study God's word thoroughly and take care not to take passages out of context. In so doing, we find that rather than refute generational sin visited upon their descendants this scripture reinforces it. A child abused by his father will not be punished for his father's sin, nor is he guilty of wrongdoing. However, if he does not forgive his father, and release him from his judgment, the iniquity pattern may continue in the child's life.

There is always a "dual" dynamic to sin. No one sins in a vacuum. They experience the effects of their sin, as do those close to them even into future generations. Jer. 31:29 illustrates this fact. Another scripture, Ex.20: 5, that may give some pause contains the phrase, "of those who hate Me." This could appear to be an "out" because we certainly don't hate God; so how can we be a target for ancestral sin? The word "hate" however, implies that any disobedience to God is evidence of hatred in the heart. We do not have to feel literal hatred in order for this scripture to apply to us. The Hebrew word for *hate* in this scripture is "sane" and it represents an emotion ranging from intense hatred to the much weaker "set against." Another use of this verb is "to be unloved." It may also indicate that someone is untrustworthy. Another meaning is "to be alienated." How many of us can say that we are never "set against God" by our actions, thoughts, or feelings? Do we love God with all

45

our heart, mind and soul? Do we truly trust God? Do we ever alienate Him by our sin? In the purest sense of the word "hate," we have all been guilty.

A good example of iniquity at work can be found in the story of King David. He participated in adultery and then murder to cover up his adulterous act. We only need to look at his own children to see sexual sin and murder coming down the generational pike. The sins of the father were passed on, with serious consequences.

In Acts 8:23, the apostles spoke to Simon saying, "For I see that you are in the gall of bitterness and in a bond forged by iniquity (to fetter souls)(Amp.)." The word "forged" means formed, shaped or produced.

A New Testament example of iniquity is in John 9:1-2 when the question is asked of Jesus, "Who sinned, this man or his parents, that he was born blind?" Jesus answers that this particular man was born blind so that God could be glorified by healing him through Jesus. Notice however that Jesus did not rebuke them for false doctrine. He merely lets them know that in this case, the man's blindness was not caused by a generational curse (or iniquity). In His response, then, Jesus (unspoken) acknowledges the concept of iniquity.

Peter Horrobin says, "Some may argue that we live in the 'days of grace' and the law is not relevant for believers. Although it is true that we do not abide by the Jewish dietary or ceremonial laws, we cannot ignore any part of the basic moral or behavioral commandment." Yes, we are under the new covenant, but far too many believers do not experience the freedom and liberty of the abundant life. Just as God heals us when we ask in prayer, He also breaks iniquity when we ask. If every mindset, health problem, temptation, etc. was corrected at salvation, there wouldn't be any need for renewing the mind and being transformed daily into the image of God

Some argue that when we become a Christian "old things are passed away," therefore there should be no consequences of our ancestor's sins in our lives. We must acknowledge that we are not given a new flesh-life when we are born again. It is only by renewing the mind and receiving healing and deliverance that we can destroy the works of sinful desires passed down our generational line.

Many, however, will not embrace this truth. The transference of iniquity, or generational curses, is soundly refuted by some—even some noted ministers. Charles Finney, the famous revivalist was one who disputed the transferring of iniquity as well as the belief in original sin. This is a common continuum among those rejecting the principle of the passing of iniquity. Many of these feel they are on the cutting edge of a new revealing of divine wisdom. Sadly, such is not the case. Let us clarify.

The term "original sin" is that belief that holds that mankind is sinful in nature because of Adam's "fall" from grace by sin. It holds that before one commits any sin they are already a sinner; and, man does not come into the world as an innocent or natural creature.

This is a foundational principle of the Christian faith from the first century church. It holds to the precept that mankind "inherits" its sinful nature from Adam and must accept Jesus as Savior and Lord to reverse this "curse." The disputing of this tenet of faith, the transference of original sin nature, is almost as old as the tenet itself. The heretical belief that man is born sinless and uncorrupted can be traced at least as far back as Pelagius, a British monk of 380 A.D. He issued various Pelagian interpretations refuting the doctrine of original sin and was in turn vigorously opposed by Augustine.

Most today who hold to some form of Pelagianism on original sin would also dispute that we can "inherit" a bent toward a type of sin (iniquity) from our paternal or maternal ancestry. They would debate that we sin <u>like</u> Adam. We are only guilty of sin we actually commit. Sadly, these individuals are relegated to a life of struggle with inward "bents" toward sinful tendencies. These powers of iniquity continually pressure them whether or not they submit to them. How tragic. And all the while, Jesus has provided a means of liberation from such destructive inner forces as well as their repetition throughout generations.

Iniquity can be found in a variety of forms in our lives—an inability to be truthful, a tendency toward addictive behaviors, broken marriages, untimely deaths, repeated rejection by others, etc. One woman approached us for counseling and deliverance because she was distressed over her "obsession with adultery." She assured us she was born again, Spirit-filled and happily married.

Although she had never committed adultery, she was "fascinated by it," much to her dismay. She found herself drawn to romance novels, songs and television shows that glorified adultery. She was perplexed and filled with shame because of the strong draw she felt to that area of sin. The final straw was her inability to minister to her best friend when her friend committed adultery. "I couldn't even pray with her or remind her of God's Word," she said. "Instead, I found myself hanging on every word, enjoying the affair vicariously." Within minutes of the first counseling session, we discovered that this client's mother, as well as grandmother, fell prey to adultery repeatedly in their lifetime. What a relief to this dear lady to find that it was iniquity at work, not some subconscious dissatisfaction with her husband or their marriage. Subsequent ministry to this woman set her free from the generational predisposition toward adultery.

Once we realize that we have within us a "bent" in a certain direction, we can go with that bend (often to the point of breakage) or do everything possible not to succumb to the predisposition. Those who never learn about their family history are doomed to repeat it. Severing cords of iniquity frees us from repeating the sinful "history" of our predecessors.

Now, for the good news. Returning to our first scripture, Isaiah 53:5 announces to us that Jesus was "wounded for our transgressions, and bruised for our iniquities!" Again, in Is. 53:11, we read that "He shall bear their iniquities." Just as the price for sin was paid on Calvary, so was the price paid to break generational curses. Our salvation was provided for along with inner healing, physical healing and deliverance. Jesus was bruised for our iniquities. A bruise is bleeding on the inside. He took "stripes" on His back so that we might walk in physical health. He took bruises **inside** His body so that the power of iniquity within us might be broken (as well as for all our descendants). When His side was pierced and blood and water flowed , we believe, the power of iniquity over humanity was pierced and burst as well.

God wants us to live an abundant life; not robbed of that abundance by iniquity. He says we are more than conquerors, not slaves to sin and defeated by this "enemy." Psalm 47:4 tells us that God "chose our inheritance for us, the glory and pride of Jacob, who He loves."

The blood of Jesus redeems us from every curse. Yet we are destroyed for lack of knowledge. It's truth that we know and understand that will set us free. The word "to know" in John 8:32 ("and you shall know the truth and the truth shall set you free") means to understand or realize. The Spirit-filled Bible reveals that this "knowing" involves an inception, a progress and an attainment (SFL Bible-Word Wealth). It is like the difference between hearing and listening. We hear truth all the time, be we must progress from merely hearing to believing and understanding. Then the freedom of that truth can be attained. Know can also describe physical intimacy. Thus if we become physically, internally intimate with God's truth it becomes part of us; one with us. We then receive its liberating effects.

In Nehemiah 1:6-11, we see Nehemiah fasting, praying and crying out to God for forgiveness. He confesses the sins that have been sinned against God and says, "Both my father's house and I have sinned." Nehemiah intercedes intensely, ever aware of God's sovereignty and that He keeps His promises. We likewise must confess our own sin as well as our father's iniquity. As we do so, God "remembers" His covenant with us. We are the seed of Abraham and his blessings are rightfully ours. What a promise we have according to Gal. 3:13-14 and 29: "Christ has redeemed us from the curse of the law, having become a curse for us..that the blessing of Abraham might come upon the Gentiles in Christ Jesus, that we might receive the promise of the Spirit through faith." Verse 29: "and if you are Christ's then you are Abraham's seed and heirs according to the promise." Through His death on the cross, Christ did for us what we could not do for ourselves. His work, not ours, removed the curse that was on us because of man's disobedience (SFLB).

In conclusion, we note again that the curse of iniquity lasts to the 3rd or 4th generation, but the blessings of obedience flow to multiple generations. The effects of good far outweigh those of evil. When we break the cords of iniquity off of ourselves, we also break them off of future generations. In effect, we are saying, "the buck stops here, Satan, and I'm destroying it, to boot!" One of our favorite testimonies is that of a lady we prayed with to break a generational curse of obesity. In a few weeks time, she called to report that her teenage son who was overweight had suddenly begun to lose quite a lot of weight. At first, she was alarmed. Then the Holy Spirit showed her that when the curse was broken over her, it also broke over her son. His appetite changed, along with his metabolism, and the weight fell off. God is good!

We are including two sample prayers so that you can break iniquity yourself now that you have gained insight and understanding. A word of caution however. We often find that demons have attached to the iniquity that has led to sin patterns. When the iniquity is severed, the demon may manifest. In those instances, you may want a deliverance minister present to assist you.

Note: In our preparation for deliverance ministry to an individual, as we complete the "Demon Groupings Worksheet" we note with each demonic group any iniquity that is present (for mother's and father's families).

From Healing through Deliverance by Peter Horrobin

"I unreservedly forgive all my ancestors for all the things they have done which affect me and my life. I specifically renounce the consequences of their sins in Jesus' Name. As a child of God, I now claim that the power of the Word of Jesus is setting me free from the consequences of all occult activity in either my father or my mother's family lines, from curses that have had an effect on my life, from hereditary diseases and from the effects of any of their sins which have influenced me. I pray this in the Name of Jesus Who became a curse for me on Calvary and died that I might be set free. Amen."

From Demons Defeated by Bill Subritzky

"Dear Heavenly Father, I come to you in the Name of Jesus Christ. I praise You, Father, and I worship You. I confess that Jesus Christ is my Lord and my Savior. I confess that I have sinned, and I also confess the sins of my ancestors, known and unknown, and renounce all of those sins. I renounce the gods of my ancestors. I repent from those sins and from all occultic activity. I forgive my ancestors and I believe that on the cross, Jesus Christ delivered me from the curse of the law. And I believe that I have been released from all curses through the Name and through the blood of Jesus Christ."

Travail

As we seek to define and investigate iniquity, we would do well to also gain understanding of a spiritual manifestation called **travail**. Psalm 7:14 points to the clear link between travail and iniquity – "Behold, he travaileth with iniquity, and hath conceived mischief and brought forth falsehood." Almost always as we minister deliverance, if the root is iniquity we will experience what is called travail.

Webster's dictionary defines travail as "very hard work; toil; labor pains." Vine's Expository dictionary of Biblical Word explains one application of travail in these terms: "In Galatians 4:19 the apostle Paul uses it (travail) metaphorically of a travailing on his part regarding the churches of Galatia; his first was for their deliverance from idolatry (vs. 8), now it was for their deliverance from bondage to Judaism." In Galatians 4:11 ("I am afraid for you, lest I have labored for you in vain") the Greek meaning for the word "labored" is "to feel fatigue, to work hard; toil; be wearied."

Travail is commonly thought of in terms of birthing or creating. The Hebrew words for travail in the Old Testament are translated " to bring forth" and "give birth to." Psalm 90:2 likens the Genesis creation to a birthing. In Galatians 4:19 Paul likens his anxiety over the Galatians to the travail of a mother at childbirth, "My little children, for whom I labor in birth again until Christ is formed in you."

In Ezekiel 4:4 we see where God lays the iniquity of the houses of Israel and Judah on Ezekiel. Symbolically Ezekiel was bearing the punishment they were actually suffering.

When the Holy Spirit hovered over Peter, He was bringing forth healing (Acts 5:15); through Elijah it was rain (I Kings 18:45); through Jesus it was salvation (in the Garden of Gethsemane); and through Paul it was maturity (Gal. 4:19).

In <u>Intercessory Prayer</u> by Dutch Sheets, he says, "God wants to go forth and hover around individuals, releasing His awesome power to convict, break bondages, bring revelation and draw them to Himself in order to cause the new birth or new creation in them. Yes, the Holy Spirit wants to birth through us."

In his book, The Mystery of Iniquity Revealed and the Power of Travailing Prayer, Rev. James Wesley Smith says, "Travail is the power of Christ within me drawn out to satisfy the afflicted soul. As He moves from within the depths of me He bears away that which is offensive to Him and unacceptable in His kingdom..." When we bear another's burden we "stake" (**Anechomai**-Greek –Col. 3:13, Eph. 4:2) ourselves to that person and allow the Holy Spirit to "carry away" their weakness or burden.

John 7 speaks of the "river of life" flowing out of us. It is the Spirit of God flowing from us. "We, the church, are God's womb upon the earth. We 'birth' the things of God-we bring forth" (Dutch Sheets, Intercessory Prayer). In Isaiah 53:11 Gods says He wants to "see the travail of His soul" (in the church). He wants to teach us how to set the captives free. Isaiah 58:6-7 speaks of the fast that God has chosen—"to loose the bands of wickedness, to undo the heavy burdens, let the oppressed go free and break every yoke." The word band refers to a fetter and pain. Wickedness is also translated iniquity. Fasting is often related to intercession and thence, often results in travail. This passage illustrates that connection.

Travail cannot and should not be separated from intercession. True intercessors often stumble upon travail without understanding what it is or its function. Prayer is not just a matter of asking the Father to do something, but rather a matter of releasing enough power by the Holy Spirit to get the job done. God's power is unlimited yet He chooses to flow that very power through man.

Elijah had to pray seven times in travail before rain came (I Kings 18). It took Daniel 21 days to get his answer (although God sent an angel the first day he prayed). Even Jesus prayed three hours at Gethsemane. Power was being released in the spirit to cause the breakthrough. Dutch Sheets says, "When we intercede, cooperating with the Holy Spirit of God, it releases Him to go out from us and hover over a situation, releasing His life-birthing energies until that which we are asking for comes forth." When we cooperate with God and pray in accordance with His will it moves God to action unleashing His power to affect a given situation.

We might think of travail as "putting our shoulder to the plow" as we strain with a brother or sister in the Lord so that they might move forward. WE may travail with them as they step into an unfamiliar spiritual area such as a new ministry. Other times, the travail may be for breaking cords of iniquity or breaking the hold of a deeply embedded sin pattern (Jer. 30:5-9)

The most disconcerting elements of travail, to those who observe them, are the intensity of the prayer, the groaning, straining, sobbing and wailing. James 5:16b says, "The fervent, effective prayer of a righteous man avails much." *Effective prayer* is characterized by earnestness, intensity (fervor) and energy. (Elijah prayed earnestly and there was no rain for three and a half years. When he prayed again, the rain fell.) The word fervent in this verse denotes being "red hot" with zeal. It is akin to the jealous anger of a husband or of God or the anger of an enemy. When we hate what God hates we will burn hot and intercede with travail over his children whom the enemy has snared and trapped. Other uses of the word *fervent* indicate, "strained, strenuously and laboring fervently." An example of this type of prayer can be found in Ezekiel 9:4 where the men of Jerusalem "sigh and cry over all the abominations that are done within it (Jerusalem)." This type prayer moves God to act in mercy and love to release His power on our behalf.

A final word before we end this very condensed, brief overview of travail. We are certainly not experts on the subject of travail, but in our experience, any spirit-filled prayer warrior and/or deliverance minister who is willing to be used by God in travail will be able to do so. Some ministers believe travail is a gift or an anointing that must be transferred by prayer and the laying on of hands. We feel no need to debate that opinion but we have seen many operate in travail who have never seen it in operation and had no idea that it had a name other than intense intercession, and have not had the anointing for travail imparted to them by ministers.

As with any intense ministry practice we recommend a "good sense" approach to travail. It is tiring at best and exhausting at worst. In some deliverances one of us may travail while the other does not. If we find ourselves getting too weary we may ask God to pass the travail to one of the other deliverance ministers present— which He does!

In conclusion let us say that we find travail to be a bit mysterious, very powerful and a huge aid in deliverance ministry. It's not something you can fake or "will" to happen. We let God stay in control of when and if travail needs to come forth. We stay available and willing –that is our part.

For more in-depth information on the subject we recommend the following books: Intercessory Prayer by Dutch Sheets, and The Power of Travailing Prayer by James Wesley Smith.

We leave the topic of iniquity and travail with this directive from the book of Joshua:

> "Now therefore fear the Lord, serve Him in sincerity and in truth, and put away the gods which your Fathers served on the other side of the river (Euphrates) and in Egypt. Serve the Lord!
> And if it seems evil to you to serve the Lord, choose for yourselves this day whom you will serve, whether the gods which your Fathers served that were on the other side of the river (Euphrates), or the gods of the Amorites, in whose land you dwell. But as for me and my house, we will Serve the Lord." (Joshua 24:14-15)

Chapter III

Soul Ties

Although the term "soul tie" cannot be found in the Bible, there are several Biblical words that have the same meaning. Some of the more common ones are: "joined" (Ps. 106:28 and Eph. 5:31) "joined and knit together" (Eph. 4:14). "Perfectly joined" (I Cor. 1:10), "yoked" (II Cor. 6:14) and "cleave"(in Gen. 2:24, Gen. 34:3, Ruth 1:14, Deut. 30:20). The word "cleave" in Scripture probably best describes a soul tie. In Hebrew, to cleave is to "bring close together, follow or adhere to one another as with glue" (Deut. 10:20).

If we define the soul as the mind, will, and emotions, we get a clearer understanding of what it is to have an attachment or tie in those areas. In his book Healing through Deliverance, Peter Horrobin defines a soul tie as "a relationship in which we are either rightfully bonded or subject to bondage." There can be Godly soul ties as well as ungodly soul ties. Godly soul ties are God's provision for healthy nurturing within relationships. Ungodly soul ties can lead to sin and misery. We need to understand that a godly soul tie can exist along with an ungodly soul tie. For example, a husband and wife may enjoy a godly relationship until the husband introduces an ungodly soul tie through adultery or physical abuse. In ministry to such a couple, the deliverance minister would break the ungodly soul ties while praying to strengthen the godly ones. An ungodly soul tie is a spiritual bonding empowered by Satan between two people or a person and an animal or possession. An unnatural attachment to a person brought about by a vow can create a soul tie. People often make vows to avoid hurt or pain. They may say, "I'll never be like my Dad," or "No woman will ever hurt me like that again." These type statements become what we call self-fulfilling prophecies. They can "set" a person for or against something. They can also dictate behavior that can hinder one from giving complete allegiance to Jesus.

Healthy soul ties can and should exist between husband and wife, parents and children, friends, church members and pastors, siblings, etc. When the relationship is conducted according to Biblical standards, you can't go wrong. Such ties help to strengthen the relationship in a Godly way.

Good soul ties are founded upon the law of love, which the

57

Bible calls the "law of Christ" (Gal. 6:2) and the "royal law" (James 2:8). The law of Christ is "to bear another's burdens" while the royal law is to "love your neighbor as yourself." The latter is the king of laws encompassing all other commandments dealing with human relationships (SFL).

Frequently, however, relational bonding in the area of the soul is not so healthy and Godly. Perhaps the best way to define ungodly soul ties is to list some examples. Remember that every soul tie is a "conduit." It is like a pipeline transferring demonic characteristics, control and influence.

Examples of Ungodly Soul Ties:

- A strong -willed woman who attempts to control her husband's life

- Domineering, chauvinistic men who demand total submission

- The young man who has never cut the apron strings with his mother

- "Daddy's girl" who continually compares her husband to her father

- The irresponsible young husband who cannot break free from former companions who were evil or immature

- A parent who won't maintain authority over and discipline his children (caused by idolizing children and fearing their reaction; or, being fearful of the child's anger – I Sam. 3:13, Is. 3:4, 12a)

- A friendship that experiences constant betrayal, manipulation, control, etc. yet the friendship is maintained in this unhealthy state (codependency)

- A church pastor who violates the trust of his members (abuse, victimization) and the members seem to be compelled to remain in the abusive church

- When one family or person runs the show at church (control)

- When a congregation of believers treats a person or group as if they are more spiritual or gifted than others

- When a person controls others through prophecy (witchcraft)

- Friendship with an angry person (Prov. 2:2)

- Bonds of secrecy (Luke 12:3)

- Membership in any secret society; secret oaths (fraternities, sororities, masons, Knights of Columbus, etc.). This establishes/uses "bonds of secrecy" to keep members from leaving the "club"

- Membership (current or former) in a legalistic, spiritually dry, or abusive church. Ties are established that either prevent one from leaving or set a pattern of membership in successive abusive/legalistic churches.

- Pornography (soul ties are established with the object of the lust, especially when masturbation is present-Gen. 34:2-3)

- Harmful gossip/slander (agreement by two parties to accomplish evil conspiracies). Often spirits of sedition and division use this soulish bonding to direct the achievement of their demonic goals: church splits and discrediting of spiritual leadership

- Gifts that create an unhealthy obligation (jewelry, money, etc.) Heb. 11:24. Such gifts are designed/desired by the benefactor to create obligation from the recipient to the giver. Resolution: Refuse to receive them or give them back if a sense of obligation or control ("you owe me") is determined to exist.

- Assistance that creates an unhealthy obligation (influential "favors," paying a fine, bailing you out of jail, etc.) This assistance comes with "strings attached" and the giver uses the gift (empowered by a soul tie) to obligate and control the recipient. Solution: Find someone else to assist you.

- Submission to ESP, hypnotism, divination, New Age healing techniques.

- Addictions: dependence on the "friend" who can meet one's need

- Places (unnatural, sentimental attachments to places)

- Pets (overly doting on them, inordinate affection) Such Soul Ties cause one to treat animals as if they were human. There is usually an underlying need for emotional healing present.

- Those who remove our fears (pastors, doctors, attorneys) Ps. 118:8-9, Heb 2:15. We can through a soul tie develop an unhealthy attraction or dependence upon a particular authority figure. This makes us vulnerable to victimization should that person be abusive.

- Abortions. Soul ties need to be severed with the fetus and a process of inner healing applied.

- Deceased people (through guilt, obligation, etc.)

- Oneself (multiple personalities)

- An overprotective spouse, parent, friend

Common spirits associated with ungodly soul ties are fear of rejection, fear of hurt, victimization, deception, dependency, mistrust, hate, jealousy, control and manipulation.

Side Effects of Unhealthy Soul Ties:

- Loss of individuality and self confidence
- Loss of clear thinking in decision making
- Loss of peace
- Loss of ability to really love others
- Loss of spiritual liberty and personal freedom
- Loss of good health
- Loss of closeness to the Father

A helpful question to ask yourself in determining the presence of soul ties is, "Are there any persons in my life that I <u>must</u> consult before making decisions?." If we fear making choices and decisions without this person's input, there is likely to be manipulation present. We're not rejecting the idea of receiving godly counsel or consulting with significant others out of consideration and courtesy. The situation we're defining here involves the element of fear and may include even the most minor decisions.

Types and Forms

The entry points created by ungodly soul ties are many, a number of them having a root in rejection. Our flesh nature often manifests itself in control. We feel secure if we can control others. This desire to control can express itself through manipulation, intimidation and domination. Many family relationships portray this dynamic. Micah 7:6 says, "For the son dishonors the Father, the daughter rises up against her mother-in-law – a man's enemies are the members of his own house."

Family members may exert control and manipulation with tears, the " silent treatment," rage and violence, guilt or shame. If you've experienced these tactics in a relationship, you've experienced witchcraft to some degree. To be free, you must repent of submitting to such control and sever the ungodly linking. It may be necessary to have limited (or even no) contact with the person in question.

A healthy family soul tie will help a child's personality develop properly as they feel the security and love necessary for sound emotional well being. An ungodly soul tie will create over dependence and stifle independence. An example of an ungodly father/son tie is found in Gen. 44:20, 30-31 between Jacob and Benjamin. "His father loves him...his life is bound up in the lad's life and his soul with the lad's soul...When he sees the lad is not with us, he will die." To feel that there is someone you cannot live without is a clear indication of an unnatural soulish attachment.

The strongest soul ties appear to be sexual ones. Soul ties established through ungodly sexual activity are a prime entry point for the demonic. If the sexual contact had a violent aspect (such as molestation or rape), a soul tie invariably develops. The tie attaches through the trauma, fear, pain, anger and shame.

In cases of sexual relationships, involving fornication, adultery or homosexuality, the relationship most often must be terminated (II Cor. 6:17). In II Cor. 6:14, we are warned not "to make alliances with them or come under a different yoke with them, inconsistent with your faith" (Amp.). A sexual union is a spiritual union first and a physical union second. It is no wonder that Satan takes advantage of sexual relationships to develop strong soul ties as well as demonic attachments.

Gary Greenwald in <u>Seductions Exposed</u> says, "God created sexual union to be whole being to whole being; spirit-to-spirit; soul-to-soul and body-to-body." Those who have formed many soul ties through fornication and promiscuity have developed fragmented souls that are scattered among all their sexual partners. They are thus unable to give themselves fully to their spouse. Their thoughts and emotions are being continually drawn back to past lovers (Prov. 6:27-29, 32 and I Cor. 6:18).

Another consequence of illicit sexual intercourse is the possible transference of evil spirits. Often, homosexuals were victims of homosexual molestation as a child or adolescent. That spirit then begins to draw other spirits to itself. These individuals may be dismayed to find homosexuals drawn to them constantly. They may eventually decide their sexual preference is biologically decided for them and thus inevitable.

Looking to the following familiar scripture with soul ties in mind gives us greater insight than before. The Bible declares that in marriage, God "joins a husband and a wife." In Matthew 19:6, Jesus says, "let not man, through divorce, put asunder what God has joined together." A divorce violently tears apart the godly soul tie intended for marriage. Some liken it to ripping apart Siamese twins who share common organs. Even if you separate them surgically and carefully, it is terribly risky and painful for both. We say this not to condemn those who have divorced but to identify why it is so intensely painful.

When we think of soul ties, we tend to think primarily of sexual partners and family members. But friendships can be powerful attachments in the soulish realm for good and bad. A biblical example of a godly soul tie is the relationship between David and Jonathan. It was said that their souls were knit together in love (I Sam. 18:1 AV). Proverbs speaks of the "friend who sticks closer than a brother," and Prov. 17:17 reminds us that a true friend "loves at all times." Just as a true godly friendship can be a blessing, an unholy alliance can be a curse. "Evil companionships corrupt and deprave good manners, morals and characters" (I Cor. 15:33). "Thorns and snares are in the way of the perverse; he who guards his soul will be far from them. Make no friendship with an angry man, lest you learn his ways and set a snare for your soul" (Prov. 22:5,24,25).

Soul ties are always present between church members; and, between church leadership and the church members. Thus, soul ties play a significant role in spiritual abuse. Put simply, when pastors join church members to themselves rather than to Jesus, an unhealthy attachment has taken place. This attachment draws people away from God and to a man. God will not share His glory, nor suffer idolatry without consequence. In some instances, the soul tie is deliberately formed by the spiritual leader, and in others, it is the people who attach to the leader. If the soul tie is strong enough, a cult may be the eventual result. All well-known cults revolve around one central forceful leader (Jim Jones, Charles Russell, Sun Yung Moon, Joseph Smith). The same is so of most false world religions: Buddhism, Islam, and Hinduism, etc.

Inanimate objects may often become the focus of a soul tie. It may come as a surprise to some that we can be soul-tied to an object. Soul ties can be formed with objects through sentimental attachment. Feeling that, "I can't live without it," or, "I just can't part with it," indicates a soul bondage that can lead to idolatry. We often form this type of attachment to family heirlooms or special gifts from loved ones. Nothing is sadder to us than seeing siblings fighting over their deceased parents' inheritance. We tend to agree with Larry Burkett (founder of Crown Ministries-Christian Financial Concepts), who says we should give our children their inheritance while we're still alive so we can see that it's spent properly.

Where we get into real trouble is with objects that are passed down to us that have occult or demonic origins or attachments. A Masonic ring is a good example. Because of what the ring stands for and symbolizes, it is dangerous to have in our possession even if it is kept in a jewelry box. For more insight and information along these lines, see the section in this book in chapter Five titled "Spiritual housecleaning."

A good rule of thumb is to strike a balance between gratitude for God's provision and being content with whatsoever state we find ourselves in. We must hold all "things" with an open hand— even our homes, vehicles, and jewelry. The loss of such items would certainly be impacting, but it should not be devastating. I Peter 5:7 is a familiar scripture, urging us to cast all our care upon Him (Jesus), because He cares for us. Our heavenly Father provides for both our daily needs and our special needs. He warns us not to make riches our refuge (Ps. 52:7) and urges us to put our hope in Him, not in wealth (I Tim. 6:17). If we trust in our riches, we will fall (Prov. 11:28). The more we gain materially, the more we find ourselves beset by things that deplete it. We should enjoy God's material blessings in moderation because we can't take them with us when we leave (die) (Eccl. 5:10-15). (Other scriptures along these lines: Mk. 4:18-19; I Pet. 5:7; I. Jn. 2:15-17). Soul ties with material possessions and wealth hinder us from this. They contribute to the operation of idolatry.

Another object of soul ties is animals. Because animals have souls, we can form soul ties with them. The spectrum can go from false compassion and inordinate affection all the way to bestiality (lying carnally with animals). Frank Hammond says, a soul tie with an animal is a perversion (Gen. 2:20 Amp.).

It's pretty easy to identify soul ties between pet owners and their pets. These animals are often allowed to eat "people food" (sometimes off the same table where the master eats); they sleep on their owner's bed, and are taken along on trips and vacations. They are constantly held and talked to as they perch in their owner's lap at every given opportunity. They are groomed and primped far beyond what's needful for good health and hygiene. They have every deluxe toy, collar, treat, etc. imaginable. Personally, we love animals and have had some great pets over the years. However, an animal should be trained and disciplined. It should not be treated like one of the children. It should not be allowed to control, manipulate or abuse anyone. Animals have their place in our lives. The problem is that, as we do with so many other blessings from God, we develop unhealthy attachments to them. Then when such a pet dies, we are devastated. Some people carry the pet's picture in their wallet. We even knew one couple that paid an extravagant amount of money to have an oil portrait made of "Fido," which they proudly hung in a prominent place in their living room.

Other expressions of soul ties with animals are pet counseling and pet cemeteries. If we do not elevate our pets to human status, then why do we have analysts for dogs and pet cemeteries for cats, dogs, birds, etc.? Something is terribly wrong. And let us add this, if this subject upsets you, we would advise you to take an honest look at your relationships—past and present—with your pets/animals. If you ask God to show you any soul ties, He will. If you feel defensive, you're probably guilty. For comparison, do some research on ancient societies that deified animals. Excavation of their cities often uncovers cemeteries with thousands of mummified animals buried with reverent "honors."

Just when you thought you couldn't be soul-tied to another thing, we identify yet another addition to people and animals. We can be soul-tied to places. Perhaps the best biblical example is Lot's wife as she fled Sodom and Gommorah. "Judgment engulfed her because her affections were with Sodom, not with God" (SFL Bible, note, Gen. 19:26). Some commentaries surmise that she lingered behind. Lot's wife was probably overtaken by fire and brimstone, and her dead body became encrusted with salt. At any rate, her soul tie to her city home cost her even her life. Her fate is a warning to us today (Luke 17:28-33). We can become so attached to a place that we resist God when He tells us it's time to leave. Sometimes, our departure is to spare us, and other times, it's to send us out to another people, place, church, job, neighborhood, etc. We can reject God's perfect will for us and refuse to leave, but be assured that we will also forfeit God's intended blessing. We may continue where we are and live within God's permissive will but we will not experience God's best for us. We may very well suffer harsh consequences as a result.

Another Biblical example of a soul tie of longing for a place is the story of the children of Egypt. After God miraculously spared His people from the horrific oppression of Pharaoh by performing miracle after miracle, they still found themselves longing for home. Exodus 16:3 finds them complaining loudly because the food wasn't as good as the food in Egypt. They accuse Moses of luring them into the wilderness to let them die of hunger. After God feeds them supernaturally with manna and quail, they again complain—this time of thirst. And again, they accuse Moses of bringing them to that place to die. In spite of God's continual miraculous provision, protection and blessing, all the children of Israel could do was whine and pout because they miss the food and drink they "enjoyed" in slavery. Are we very different? We're so spoiled that we grumble and complain when we're in another state or country, and can't find our favorite foods or drinks in the restaurants. There's nothing wrong with partiality to your city or part of the country, but when we refuse to live anywhere else there is something wrong. Our pride in a certain place can make us critical of other places. We must be salt and light everywhere we go—we are ambassadors for Christ. True ambassadors develop a love and appreciation for the place to which they are sent. It truly becomes a home to them. In truth, our home and our place is with God—wherever He may lead us. Soul ties to places sabotage our ability to follow God.

Steps to Freedom and Victory:

❏ Repent to the Lord. Even if the sin was committed in ignorance, it still requires forgiveness. Remember, Satan is a
legalist.

❏ Forgive all others. We must release others from our judgment, remembering that vengeance is the Lord's. He will
repay.

❏ Declare each demonic soul tie destroyed in Jesus' name, and
confess that Satan has no legal right to you in those areas. Be
as specific as possible calling out names as you can. In other
words state the name of the person (or place or thing) with
whom you have the soul tie and speak it canceled.

❏ Confess and cancel any ungodly vows made in relation to
the soul tie.

❏ Command the evil spirits associated with the soul ties to
leave you in the Name of Jesus. The most common ones we
find are: control, manipulation, domination, dependency, co-
dependency, victimization/abuse, persecution and martyr-
dom and longing.

❏ Restore the fragmented soul (use the following prayers).

Prayer to break Soul Ties:
From <u>Healing through Deliverance</u> by Peter Horrobin

<u>General</u>

In the name of the Father, Son and the Holy Spirit. I break all ungodly spirit, soul and body ties that have been established between myself and _____. I sever that tie with the sword of the Spirit and I ask you Lord to remove from me all influence of this person. Draw back to me Lord every part that has been wrongfully tied in bondage to another person.

<u>Sexual</u>

Father, in the name of Jesus, I submit my soul, my desires and my emotions to your Spirit. I confess as sin all my promiscuous, premarital sexual relationships and all sexual relationship outside of marriage. I confess all my ungodly spirit, soul and body ties as sin. I thank you for forgiving me and cleansing me right now!

Father, thank you for giving me the keys of your Kingdom, the keys of spiritual authority. What I bind is bound and what I loose is loosed. In Jesus' name, I ask you to loose me from all soulish ties to past sexual partners and ungodly relationships. Please uproot all the tentacles of sexual bondage, of emotional longings and dependencies, and of enslaving thoughts. I bind, renounce, and resist any evil spirits that have reinforced those soul ties or may have been transferred to me through evil associations.

Please cleanse my soul and help me to forget all illicit unions so that I am free to give my soul totally to you and to my mate. Father, I receive your forgiveness for all past sex sins. I believe I am totally forgiven. Thank you for cleansing me from all unrighteousness. I commit myself totally to you. By your grace, please keep me holy in my spirit, soul and body. I praise you. In Jesus' name, Amen.

Breaking Soul Ties

It is our practice when breaking soul ties to have the client place their hand over their abdomen-navel and the same sex member of our deliverance team places their hand over the client's. Soul ties seem to operate much like an umbilical chord. We then lead them in a prayer to break soul ties. Something miraculous happens in the spirit realm when this ministry takes place. Many times, the person on the other end of the soul tie will have a literal, physical sensation at the same time the soul tie is severed. Most times, that individual is not aware that our client is receiving ministry. They sometimes report aches and pain or nausea at the exact moment the soul tie was severed. It's as if their "lamp" has no "outlet" which they can plug into in order to "light up." It's disconcerting for them.

Just as in all deliverance ministry, the individual on the receiving end is responsible to "walk out" their newfound freedom. Old soul ties can reform and unhealthy new ones can attach. We must change our former patterns of behavior and habits and learn how to have healthy, productive relationships. When that is impossible because of the other person's unwillingness, we can still refuse to allow old, harmful ways of relating to continue. This may require the termination of unhealthy relationships that cannot be redeemed due to refusal to change by the other person(s) involved.

"Squeezing Soul Ties"

Although we do not have the authority (without their consent) to break ungodly soul ties between two other people, we do believe that soul ties can be "squeezed" in the spirit realm through prayer. A warning at the onset—you must have clear direction from the Holy Spirit before praying such a prayer. Otherwise, you'll be bordering on witchcraft. We must never pray a manipulative prayer. Some cases are clear-cut because the Bible calls certain unions sinful (e.g. homosexuality, fornication, adultery, etc.). We can know we're praying God's will when we pray that the sinfulness passing back and forth between two individuals be restricted to a trickle. In our experience, we've seen one or both such persons "come to their senses" after we've prayed to squeeze the ungodly soul ties. After that point, repentance came and the ungodly soul ties were allowed to be broken. We find that these prayers must be prayed on a daily basis to be effective. In such manner we progressively weaken the "ties." Where we must be careful is in gray areas. If I don't like the guy my sister is dating, can I pray and squeeze the soul tie so they'll break up? What about a woman married to a controlling, chauvinistic man—wouldn't it be God's will to dry up that soulish connection that makes her submit to abuse? I repeat. We MUST be clearly led by God's Spirit and His word before we pray such a prayer. The Holy Spirit will give us insight and direction as to when it's allowable to "squeeze" a soul tie.

Demons and Soul Ties

As we have previously stated, the term "soul tie" is not found in the Bible verbatim; yet it quite aptly labels a very real phenomenon that takes place in the spirit realm. It is important to note that demons can and often do enter through ungodly soul ties. When there is an unhealthy bonding, demons can travel through the soul tie. Soul ties act like a 'demonic tube' along which demons can move, or through which power and control can be exercised. Think of it as a type of umbilical cord in the spirit realm. Through this cord, " sustenance" (good or bad) flows. As long as the cord remains intact, there is sustained life on both ends. Blessings can flow through, but so can curses. Just as you need to be prepared for a demonic manifestation when you cut cords of iniquity, you will often see a demonic manifestation as you sever ungodly soul ties. Remember, through soul ties a spiritual channel is formed.

Freedom from Soul Ties

It is such a blessing to see the freedom that comes to those who break soul ties. Many report that they finally "see" the relationships for what they are. This often leads to confirmations, new choices and decisions, and, sometimes, termination of the relationships. The point is, after the unholy alliance is broken, the individual has the power and desire to do God's will in their relationships.

We have to learn to allow the living two-edged sword of God's truth in the Word to be between us and any close relationships—no matter who it is! In Luke 14:26, 33, Jesus urges us to break the unholy alliances and soul ties that keep us in constant turmoil. Don't behave like a thermometer! A thermometer reflects the climate around it. A thermostat <u>controls</u> the climate around it.

Since those we are soul tied to are so influential and important in shaping our lives, we should carefully examine our relationships with others. Our goal should be to have the healthiest relationships possible. Some relationships we cannot choose (like family, co-workers, etc.) but even in those, we can refuse to be victimized or abused or co-dependent and enmeshed. Be a "thermostat" and maintain healthy godly boundaries in your relationships. Set the temperature for the climate of your relationships.

Certainly, in the choice of friends, we should be very particular. The friendship should be balanced in that both individuals give, love, and share. A good friend should encourage you. They should have your best interests at heart and be supportive of your plans and dreams. Ecclesiastes 4:9-12 gives a good discourse on the value of a friend. Overall, the best form of countering/resolving ungodly soul ties is never to form them. We must educate ourselves as to their operation and effect. Then we must be alert to avoid their formation within us. The Word states in III John 2 that God desires for His children to prosper and be in good health even as their **soul** prospers. How can our souls fully prosper when ungodly soul ties connect them to people, places, things or animals bringing inordinate affections? Christ has made us free. Let's not "be entangled again with a yoke of bondage" (Galatians 5:1) through unhealthy, demonic soul ties. Break them and "stand fast in the liberty by which Christ has made (you) free."

Chapter IV

Curses and Inner Vows

The effect of curses is a vital issue that must be addressed if an individual's complete deliverance is to be achieved. This chapter deals with curses, their impact upon an individual, and guidelines for canceling their effects.

Sadly, our western civilization (and the western mindset it produces) tends to deny not only the reality of deliverance but that of curses as well. As Francis Macnutt states: "The idea of being cursed is seen as even more superstitious and primitive, even in many fundamentalist or conservative churches that claim to be based solely on scripture." Many churches have abandoned much of the teaching on blessings as well as curses. This is amazing when these teachings occupy such a central position in the Old and New Testament. Yet, these churches would view such teachings as simplistic, base, and primitive. Such viewpoints could not be more distant from the biblical truth. The principals of blessings and curses are as integral to full scriptural truth as those of deliverance and healing.

Before looking at the biblical record let's examine some definitions of curses from various sources.

Webster's New College Dictionary states: "To curse is to call on God or the God's to send evil or injury down on a person or thing. A profane, obscene or blasphemous oath, imprecation, etc. Evil or injury that seems to come in answer to a curse or any cause of evil or injury. To bring evil or injury upon, to damn. Curse is the general word for calling down evil or injury on someone or something." "Imprecate" and "anathematize" are synonymous with curse and share the meaning of cursing prompted by great anger or abhorrence and the calling down of calamity upon someone especially from a desire for revenge. Anathematize carries the specific reference to a formal utterance by one in spiritual authority to solemnly condemn. Anathema is usually considered the opposite of what would bless someone and is usually devoted to evil.

Merriam-Webster's Collegiate Dictionary states: *Curse* – a prayer or invocation for harm or injury to come upon one; evil or misfortune that comes as if in response to imprecation or as retribution; a cause of great harm or misfortune. To call upon divine or supernatural power to send injury upon; to execrate in fervent and often profane terms and having great evil upon; afflict.

Vines Expository Dictionary states: *Curse* – a malediction, an imprecation uttered out of malevolence or pronounced by God in righteous judgment; as upon a land doomed to barrenness (Hebrews 6:8). *Anathema*: signifies to be devoted to destruction. Retaining the disfavor of Jehovah. To bind by a curse. Something that has been utterly cursed and designated for destruction. Something that has been verbally and formally assigned for evil purposes and declared as fit only for malady.

Frances Macnutt offers these definitions in his book, Deliverance from Evil Spirits: "*to curse* is to call upon divine or supernatural power to send injury upon someone; *to hex* is to affect as if by an evil spell or to practice witchcraft; *to cast a spell* is to repeat an incantation that is meant to have power to influence, charm, or bewitch someone." All three practices are interrelated within the arena of curses.

SCRIPTURAL RECORD

Now, let's examine the basis of scripture in verification of the concept of blessing and cursing. Being "joint heirs with Jesus," God's desire is to bless us as His children. However, we may knowingly or unknowingly commit acts that cause gaps in the protective hedge God provides for us. These acts give Satan legal access to bring evil effect upon us, and hinder God's efforts to bless us.

A foundational scripture for understanding blessing and cursing is Deuteronomy 30:14-20 "But the word is very near you, in your mouth and in your heart that you may do it. See, I have set before you today life and good, death and evil. In that I command you today to love the Lord your God, to walk in his ways and to keep his commandments, his statues and his judgments that you may live and multiply; and the Lord your God will bless you in the land that you go to possess. But if your heart turns away so that you do not hear, and are drawn away, and worship other Gods and serve them, I announce to you today you shall surely perish; you shall not prolong your days in the land which you cross over the Jordan to go in and possess. I call heaven and earth as witnesses today against you, that I have set before you life and death, blessing and cursing; therefore choose life, that both you and your descendents may live; that you may love the Lord your God, that you may obey His voice, and that you may cling to Him, for He is your life and the length of your days; and that you may dwell in the land which the Lord swore to your fathers, to Abraham, Isaac and Jacob, to give them."

As you can see from this foundational passage regarding both blessing and cursing, God's desire is to bless His children. As a father would, He desires the best, and what is good, for his "family." But just like our own children, who may make choices bringing harmful consequences, we may knowingly (or out of ignorance) make choices that bring us harm spiritually. And just as in our life in the natural (where there are potentially harmful individuals and situations), there are forces that exist in the spiritual dimension that are pre-determined to bring us harm because we are God's children.

Scripturally, the reason for these spiritual dynamics at work in our lives originates in the actions, and subsequent consequences, of Adam and Eve. Eve's falling prey to the snare of Satan's temptation and lies, and Adam's irresponsibility and abdication of authority, brought sin and consequential curses into humanity's existence. For Eve: There would be multiplied sorrow related to conception; pain in childbirth, and submission to the husband's rule, (Genesis 3:16). The Spirit Filled Life Bible notes: The woman is not directly cursed but comes under God's general curse. There became a major marring of her appointed roles of wife and mother with great suffering in maternity. For Adam: Much toil to bring forth food from the "cursed" ground. This toil will be very strenuous with much sweat and last for the whole of Adam's life. Again, the Spirit-Filled Life Bible notes that Adam is spared a direct cursing, his major mistake being that he heeded the voice of his wife rather than the voice of God. As the one having the greatest responsibility, his sentence is the longest and the most comprehensive. His role as laborer/provider being marred, his work will forever be completed with difficulty. This lifelong toil will then end in physical death. The serpent: used by Satan as a "corporeal" instrument for Satan to work through in tempting Eve, the serpent comes under a direct curse from God. In

Genesis 3:14 God says to the serpent, "You are cursed more than any beast of the field. On your belly you shall go, and you shall eat dust all the days of your life. And I will put enmity between you and the woman...between your seed and her seed; He shall bruise you head and you shall bruise his heel."

This last, speaks prophetically of the war that is initiated between Satan and God's "seed," the woman (and later Jesus). It reveals that there will be mutual warfare resulting in bruising affected on both sides. However, ultimately, Satan's authority/head-ship (his head) will be crushed (bruised) by Jesus, the seed of the woman. Jesus is referred to as the last Adam. In order to free us from this "generational curse" Jesus was "bruised" for our iniquity (Isaiah 53:5). This was discussed at length in the chapter on "Iniquity."

In doing this, Jesus reversed the curse upon mankind resulting from the fall of Adam. We still experience a limited physical lifetime but we can live that life in victory over curses and, through Jesus, receive eternal life. The Spirit Filled Life Bible comments: "In its most specific sense the Lord Jesus had trampled Satan at the cross. In it's wider sense, the human race will eventually completely triumph over the evil one. Romans 16:20 states: " and the God of peace will crush Satan under your feet shortly." "Crush in the Strong's Concordance (#4937), **Suntribo**, means "To trample upon, break into pieces, shatter, bruise, grind down, smash. This refers to Genesis 3:15." Our victory is a continuation of Christ's victory on Calvary when he bruised the head of the serpent. **Suntribo** points to present victories over the powers of darkness as well as the ultimate destruction of Satan's kingdom at Christ's second coming. Until then, parts of

Satan's demonic strategy is to either cause us to commit some act that will bring the consequences of God's discipline against us or to launch direct curses against us himself. This he does in a variety of ways that we will discuss. Usually, Satan maneuvers us into some position that makes us vulnerable to curses through gaps created in our "protective hedge." Ecclesiastes 10:8 says, "He that diggeth a pit shall fall into it; and who so breaketh a hedge, a serpent shall bite him.

If we are not careful to maintain our walls of defense (discussed in detail in "Maintaining your Deliverance," chapter 7), Satan will send demonic serpents to bite (or bruise) us. Many times this will be in the form of curses. Let's look now at what some types or kinds of curses are.

Rebecca Brown in her book, Unbroken Curses, identifies three types of curses:

1. Curses from God
2. Curses from Satan (and his servants) with the legal right to curse
3. Curses from Satan (and his servants) without the legal right to curse

She states in amplification of points 2 and 3 that Satan is a legalist. She explains that we often give Satan a legal right before God to attack us by knowingly and unknowingly opening a spiritual "doorway" that gives him an access point into our lives. Quoting Rebecca Brown: "Most curses come from this source. It is only as that legal right is removed through repentance and cleansing that we then break a curse."

An example describing this process (as related in Unbroken Curses) is the account of Israel's first defeat at Ai due to Achan's sin. In the defeat at Ai, thirty-six of Joshua's men were killed as the army of Israel fled in defeat. These men had done nothing wrong themselves and were being obedient to God. Yet they died in battle as a result of their army's defeat that was a result of one man's disobedience/sin.

Why? As Joshua asked, "alas Lord, God, why have you brought this people over the Jordan at all; to deliver us into the hand of the Amorites, to destroy us?" and God answered, "Israel has sinned, and they have also transgressed my covenant which I commanded them. For they have even taken some of the accursed things....and they have also put it among their own baggage... neither will I be with you anymore unless you destroy the accursed from among you"(Joshua 7:10-12). Note how God speaks to Joshua of Israel's sin as in the plural.

It was one man, Achan, who sinned by disobeying God. Yet,

the entire people of Israel were cursed. "Accursed objects" in the camp gave Satan and his servants legal right to attack and defeat the children of Israel. This is why the sins of a ministry within a given body of believers may bring negative consequences upon the body as a whole. If not identified and corrected the "curses" that result can hinder greatly the plan and purpose of God for that specific fellowship of Christians. They may bring effect upon the entire body. Just as God told Ezekiel regarding Israel, "Again when a righteous man turns from his righteousness and commits sin, and I lay a stumbling block before him, he shall die; because you did not give him warning, he shall die in his sin, and his righteousness which he has done shall not be remembered; but his blood I will receive at your hand. Nevertheless if you warn the righteous man that the righteous should not sin, and he does not sin, he shall surely live because he took warning; also you will have delivered your soul." Ezekiel 3:20-21

Our disobedience of God causes us not only to sin but it gives Satan a legal right to assault us/curse us. God is a completely just God. If we give Satan a legal right to attack us, God will not interfere. Often we believe that a "just" God <u>will</u> interfere. Often we believe that a just God would not hold us accountable for something we did out of ignorance. We think "He will not allow a curse to have effect upon us as a result of something we did not know was wrong."

Derek Prince states in his book <u>Blessing or Curse: You can choose</u>, "multitudes of people today, many of them churchgoers, through ignorance have trespassed in the area of the occult and have become involved in sin. Until they recognize the true nature of what they have done, they must continue under the shadow of the curse God has pronounced on all who turn away from him to false Gods. Furthermore, the same shadow may continue to rest over the lives of the next four generations of their descendants."

Prince states that Christians often respond, when confronted with such issues, that they didn't know they were doing anything wrong. He points out I Timothy 1:13-15 where Paul describes himself as the "chief of sinners" for sins he had committed out of "ignorance in unbelief." Prince states that ignorance does not absolve us from the guilt of our sins, but that it may dispose God to show us mercy if we turn to him.

The truth is that God has established his word as our guide and God holds us accountable for all that is in it. Satan knows God's word also and uses it to justify legal ground to attack us even if we are not aware that it's wrong (for example, to consult a psychic or Ouiji board).

Such activities give curses access to our lives until, through knowledge/revelation, we learn to cancel their effect. Rebecca Brown says that the first two types of curses can be broken only after repentance from the sins responsible for bringing the curse to bear (Joshua 7:12-13). The third type of curse listed may be easily broken through confessing in Jesus as our Lord and Deliverer.

Additionally, Rebecca Brown states that there are two purposes for curses. First, Satan uses curses against us to bring us injury, loss, destruction and even death. Second, God uses curses as consequences, in order to gain a person's attention to turn them from evil ways and toward God (thus purifying their life). If the person does not respond to this they may eventually be destroyed through tragedy or death (this can be effected upon a Christian who becomes deeply backslidden). I Corinthians 5:4-5 states " deliver such a one to Satan for the destruction of the flesh, that his spirit may be saved in the day of the Lord Jesus."

Rebecca Brown states further that curses from Satan always involve demonic spirits. The curse is the sending mechanism and the demons bring about the fulfillment of the curse. She says that types of curses from God may include direct injury and destruction through catastrophic weather, disease, lack of fertility and economic collapse. God may also bring people who are Satan's servants to conquer and destroy-such as invading foreign armies, etc.

Francis Macnutt in his book Deliverance from Evil Spirits classifies curses as "those that come on us from outside sources," and, "those that come on us through some present cause." He categorizes curses from the outside as, primarily, curses descending upon us from past generations (iniquities)/ancestral sins.

We have covered the subject of "Iniquity" in depth in chapter 2. Francis Macnutt lists three main "roots" of generational curses:

1. Family involvement in the occult- especially warlocks/witches in the family linkage
2. If the family has been cursed by someone else.
3. If the family has been deeply involved in ungodly spiritual activity.

Macnutt states that the result of these ancestral curses is to block the family from receiving God's full blessings through multiple disasters targeting the family. He notes that the Greek goddess, Nemesis, was assigned to "haunt" particular families to pursue and destroy them.

Let's now turn to what Francis Macnutt calls curses from "present causes." These, simply put, are curses resulting from sources existing and occurring in our present life. We will cover types of curses from present causes as we discuss the sources of curses. Francis MacNutt determines their origin first in the activities of occult groups who target Christians/Christian leaders for curses; second in the acceptance (even out of ignorance) of occult practices within traditional religions; and third in various cultural teachings/practices rooted in the occult or superstition.

The most obvious of these would be curses directed by or originating from a network of witches and Satanists. Not only does Satan have a host of demonic beings to do his bidding (Ephesians 6:12), but he has human devotees as well (witches, warlocks, mediums, Satanists, occultists etc.). In various cultures those most skilled in Satanic "arts" and practices may be called witch doctor, medicine man, shaman, tohanga, wizard kahuna, priest or priestess. These human practitioners regularly direct curses at Christians, ministers, Christian leaders, churches and ministries.

Derek Prince states that this process involves fasting and satanic prayers and witchcraft spells cast for:

1. The rise of the Antichrist.
2. The fall of ministers, leaders and missionaries.
3. Destruction of ministries and works of God
4. Complacency and apathy among Christians; pastors seeking "peace" despite the presence and practice of sin; churches to

reject Full Gospel truths/messages.
5. Christians to cease fasting and prayer
6. Christians to ignore the gifts of the Holy Spirit.

Francis Macnutt, in his book on deliverance also identifies Satanists/occult involvement as a source of curses. He lists the following ways Christians may come under their effect.

1. Targeted by covens/occult groups. This may result in depression, illness, obsessive desires, sexual sin.
2. Occult elements in traditional religions. Many of these mix moral teaching with demonic practice. It should be noted that practices such as Yoga and martial arts cannot be "Christianized."
3. Accepting certain teachings, philosophies, etc. as "good" simply because they are spiritual. The flip side of this "over acceptance" is to dismiss the existence of the demonic realm as primitive superstition.
4. Acceptance of cultural teachings and beliefs that have origins in superstition.
5. Direct practice of superstitions, astrology, psychic "reading" etc.

To illustrate how these groups project curses at Christians, Derek Prince categorizes the traditional practice of satanic arts into three broad areas. One is the "Power" branch that includes the practice of witchcraft/Satanism and seeks to bring effect upon Christians through rebellion, manipulation, intimidation, and domination. A second area he terms the "Knowledge" branch. This is rooted in various forms of divination such as soothsaying, palm reading, fortune telling, new age practices, E.S.P., astrology etc. Finally, a third category of demonic practices comes under the branch of "Physical Objects." This branch utilizes things like tarot cards, crystal balls, new age crystals, Ouiji boards, etc. Included in this list would be rosary beads like those used in Catholic prayer. These are patterned after Hindu "Malas" which are strings of beads used as an aid in reciting a Mantra. This branch may overlap or combine with either of the other two branches.

So then, how do we as Christians and churches counter such satanic activity? Derek Prince identifies several Christian actions that will serve to release God's favor over his people. These will facilitate God's active stand against Satan's attack toward any given body of believers. These Christian actions reach out to God and prompt His heart of love for Hs people to initiate an active defense of His children. It releases into the heavenlies the marching cry of Moses, "Let God arise and His enemies be scattered. Qumah Adonai." It brings about God's corresponding action on behalf of His people.

These actions are:

1. The people must be moving in the fulfillment of God's plan for them.
2. Christians must be guided by the "cloud by day" and "fire by night" in this day represented by the Holy Spirit (Romans 8:14).
3. We, as a nation, must be under God's discipline/direction, with God-appointed leaders and God-given laws - - crucial in light of terrorist activity in this historical time.
4. Our relationships must be ordered according to a divine pattern. We must exhibit a divinely harmonious pattern of relationships. Numbers 24:5-6 is a visionary description of this.

Derek Prince states, "We must become a community divinely ordered, disciplined and guided, living in harmony with one another. Christians who are living in discipline and obedience to God and in harmony with each other can look to God for protection against Satan. Christians who are undisciplined, disobedient and out of harmony will forfeit their claims on God's protection and blessing." Such Christians will, as a result, become vulnerable to Satan's attack in the form of curses.

Derek Prince states further, "In the strategy of Satan against God's people he first launches a frontal assault. If and when that should fail he will try indirect, deceptive tactics to entice, through subtlety, the body of believers into immorality and idolatry." Satan reasons "Why pronounce curses on a people who have brought God's judgment on themselves through disobedience and corporate sin?"

Remember, as stated previously, that ignorance does not absolve us from the consequences of sin. Satan and his demons have no regard for your motives for occult or sinful practices. Satan is a legalist. He is looking for an "in road," or a legal right, to oppress you and bring curses upon you. Even innocent "dabbling" in horoscopes, Ouiji boards etc. will give Satan and his followers an avenue of approach to oppress and curse us. Involvement in the occult, even by ignorance, is always connected to worship of false Gods (and thereby expressly forbidden by God). We are seeking knowledge through alternate means (divination) that should only come from God.

There is resident within such practices a desire to control other people or circumstances. Seeking power through supernatural means other than God is witchcraft and/or spiritualism. As Derek Prince states, "Such involvement with spiritualism invariably curses the descendants as well as the person directly involved."

Remember, I Peter 5:8 states: "Be sober, be vigilant. For your adversary the devil goes about as a roaring lion, seeking whom he may devour. Resist him, steadfast in the faith." One means of resisting Satan and avoiding his curses is to be knowledgeable regarding his "access" points.

Following are typical means Satan uses to unleash curses against us.

1. Various symbols of the Satanic, Demonic or Pagan religions. These include hex signs like those used on barns/houses such as in Pennsylvania Dutch culture; five pointed stars called "Pentacles" or "Pentagrams" used by Satanists and witches and also in the "Eastern Star"(female branch of the masons). A number of Masonic Symbols are occult in origin. We will discuss free masonry in more detail in a subsequent section. Other well-known occultic signs are Irish Shamrocks, Lucky Stars and Astronomical signs (used in astrology), Unicorns, Dream Catchers (American-Indian

85

spiritualism), Kokopeli (American-Indian spiritualism), Yin Yang (Eastern mysticism sign of universal energy/force flows) and lightening bolts. Numerous books contain detailed lists of such objects. See the bibliography for a list of some of these.

2. Objects that may become cursed through proximity to a person engaged in sinful or occultic activity, or who are under demonic influence themselves. Jewelry inherited in a family is a typical means of transferring curses from generation to generation. Also various items of clothing and furniture: Grandmother's coat/shawl or comforter, Grandfather's bed or bedroom suite. Previous owners could have been involved in any number of addictive and compulsive or sinful activities (demons of sexual sin can inhabit a bed for example). Infirmity spirits are also typically transferred through various pieces of furniture or items of clothing that were owned by relatives (especially if they died from sickness or disease). Soul ties are often maintained through gifts or items of clothing received from someone who is/was controlling, dominating or manipulating.

    Children's toys, if occult in origin, will bring curses to the child and home. For an in-depth study on that topic read <u>Turmoil in the Toy Box</u> by Phil Phillips. In all of this we remind you of Achan who brought defeat to the entire army by hiding cursed objects in his tent (Joshua 7:16-26).

3. Cursed places may also loose demonic attack against individuals who inhabit them. When a violent crime or tragic death occurs in a house, the demons present in the person may remain to dwell in the home. This is what many believe is a ghost. In reality, it is a demonic "familiar spirit" that has inhabited the person and knows how to mimic them in appearance and sound. Be aware that human spirits do not roam the earth or remain in a building as ghosts. A human spirit, upon the death of the person, goes to heaven or hell, depending upon the person's salvation or lack thereof. Mediums who *appear* to contact "Uncle Bob" or "Aunt Bess" are actually communicating with that person's *famil-*

iar spirit (who by the way, has no contact with them whatsoever in the afterlife).

Locations where Satanic rituals or occult practices have taken place (especially repeatedly) will also be cursed and maintain the presence of demonic spirits. Thus anything built on such sites (or any activity conducted there) is vulnerable to demonic attack/operations. Many homes and subdivisions built over pagan burial sites will experience demonic activity as a result.

4. Oaths spoken by an individual may bring them under the effect of curses and demonic influence. Matthew 5:34-36 and James 5:12 forbid such oaths. It is a form of idolatry and can establish soul-ties with the people and organizations that administer the oath.

Many who have been in fraternities or sororities or various civic lodges have spoken such oaths. Organizations such as the Masons and Shriners require members to swear oaths. Other sources of such oath swearing are the Hippocratic oath and even the Order of the Arrow (a service branch of the Boy Scouts of America).

Regarding the Masonic Lodge and Shriners, these are one of the largest groups today (in terms of members) that are accepted as beneficial to society; and yet, have roots of the occult in their origins and practices. For an in-depth study of the Masons read: Free Masonry: An Interpretation by Martin Wagner or Ron Campbell's book, Free from Masonry. These thoroughly document the fact that the Masonic lodge is steeped in occult practice and ritual (particularly Egyptian). It is not an organization that is conducive to Christianity in spite of its portrayal as a benefactor of society. Masonry is, at its core belief system, a false religion—-complete with it's own revelations, temples, altars, religious symbols, confession of faith, priests and false God (called a "creative principle," "the great architect"). Some researchers say this false God named "Jubelo" is a composite of Jehovah, Baal and Osisris: Ju-bel-o.

Tragically, many Christians, as well as ministers, are duped into membership believing the Masonic Lodge is a harmless and beneficial expression of community service.

And, it should be likewise noted, its sister lodge, the Shriners, is an equally deceptive and spiritually harmful organization as well as its female counterpart, the Eastern Star.

To be free from the effect of involvement in such groups one must make a verbal renunciation and repentance to God for involvement in the group; and, then, one must get rid of/destroy all materials, symbols, books, etc. acquired through the association. Derek Prince calls them "marks of your association." Some ministers advise a formal letter of resignation from the Lodge that includes a statement of repentance and truth-telling be sent to the past member's Lodge.

5. Involvement in obvious cults (and "cultish" religious groups) can bring curses upon an individual. Groups such as the Mormons (Church of Jesus Christ of Later Day Saints), Jehovah Witnesses (Watch Tower Society), Unification Church (Rev. Sun Myung Moon), Unitarian Universalist Church, Scientology (L. Ron Hubbard and Dianetics), and, the Way International, to name only a few, do not practice the tenets of Orthodox Christianity and deny various fundamental Biblical truths. Involvement with such groups will leave an individual open to curses as discussed here.

Additionally, certain denominational groups though not considered cults, are prone to intense legalism and strict control that may leave a person a victim of spiritual abuse. Examples of such would be "oneness" Pentecostalism (U.P.C.) and Seventh Day Adventism as well as certain "Primitive Holiness" church groups.

Cults, at times, may develop from churches that slip into legalism and intense control by a dynamic leader. Examples would be Jim Jones and his "Peoples Church," David Koresh and "The Branch Davidians" and Herbert Armstrong's "Worldwide Church of God" (though this last group has undergone major positive reform following Armstrong's death). The first two groups ended in terrible tragedy and mass suicide.

6. It is sad to need to include this last pathway for cursing but it is a subtle and rapidly growing trend among churches and Christians. We refer to the growing practice of churches hosting and promoting martial arts "clubs" and yoga meetings. This is conducted with the mindset that only the physical fitness aspects are practiced.

This is clear deception. These oriental practices have at their roots Eastern Mystical belief systems. They cannot be separated from them with only the "non religious" aspects adhered to for physical benefit. Calling these groups "Christian" does not negate what they inherently are: forms of Eastern Religion. As the old adage goes: "If it walks like a duck and quacks like a duck, it's a duck." Yet countless Christians are exposing themselves to practices that can bring them under the effects of a curse due to their involvement with forbidden occult practices (i.e. yoga and marital arts).

Self imposed curses and inner vows

Another means of bringing evil effect upon oneself is through the means of spoken "self curses" and by inner vows.

Scripture is very clear regarding the power of our words. The main vehicle for both blessings and curses is our words. God has given us a power, in His image, to speak a blessing or speak a curse. Remember how the book of Genesis accounted God's creating all things… "then God said, Let there be light, let there be a firmament, let the waters gather," etc. God said and creation <u>was</u>.

In like manner we can speak evil or good with consequential effect, corresponding to our words. These words may be directed upon ourselves as well as upon someone else.

Words spoken evilly against our own self form the base upon which "self curses" may operate.

Scripture speaks to this: "Death and life are in the power of the tongue" (Proverbs 18:21). "Even so the tongue is a little member and boasts great things. See how great a forest fire a little fire kindles!…with it we bless our God and Father, and with it we curse men, who have been made in the likeness of God. Out of the same mouth proceed blessing and cursing. My brethren, these things out not to be so" (James 3:5-10).

Through various circumstances and experiences, often reinforced by others opinions, we develop mindsets that lead us to pronounce self-curses, inner vows and judgments upon ourselves.

A "self curse" usually results from an observation about ourself arising from a negative experience or comment from others (especially parents). Our physical characteristics or physical/mental actions can lead to such curses upon ourselves as: "I am so stupid. I can't speak well. I am such a klutz. I am so uncoordinated. I hate my skinny, unshapely legs. I hate my red, brown, black, blond, straight, curly, etc. hair. I hate my big nose, large lips or big/small feet. I hate my large breasts. Men stare at them. I hate my small bosom. I never attract guys."

In our minds, often reinforced by the cruel words of others, we just don't (and never will) "measure up" to self-imposed standards. "Inner vows" often result from such experiences and shackle us for life to subsequent experiences that bring continual pain and emotional harm ("soul hurts" or "soul wounds").

Peter Horrobin in <u>Healing through Deliverance</u> describes Inner Vows as arising from a self curse. He says, "An inner vow is actually a self curse in which we vow not to allow (harmful) things to happen again, no matter what. Inner vows cause us to live our life in a way that is contrary to God's plans and purposes. We limit our potential mentally, emotionally and spiritually when we make an inner vow. In essence we invite the enemy to control us in that area. Inner voices state, "I'll never forgive (myself) (God) (them) etc. I'll never speak to _____ again. I'll never let anyone hurt me again. I'll never trust (leaders), (teachers), (pastors), (women/men), etc. again."

In regards to inner vows, John Sandford says in <u>Deliverance and Inner Healing</u>, "Inner vows are determinations that become 'computer programs' within our nature. They energize our brains to produce repeatedly whatever the vow calls for. These vows are called 'inner' because we make them as children and then forget them. They actually have more power by virtue of their hiddenness. Inner vows resist change. We can determine with our will to act differently, but these vows haul us adamantly back to habitual practices. We can receive Jesus as Lord and Savior, but find ourselves defeated continually."

In his book <u>Blessing or Curse</u>... Derek Prince lists 7 effects of curses and examples of self-curses that bring the effect to an individual. These follow:

1. Mental or emotional breakdown
   "It's driving me crazy!"
   "I can't take it anymore."

2. Repeated or Chronic Sickness (especially Generational)
   "Whenever there's a bug, I catch it."
   "I'm sick and tired of ..."
   It runs in the family. Guess I'm next."
   "Everyone in our family gets _____ at my age."

3. <u>Barrenness, Miscarriages, Female Problems</u>
   "I'll never get pregnant!"
   "I've got the 'curse' again, (sigh)."
   "I am afraid I'll lose this one, too."
   "All the women in my family have problems with
   _____. Me too."

4. <u>Marital Breakdown</u>
   "I always knew my husband/wife would leave me."
   "Our family always fights like cats and dogs."

5. <u>Financial Difficulty</u>
   "We never make ends meet."
   "Our family has always had poverty."
   "I can't afford to tithe."

6. <u>Accident Prone</u>
   "I knew there was trouble ahead."
   "I am always so clumsy."
   "If anyone will have an accident I will."

7. <u>Suicide and Untimely Death</u>
   "What's the use of living?"
   "Over my dead body!"
   "This is killing me."
   "I'd rather die than _____."
   "All the men/women in our family die at an early age."

To cancel the effects of inner vows and self-imposed curses, Francis Macnutt says, "**Repent** of what we have said. **Renounce** what we have done. – **Turn** from it."

Derek Prince says to be free from such curses we must "Repent-Revoke-Replace." He states that , First, we must recognize that we have made a negative confession about ourselves and we must repent of it. Second, we must revoke it, that is, "unsay" or cancel it. Third, we must replace our previous wrong confession with the right one.

<u>Soulish Talk and Soulish Prayers</u>

Derek Prince, in his book <u>Blessings and Curses</u>, identifies two other ways Christians may bring curses upon themselves. These are by means of Soulish Talk and through Soulish Prayers.

In essence, Soulish Talk and Soulish Prayers are those rooted in or directed by what scriptures term "Psuchikos" or "of the soul and the senses: sensual as opposed to spiritual."

Prince states, "Before Adam's fall man's spirit related upward to God and downward to his soul (man being a tripartite being: Body, Soul, Spirit). God communicated directly with man's spirit and through that spirit with that person's soul. As a result of the fall of Adam, man's spirit was cut off from God and the soul began to express itself independently of the spirit, seeking preeminence."

In the New Testament, the term "soulish" denotes the activity of man's soul when it is not in proper relationship to the spirit. This creates a condition in man that is in opposition to God's highest will for us.

I Corinthians 2:14-15 describes this condition as follows: "But the natural man does not receive the things of the spirit of God, for they are foolishness to him; nor can he know them, because they are spiritually discerned. But He who is spiritual judges all things, yet He himself is rightly judged by no one." Jude 19 adds this: "These are sensual persons, who cause divisions, not having the spirit."

From these passages we observe that "soulish" (natural) and "sensual" are opposite terms from "spiritual." The person who is "spiritual" operates directed by God's will through knowledge revealed by God to their spirit. This is "supernatural." The "natural," "soulish" and "sensual" person is out of harmony and agreement with God's will for them. They cannot comprehend fully the supernatural.

As Prince says, "A soulish person will endeavor to understand spiritual truth by means of the soul and the natural (which they cannot do.) The spiritual person, however, is united with God in the spirit. They are thereby able to comprehend and receive spiritual insight directly from God."

Prince says that this results in the following condition for the soulish Christian. "Taken together these passages (of scripture) present a consistent picture of a person described as 'soulish'. He is apparently one who associates with the church and wears a veneer of spirituality. At the same time, his soul is not rightly related to God through his spirit. In spite of the faith he professes, he is in reality a rebel, out of harmony with God and the people of God. He is incapable of apprehending spiritual truth. His rebellious attitude and conduct grieve the spirit of God and cause offense in the body of Christ."

The core problem in this condition is one of rebellion. In some way this person described is disobedient and rejects God's authority. This restricts them to the realm of earthly values and motives (in the arena of the soul) and hinders their spirit from connecting with God and the things of heaven. This produces a corrupted form of demonically influenced, counterfeit wisdom that is expressed in the words of Christians as, "soulish talk." Derek Prince explains it thus, "At the same time, his soul-out of harmony with God-is exposed by its rebellion to the influence of demons, which his blunted 'spiritual' senses cannot identify. The outcome is a form of wisdom that appears to be 'spiritual' but is, in fact, 'demonic'." When expressed verbally, the result is "soulish talk" which, as Jude 16-19 states, results in grumbling, complaining, and walking according to one's lusts and divisions. Such was the case of the Hebrews under Moses. They were soulish and lusted for things left behind in Egypt. Ultimately it cost them all, except Joshua and Caleb. They alone were allowed to enter the Promised Land.

The book of James, for the most part, devotes itself to addressing this form of corrupt, counterfeit, demonic wisdom that is resident within the words used by some Christians. It's object will be other Christians and causes the effect of curses both upon the person spoken about and the person speaking.

Titus 3:2 urges us to "speak evil of no one." The term "no one" includes all others, including non-Christians as well as Christians. The word, in Greek, for "to speak evil" is **blasphemos** from which we get "Blaspheme." Are you aware, then, that we can Blaspheme (speak evil) against not only God but other Christians and all others. Christians are expressly forbidden to do so. Doing so will result in the bringing of curses upon one's own self. Further, Christians are directed to refrain not only from evil talk (blasphemy) but any harmful talk (even truth) against one another.

James 4:11 directs that we "do not speak evil about one another, brethren." "Evil" in this case is the Greek word Katalalo which means to speak against another, even the truth. This, then, leads us into instructions against such talk that would be defined "gossip." As Christians, to gossip is to engage in soulish talk and place us under the effect of curses ourselves. Thus, soulish talk includes blasphemy, speaking against others, gossip, and all critical talk.

In summation, Derek Prince warns: "The danger of this kind of talk is brought out by the descending order of adjectives in James 3:15: 'earthly, soulish, demonic'." Christians who permit themselves to gossip about other people are directly disobedient to God's word..before they realize what is happening, they have slipped from the 'earthly' to the 'soulish'.. to the 'demonic'. (Their words) are in fact channels through which demonic forces are directed against other members of Christ's body. The believer who is guilty of this kind of speech actually defiles both himself and that part of the body of Christ to which he is related. We would do well to heed the warning presented in this vital revelation expressed in Derek Prince's insightful teaching. In our ministry we are deeply grateful for his discernment and expression of such truth!

Soulish Prayers

One final source of curses is what we call "Soulish Prayers." These are those prayers spoken out of soulish intent, almost always by those soulish Christians depicted in the last category ("Soulish Talk"). Again, we thank Derek Prince for his teaching on this issue, which we summarize here.

These prayers, like soulish words, flow from a motive of accusation and control, as well as envy, self-seeking, resentment, anger, bitterness, criticism, false judgement, and self-righteousness. Those individuals influenced in particular by the demonic groups (see appendix) of Bitterness, Retaliation, Rebellion, Control, Accusation and Religious Spirits, will pray destructive, curse-filled, soulish prayers.

Godly prayers would be in keeping with those contained in Gal. 6:1-5; Eph. 1: 15-20; Eph. 3:14-19; Phil. 4:8-9; and Col. 1:9-12. Soulish prayers in contrast are condemning, dominating, and manipulating. They follow the lead of Satan who is the "accuser of the brethren." Such prayers carry poison and are laden with curses.

If one is guilty of such prayers, they must repent, seek God's forgiveness, and possibly that of those affected by the prayer. Then, they must be on guard to renounce all future temptation toward such praying.

Most importantly, individuals caught in the syndrome described by James, Chapter 3 (that leads to soulish talk and prayer) should seek earnestly to develop a spirit directed soul (mind, emotions, will). They must endeavor to allow the Holy spirit to transform their mind and bring maturity to the soul as stated in Romans 12:2, "And do not be conformed to this world, but be transformed by the renewing of your mind, that you may prove what is that good and acceptable and perfect will of God."

Categories and Causes

In closing this section regarding causes and sources of curses we offer these excellent lists compiled by Derek Prince in his book Blessing or Curse. We heartily recommend this book as an in depth study on the topic of curses. It is one of the most comprehensive to date and is an essential reference for ministry. These lists are a composite of individual chapters in his book. This list is in two parts. The first contains general causes of curses and part two lists "curses from other causes" (or from other sources) mentioned in Scripture.

Part I

1. Acknowledging/Worshiping false Gods
2. Involvement with the occult
3. Disrespect for parents
4. All oppression or injustice against the weak and helpless

5. All illicit or unnatural sex acts
6. Anti-Semitism
7. Legalism, carnality, apostasy
8. Theft or perjury
9. Withholding money, material resources from God
10. Words spoken by those in spiritual/relational authority
11. Self imposed curses
12. Pledges/Oaths of allegiance to ungodly associations
13. Curses proceeding from servants of Satan
14. Soulish talk
15. Soulish prayers

Part II (curses for other causes)

1. Curse on the people of Menoz in not joining Barak as the leader of God's army (Judge 5:23)
2. Curse by Jotham on those who murdered the sons of Gideon (Judge 9:57)
3. Curse on Jezebel for withcraft/immorality (I Kings 9:34)
4. Curse on those rejecting God's commandments due to pride (Psalm119: 21)
5. Curse on the house of the wicked (Proverbs 3:33)
6. Curse on the earth due to defilement of its inhabitants who change and transgress God's laws/covenant (Isaiah 24:6)
7. Curse on the people of Edom for enmity and treachery against Israel (Isaiah 35:5)
8. Curse on false prophets who promise peace to people who disobey God (Jerimiah 29:18)
9. Curse on false prophets who commit immorality (Jerimiah 29:22)
10. Curse on Israelites who went to Egypt in defiance of God's warning (Jerimiah 42:18)
11. Curse on anyone who fails to carry out God's judgment on His enemies (Jerimiah 48:10)
12. Curse on the blessings of priests who reject God's discipline (Mal. 2:2)
13. Curse on "goat" nations who show no mercy to brothers of

Jesus (Matt. 25:41)
14. Curse on people who are taught the word of God but do not produce fruit (Heb. 6:8)
15. Curse on false teachers guilty of covetousness, deception and immorality (II Peter 2:14)

Effects of Curses

We now come to the specific effects of curses. We list here a compilation from several sources, again to provide a more comprehensive and cross-referenced presentation. A review of these effects may help to provide a fairly accurate determination as to whether or not one is experiencing the results of curses. Bill Subritzky in Demons Defeated lists six "results of curses":

1. Mental and emotional breakdown
2. Chronic sickness
3. Miscarriages or female problems
4. Breakdown of marriage: family alienation
5. Financial drain
6. Accidents

Derek Prince offers this list of the indications that a curse is at work. He states, "The presence of only one or two problems would not necessarily be sufficient, by itself, to establish conclusively the working of a curse. But when several of the problems are present, or when any one of them tends to recur repeatedly, the probability of a curse increases proportionately. In the last resort, it is only the Holy Spirit who can provide an absolutely accurate diagnosis."

1. Mental/Emotional breakdown (Deut. 28:28,34,20,28,65)
2. Repeated/Chronic sickness (Deut. 28:21,22,27, 35, 59,61)
3. Barrenness, Miscarriages, female problems (Deut. 28:18)
4. Breakdown of marriage/family alienation (Deut. 28:41; Mal. 4:5-6)
5. Financial Insufficiency (Deut. 28:17,29,47-48)
6. Accident prone (Deut. 28:29)

7. Suicides, Unnatural/untimely deaths (Deut. 28 throughout)

The following is a summary of Deuteronomy 28 with specific verses noted corresponding to each curse listed.

1. Poverty – Financial problems – Verse 17
2. Barrenness, impotence, miscarriages, female problems – Verse 18
3. Untimely, unnatural deaths – Verses 22, 27
4. Failure – plans/projects meet disaster – Verses 20, 38-40
5. Sickness/Disease – including chronic and hereditary – Verses 21, 22, 27, 59, 61
6. Life traumas – one crisis to another – Verses 29, 31
7. Mental and emotional breakdown – Verses 28, 29
8. Family relationship breakdown – Verses 32, 41, 54, 56, 57
9. Hindered in hearing from God and relationship to God – Verse 23

Freedom from Curses

Having determined that there is evidence of a curse and its effects, what can be done? This section presents the steps and prayers that will cancel the effect of curses.

Ultimately, Jesus has paid the price and achieved the victory for us over curses. It is only through faith in Him that we can be free/remain free from curses. Isaiah 53:5 says, "But He was wounded for our transgressions, He was bruised for our iniquities; the chastisement for our peace was upon Him; and with His stripes we are healed." Galatians 3:13 says, "Christ has redeemed us from the curse of the law, being made a curse for us: for it is written, 'Cursed is everyone that hangs on a tree; that the blessing of Abraham might come on the Gentiles through Jesus Christ; that we might receive the promise of the Spirit through faith."

Essentially, to be free of a curse(s) one must first ask God to identify the source of the curse(s) operating. Second, through prayer and repentance and forgiveness we must "break" the curse's power (canceling its effects) – Remember, as in self-imposed curses, <u>Repent</u>, <u>Revoke</u>, <u>Replace</u>. Third, we must deal with demonic activity (indwelling) resulting from the curse. Fourth, we must thank God for freedom and receive His blessings.

The following are prayers from various ministries to break the effects of curses:

Roger Miller, Trumpet of Gideon ministries:

> "In the name of Jesus Christ, I now rebuke, break and loose myself and my children from any and all evil curses, charms, vexes, hexes, spells, jinxes, psychic powers, bewitchment, witchcraft and sorcery that have been put upon me or my family line from any persons or from any occult or psychic sources. I <u>cancel*</u> all connected or related spirits and command them to leave me. I thank you Lord for setting me free."

The following prayer is used by Peter Horrobin of Ellel ministries to break connections and cancel curses associated with generational curses/iniquity:

> "I unreservedly forgive all my ancestors for all the things they have done which have affected me and my life. I specifically renounce the consequences

<u>*Note:</u> We would substitute "break contact with" for "cancel.

of their sins in Jesus' name. As a child of God I now claim that the power of the blood of Jesus is setting me free from the consequences of generational sins. I claim my freedom from the consequences of all occult activity on either my father or my mother's family lines (at this point it is important to specifically name any known occult activity, e.g. 'spiritualism'), from curses and pronouncements that have had an effect on my life; from hereditary diseases, and from the effects of any of their sins which have influenced me. I pray this in the name of Jesus, who became a curse for me on Calvary and died that I might be set free. Amen."

This next prayer is one we have used to sever "Cords of Iniquity" (links to generational curses) and cancel the effects of resultant curses.

"In the name of Jesus Christ I confess all the sins of my forefathers, and by the redemptive blood of Jesus, I now break the power of every curse passed down to me through my ancestral line. I confess and repent of each and every sin that I have committed, known or unknown, and accept Christ's forgiveness. He has redeemed me from the curse of the law. I choose the blessing and reject the curse. In the name of my Lord Jesus, I break the power of every evil curse spoken against me. I cancel the force of every prediction spoken about me, whether intentionally or carelessly that was not according to God's promised blessings. I bless those who have cursed me. I forgive each person who has ever wronged me or spoken evil of me. In the name of Jesus, I command every evil spirit related to curses to leave me now."

Rebecca Brown, in her book <u>Unbroken Curses</u>, details the following steps to freedom from curses:

<u>"If the curse is from God, follow these steps:</u>

<u>Step 1</u>: Acknowledge your own sin and the sins of your forefathers. Then confess them to God and repent for them, asking for forgiveness and cleansing. Separate yourself from sin and those things which displease God. Change your life!

<u>Step 2</u>: Ask God to remove the curse placed on your life.

<u>Step 3</u>: Command any demons that came through the sins to leave you at once in the name of Jesus."

<u>"If the curse is from Satan and he has the legal right to do so, these are the steps to take:</u>

Step 1: Confess and acknowledge the sin that gave Satan/his servants the right to curse you. Repent and ask God for forgiveness and cleansing.

Step 2: Speaking out loud, take authority over the curse in Jesus' name and command it broken.

Step 3: Command all demons associated with the curse to leave you in Jesus' name."

"If Satan has cursed you without legitimate right, do the following:

Step 1: Speaking out loud, take authority over the curse and command it broken, in Jesus' name.

Step 2: Command all demons associated with the curse to leave, in Jesus' name."

Derek Prince in, <u>Blessing or Curse</u>, directs the following steps and prayer to be free from curses/effects.

> "All who desire to pass from curse to blessing must go through the same door. First, there must be a clear recognition of the issues God sets before us. Then there must be a simple, positive response: 'Lord, on the basis of your word, I make my response. I refuse death and curses, and I choose life and blessings'."

Once we have made this choice, we can go on to claim release from any curses over our lives. In bringing people to this point of release, however, lead them through the seven stages outlined below:

1. Confess your faith in Christ and His sacrifice on your behalf.
2. Repent of all your rebellion and your sins.
3. Claim forgiveness of all sins.

4. Forgive all others who have ever harmed you or wronged you.
5. Renounce all contact with anything occult or satanic.
6. Pray this prayer of release:

Lord Jesus Christ, I believe that You are the Son of God and the only way to God; and that You died on the cross for my sins and rose again from the dead. I give up all my sins before You and ask for Your forgiveness— especially for any sins that exposed me to a curse. Release me also from the consequences of my ancestors' sins. By a decision of my will, I forgive all who have harmed me or wronged me—just as I want God to forgive me. In particular, I forgive.....(name persons) Lord Jesus, I believe that on the cross You took on Yourself every curse that could ever come upon me. So I ask You now to release me from every curse over my life—in Your name, Lord Jesus Christ! By faith I now receive my release and I thank You for it.

7. Believe that you have received and go on in God's blessing."

<u>Lay Hold of It</u>

In closing this chapter we call your attention once more to the words of Matthew 11:12. From the Amplified Bible: "and from the days of John the Baptist until the present time, the Kingdom of Heaven has endured violent assault, and violent men seize it by force (as a precious prize – a share in the Heavenly Kingdom is sought with most ardent zeal and intense exertion)."

Against much satanic opposition we must take hold of the blessings God intends for us. We must seize them for ourselves and break the demonic handhold that would keep them from us. Identifying and breaking the effect of curses designed to rob us of those blessings is part of "taking hold" of the Kingdom of God—as is deliverance itself.

Remember, Jesus words "if I cast out demons by the finger of God, then is the Kingdom of God come upon you." (Luke 11:20).

Note the next verses, 11:21-22 (from the Amplified Bible). "When the strongman, fully armed, (from his courtyard) guards his own dwelling, his belongings are undisturbed (his property is at peace and is secure). But when one stronger than he attacks him and conquers him, he robs him of his whole armor on which he had relied and divides up and distributes all his goods as plunder (spoil)."

What if the strongman's "goods" are those robbed from **you**? What if his place of dwelling has been "poached" from **your** house (body)? Isn't it time to take it **all** back? Isn't it time to remove the power of all his devices of curses (keeping up the fence around them); and, by "the finger of God" cast him out and take **your** "goods" from him?

Hopefully, you will utilize the knowledge and insights in this chapter to destroy any barriers to **your** blessings established by curses; thereby opening the way to full deliverance, abundant living, and possessing your Godly inheritance to the fullest.

Chapter 5

The Deliverance Process and Preparation

PERSPECTIVE

The practice of deliverance ministry as we conduct it, is a process combining general counseling, identification of deliverance needs, teaching, specific deliverance and inner healing. The total practice is very intensive and usually takes 6-8 weeks to complete.* As a result, we describe our ministry as "head to toe deliverance." Our goal is to achieve as much freedom for the person as possible, allowing of course for the guidance and sovereignty of the Holy Spirit. Deliverance often occurs in layers involving one primary session where 80% freedom is usually attained, followed by several sessions to address the remaining 20%. All of this is, of course, subject to the direction of the Holy Spirit as He interacts with each individual to accomplish deliverance. Our objective is total freedom for the whole person-body, soul and spirit. As a process it is very similar to that of Noel and Phyl Gibson or Peter Horrobin and Ellel Ministries.

Each of us is a unique individual and as always the Holy Spirit relates to each person in a way uniquely oriented to individual and specific needs. Over the years we have applied this system of deliverance in ministry to hundreds of individuals. The results, in terms of life-changing effect, have been amazing; with most experiencing complete freedom from demonic indwelling. Successful deliverance is contingent upon each person's will and cooperation with the deliverance process.

As we have freely received, so likewise we offer to you this proven method for deliverance. Each candidate for deliverance is asked to read <u>Pigs In The Parlor</u>, by Frank Hammond. This book carries a particular anointing upon it that is very conducive to preparing individuals for deliverance. Our early training in deliverance ministry was based on the teaching of Frank Hammond. As a result this book forms the base from which we have developed our own respective deliverance ministry. Reading <u>Pigs In The Parlor</u> helps individuals to grasp more quickly the process of deliverance as we practice it.

During the initial intake session the need for deliverance is determined, basic intake information is recorded (past and present family history, etc.), and an overview of the origin of Satan and demons is presented. Sometimes it takes the first two sessions to achieve these objectives. Sessions are normally one hour long.

* As a result of the expansion of our ministry center we do offer an intensive three-day deliverance process on request. This is a resident process with sessions scheduled morning, afternoon and evening.

The remainder of the "preparation" sessions are spent completing the "Deliverance Checklist" and "Demon Grouping" worksheet, determining entry points, identifying demonic strongholds and reviewing the "Preparation for Deliverance" hand-out. The final deliverance session is then scheduled at a specified time allowing 2-4 hours for completion.

SCRIPTURES

The following list of scriptures is helpful for preparing individuals for deliverance. They should meditate on these continuously and allow them to soak deep into their spirit. This will have the effect of weakening the demonic "strongholds" within. Be aware that it can have the effect of causing spirits to manifest prior to the time for the final deliverance session. If so, you will need to bind the demonic spirits away from you in the name of Jesus. This prevents their early manifestation. In the final deliverance session the spirits will be loosed prior to commanding them to leave. By determining when demons will be allowed to manifest you provide more time for the client to be "educated." This will prove vital later for the client to maintain their deliverance.

• Isaiah 53:5-4	• Ephesians 6:10-18
• Luke 4:18,19	• Philippians 1:6
• John 8:36	• Philippians 4:4-9
• John 10:9-10	• Colossians 1:9-16
• Romans 8:28-39	• James 4:7
• Romans 16:20	• I Peter 2:9-10
• II Corinthians 3:18	• I Peter 5:6-11
• Galatians 2:20	

KEYS TO DELIVERANCE

There are several foundational elements that are common to successful deliverance ministry. The absence of any one of these will greatly hinder and often terminate the process of deliverance. These are contained in chapter 7 of Frank Hammond's book, <u>Pigs in the Parlor</u>.

A. <u>Honesty</u>: One cannot expect God to impart deliverance unless one is <u>open to truthful self-examination</u>. Demons seek to hide in the dark recesses of the soul (mind, will and emotions) and the body. They must be identified by self-examination and exposed to God's light of truth. <u>Unconfessed sin will grant legal right for demons to remain within</u>. One must seek, and allow God to illuminate by the Holy Spirit's power, every ungodly act and mindset through which demons have entered. Honesty will allow the revealing of every demonically dark area of one's inner self so that deliverance might be achieved in that area.

B. <u>Humility</u>: The essence of humility is dependence upon God. For the most part our own pride, rebellion and stubbornness is what grants access to the demonic. Self-will and anti-submission lead us to depend on demonic means of empowerment. Often, we aren't even aware this is what is

occurring. Reversing the process requires our acknowledge-
ment of our need for God. As we desire His reign and
control over our lives we begin to move toward His freedom
and abundant life. The deliverance process is very humbling
as we realize our inability to defeat demonic invaders in our
life without God's power. We must be willing to humble
ourselves and submit to God's supernatural deliverance
ministry as it is administered by His faithful, Spirit-filled
servants. James 4:6-7 says: "God gives grace to the humble.
Submit yourselves therefore unto God. Resist the devil and
He will flee. Draw near to God and He will draw near to
you."

C. Repentance: Repentance, by definition, means, "to turn
   from." One must determine to walk away from sin and death
   and into godliness and life. We must cease to practice sin.
   With God's help we must determine to stop performing
   those sinful actions and behaviors identified through the
   deliverance process. Repentance goes hand in hand with
   confession and renunciation. Total victory may come only
   following deliverance, but, we must previously renounce
   these sinful acts and determine by our will to gain victory
   over them. Frank Hammond states: One must "fall out of
   agreement" with evil. One must then come into agreement
   with God. The purpose for deliverance is to grow in Christ
   likeness (II Cor. 3:18). It is not some miracle cure for one's
   problems or a "quick fix." Repentance is a conscious choosing for the things of God and a life lived following after
   Jesus Christ and His righteousness.

D. Renunciation: This is the forsaking of evil and the intent to
   demonstrate repentance. It is a total disgust with sin, evil
   and the things of Satan. Renunciation is making a clear
   break with Satan – a disfellowshipping with darkness – a
   parting of the ways with evil – a disengaging with the
   demonic. We have candidates for deliverance pray a prayer
   which states, " I renounce you Satan and all your works in

my life." Renunciation says to Satan, "You and I are quits and I intend to demonstrate this to you at every opportunity." We also have individuals verbally renounce in our presence, before God, all those activities listed on the "Deliverance Checklist" This commits them to renunciation, sets their will for deliverance, and notifies Satan and his demons of these facts.

It should be noted that the act of repentance and renunciation, within the

context of deliverance, does not in any way say that the work of salvation in a person's life is incomplete. All past sins are covered at salvation by the blood of Jesus. They **are** forgiven. Repentance and renunciation within deliverance ministry first seeks forgiveness for repeated sins subsequent to salvation. Repentance and renunciation then serves notice on Satan and his demons that the work of the cross in the person's life is now being enforced through deliverance at any contact point created by a person's past and present sins. Remember, Satan is a legalist and opportunist. He and his demons will use the fact of past sins committed to continue to operate in a person's life until he is served an "eviction notice" by means of deliverance. Repentance and renunciation in this context present his demons with the person's "intent to evict."

E. <u>Forgiveness</u>: This area, together with unconfessed sin, are the two greatest hindrances to effective deliverance. Matthew 6:14-15 says: "for if you forgive men their trespasses, your heavenly Father will also forgive you your trespasses." We ask each deliverance candidate to make a list of those they need to forgive. At the start of the deliverance session we ask the person receiving deliverance to choose to forgive by name those on their list. The manifestation of deliverance often begins here with weeping and release. It should be noted that if bitterness, anger and resentment are strongholds in a person's life, the act of forgiveness is especially crucial to the success of their deliverance. As Frank

Hammond states: "No deliverance minister can effect deliverance unless the candidate has met God's 'conditions' ."

F. Prayer: The entire process of deliverance is a process of prayer. Both the candidate and the ministers are in continual prayer for God's power, released by the Holy Spirit, to effect deliverance. The promise of Joel 2:32 is a constant supplication, "whosoever shall call upon the name of the Lord shall be delivered." The entire practice of deliverance is bathed in prayer – both preparing for and conducting the actual deliverance session. If possible, those knowledgeable of deliverance should be solicited to pray for the candidate – family, spouse, friends, church members, etc. Corporate prayer greatly limits the power of the enemy in trying to prevent the deliverance. Be wise, however, in the selection of those who are to pray. Be sure they have knowledge of deliverance and can pray, therefore, effectively.

G. Warfare: Deliverance, while linked to physical healing and inner healing as ministry, in practice is enjoined with spiritual warfare: The strongman and his followers are being evicted from their home; "Goods" are being taken back and restored to the candidate. Demons are being kicked out; forcefully and without comprise. This is warfare in no uncertain terms. In accordance with Ephesians 6:10-12, spiritual warfare is being conducted using the Christian's weapons of submission to God, the blood and name of Jesus, the Word of God and our testimony as a believer (Rev. 12:11). Demonic sprits are being identified, then forcefully commanded, by faith, to "loose and go." The battle is entered with determination and with the assurance that Jesus **never** fails.

Both prior to and during the deliverance, the candidate must cultivate a spiritual warfare attitude and mindset. This helps them to set their will in preparation for ousting unwelcome demonic occupants. "Enough is enough! No more, devil!" must become the candidate's heartfelt cry from deep within their spirit. In most cases, the greater the candidate is determined to have deliverance, the easier the deliverance session will be. Derek Prince calls this their degree of "desperation."

Military Commands

As we have gained knowledge and experience in deliverance ministry, the Holy Spirit has used certain parallels with the natural to teach us principles of the supernatural. One such parallel has to do with the comparison of specific military commands to the stages of the process of deliverance. This is in keeping with the spiritual warfare nature of deliverance as stated in Matthew 11:12, "the kingdom of heaven suffers violence and the violent take it by force." As we have said, we are in a spiritual war. Ultimately, the war has been won by Jesus Christ on the cross and declared with His resurrection. His kingdom has been established in Spirit. It is left to us, the body of Christ, to enforce and advance that kingdom and its principles throughout (to the ends of) the earth. We will be countered in that effort by satanic and demonic opposition. With Spirit force, by the power of the Holy Spirit, we can overcome that opposition. Remember, we have the weapons of Revelation 12:11, "and they overcame him by the blood of the Lamb, and by the world of their testimony and they loved not their lives unto death."

Having said this, let's look at these military commands as they relate to the process of deliverance. In the conduct of military guard duty, as military security is established, sentries are instructed in the use of certain verbal commands. The first of these is the command **"Halt! Who goes there?"** This command is a warning to the "trespasser" to cease forward movement for the purpose of recognition/identification by the sentry. The question demands a verbal response as to the identity of the one being challenged. In like manner, the first phase in the process of deliverance is **preparation** for a deliverance session. A candidate for deliverance agrees to "stop" and submit to a period of preparation for deliverance. This is a time when they "Halt" or curtail ministry involvement for a season so that maximum attention may be directed toward receiving deliverance.

This is also a time of seeking to identify the origin and nature of demonic spirits present within a person and the development of a specific strategy for the person's deliverance session. Demons are bound during this phase, from their usual cycle of operation, in order to determine systematically, "Who goes there?"

The candidate for deliverance often gains great insight during this phase as to the specific means by which demons have operated in their lives. This is particularly useful to the person in remaining free following deliverance.

A second command taught to sentries is **"Advance and be recognized!"** This is used following compliance with the first command. It is an order for the one challenged to slowly step forward and demonstrate their true identity. It is a time for the sentry to establish, without any doubt, the identity of the one being challenged.

In relation to deliverance, this would cover the final conduct of the preparation for deliverance and often the first part of the actual deliverance session. Through prayer and the Holy Spirit's discernment, the exact identity of demons present is determined. Combining this with knowledge gained in sessions with the candidate as to how the demons entered, the act of deliverance is undertaken and effected.

Often, demons will begin to sense the time of deliverance as it approaches. They will either withdraw into a low-keyed, very subdued state (to try to fool the "host" into believing they are not there or have already gone) or they will operate stronger (to intimidate the "host" with hopes of shutting down the deliverance). If the latter is the case, this allows the deliverance minister (while maintaining control) to confirm recognition of the demonic spirits as they seek to operate to a limited degree. This can serve to facilitate the process of "recognition" during the preparation period.

A final command that was taught historically to sentries and soldiers was **"Stand and deliver!"** It is not used in modern times but in the past it was a challenge to engage in combat, hand-to-hand. Today, military guards are given authority without additional commands to use appropriate force if the first two commands are disregarded. In past days, where hand-to-hand combat was more prevalent, the enemy was ordered to "Stand and deliver!" This meant, "Put up your dukes! or "En Garde" or "come out fightin'!" It was a challenge to engage in hand-to-hand combat.

As it relates to deliverance, this command depicts the final deliverance session. The enemy is on notice that his time of influence and habitation with the candidate is at an end. His presence will no longer be tolerated. He is being forcefully evicted from his house, as would a trespasser. We take our "stand" and "deliver" the candidate from demonic indwelling. (This is where we derived the title to this book.) As we have stated, this is a New Testament directive to Christians as we demonstrate the truth that the kingdom of God has come upon the earth. Having rejected all prior opportunities to exit, the demonic intruder is now ordered, in the name of Jesus Christ, to "loose and go!"

Standing Firm

As stated, the Holy Spirit often speaks to us of spiritual precepts by means of illustrations from the natural realm. Reflecting on the process of spiritual warfare and deliverance we are reminded of an illustration that has inspired us deeply. It has reminded us that we must maintain an unceasing commitment to executing offensive warfare against Satan. Thereby we continually dispossess him and his forces of the Promised Land intended for God's people. Further, we must be doubly committed to give up **no** ground to the enemy – to "give no place to the devil."

As we present the following, read it and reflect on it with the eyes of the Spirit. Allow the implications for spiritual warfare and deliverance to penetrate deep within to be grasped with spiritual hands. Though it is an account of natural, earthly warfare, it is charged with a message for supernatural warfare. Lay hold of that message and let it motivate you to victory in spiritual warfare.

In the summer of 1863, in the midst of the American Civil War, the armies of the Confederate South and the Union North engaged in battle at a small town in Pennsylvania called Gettysburg. The objective of the South was to invade the North, engage in battle, and defeat the primary Union Army defending Washington, D. C. They could then demand an end to the war (invading Washington if needed). The intent of the North was to crush that effort with a decisive victory over the Confederacy, affecting permanently its ability to wage warfare; and, hopefully, breaking the South's will to continue the war.

As the battle was enjoined around the town of Gettysburg, the opposing forces fell into lines of battle South and West of the town. The Union forces were entrenched on higher ground over a series of ridges running roughly North to South and overlooking the Confederate position.

The Union's southernmost position was anchored on a ridge top known as "Little Round Top." The crucial defense of this position was assigned to the 20th Main Regiment. This unit was commanded by Col. Joshua L. Chamberlain, a college professor who resigned his position to volunteer to fight in the war. He was a deeply moral leader and a devout Christian.

The Confederate Army's plan as the battle unfolded on the second day was to attack and occupy Little Round Top. The Confederate forces would then use it as a launching point to sweep around the flank of the Union Army and defeat it.

Colonel Chamberlain's orders were simple: to hold his position on "Little Round Top" at all costs. He was told there could be no retreat _ to retreat would mean the flanking and defeat of the entire Union Army. He was instructed by his superior officer, "You are the extreme left flank of the Union Army. You must hold!"

As the assault was launched against him he commanded some 250 men against a Confederate force of around 1200 men. The attack came in successive waves with each wave of Confederates coming farther to Chamberlain's left around the hilltop. Five assault waves in all were repelled at greater and greater expense of his men and, worse, his ammunition. His line was bent back on itself around the ridge top until it formed a right angle to itself in order to defend the position. Fighting at times was brutal hand-to-hand combat. Finally, that which Chamberlain feared was reported to him _ "Sir, there is no more ammunition!" His officers reported. "Sir, you know we cannot repel another wave. We must surrender."

Now, with only about 100 men left, and no ammunition available (and no hope of resupply), Chamberlain watched in dismay as the Confederates gathered themselves for another assault. With incredible resolve and calm in an impossible situation he assessed his options and ordered the unthinkable, "If we stay here with no ammunition we cannot shoot. If we retreat, the position is overtaken, the flank caves in and the battle is lost. We cannot do that either. There's only one other option_a bayonet charge against the enemy. So **fix bayonets!**"

As the Confederates moved up the hill in a final assault, they were shocked and terrified at the sight of the Union defenders charging down the hill toward them with fixed bayonets. Surprised and shattered they turned and ran with Chamberlain's shouting men following.

In all, over 400 confederates were taken prisoner by Union troops with empty rifles. Colonel Chamberlain was awarded the Medal of Honor for leadership in this action. He fought in numerous other engagements of the Civil War, rising to the rank of Major General and becoming a true hero. He was, like Gideon in the bible, a mighty man of valor.

Like Gideon, he led his small force in defeat of a much larger force. Like David, he defeated the Giant. His victory was due in part to his resolve to never surrender to the enemy and resist with every means at hand. Like Chamberlain and like Gideon and like David, we too must carry the battle to the demonic forces opposing us. At times, small in number and low on ammunition, we can still defeat the enemy through determination, courageous selfless action, and God's anointing_"The sword of the Lord and of Gideon!"

Surrender to Satan is not an option. Giving up that which God has intended for us is not an option either. And we must determine, radically, to resist the enemy with all that we have. Remember, God has promised us that the devil **will** flee in the face of a determined counter-assault.

Gideon's men shouted, "the sword of the Lord and of Gideon!" David shouted at the giant, Goliath, "but I come to you in the name of the Lord of Hosts, the God of the armies of Israel, whom you have defied. This day the Lord will deliver you into my hand, and I will strike you and take your head from you."

Our cry today to the enemy, like Chamberlain's, is always, **"Bayonets!"** To every boasting insult hurled at us by Satan we reply, **"Bayonets!"** To every scheming plot and ploy of the enemy's demons, we shout, **"Bayonets!"** To every spear and arrow of fear and deceit and accusation launched at us, we raise our shield of faith, lift our sword of the Spirit, shout, **"Bayonets!"** and run to meet the enemy in the name of the Lord of Hosts.

For God has promised us His refuge by His power in the midst of the battle. Psalm 91 states, "surely He shall deliver you from the snare of the fowler and from the perilous pestilence. He shall cover you with His feathers and under His wings you shall take refuge; His truth shall be you shield and buckler. You shall not be afraid of the terror by night, nor of the arrow that flies by day, nor of the pestilence that walks in darkness, nor of the destruction that lays waste at noonday. A thousand may fall at your side, and ten thousand at your right hand; but it shall not come near you."

So, blow the trumpet in Zion, and sound an alarm on the holy mountain! Sound the war cry. Prepare for war and wake up the mighty men! Let all the men of war draw near and prepare for a catastrophic (for the devil's forces) counterattack! Sound the Shofar of God's justice on **your** behalf and you will be amazed to discover what the servant of Elisha saw in II Kings 6:15-17. As the prophet prayed, "Lord open his eyes that he may see," the servant saw horses and chariots of fire surrounding the enemy's army. You, too will come to know as Elisha said, "Do not fear, for those who are with us are more than those who are with them."

Sound a blast on the trumpet of attack against satanic forces opposing you. You will hear, as David did in II Samuel 5:24, the sound of angelic armies marching across the tops of the mulberry trees marching to your assistance marching in your defense. Then as David did, you will go up against the enemy as the Lord goes before you to strike the camp of the enemy. You will experience the Lord as a "man of war" (Exodus 15:3) as Moses did against Pharaoh when the waters of the sea swallowed the enemy up! And you will experience God as the "Lord of the breakthrough," again as David did (in II Samuel 5:20). You will then be lead to declare as he did, "The Lord has broken through my enemies before me, like a breakthrough of water." Shout the name of Baal Perazim ("Lord of the breakthrough") as you attack the enemy unconditionally and zealously.

So, seize your deliverance! Seize your inheritance! Take it forcefully from the demonic hands of those devilish forces holding it captive. Launch the righteous assault and the gates of hell shall not prevail against it! And to the enemy, always, we say, **"BAYO-NETS!"**

WE LIFT UP A SHOUT

Steve Fry
We march to the tune of a love song
Singing the King's jubilee
Anointed to enter the Hell Gate
Anointed to set captives free.
We lift up our banner of worship
And Jesus, our champion, we praise.
An army of worshippers stands by His side
Baptized in His fire revealing His glorious light.

We lift up a shout, a victory shout!
For we've overcome by the blood of the Lamb
And the word of our mouth. We've declared war,
In the name of the Lord. We've laid down our lives
That the triumph of Christ may resound in the earth.

We sing the high praises of heaven
And fight with the sword of the Word
To bind every stronghold of Satan
Preparing the way for the Lord.
We lift up a standard of worship
That shatters the darkness with light
And god will arise on the wings of our praise
And march as a Warrior who's mighty and able to save.

We lift up a shout, a victory shout!
For we've overcome by the blood of the Lamb
And the word of our mouth. We've declared war,
In the name of the Lord. We've laid down our lives
That the triumph of Christ may resound in the earth.

From the album "Bless the Lord," 1986 Bird Wing Music—a division of
Sparrow Corp. and BMC Songs, Inc. ASCAP

Deliverance Preparation Handouts

In preparing a person for deliverance, the following two hand-outs are given during the last pre-counseling session. One is an overview of the deliverance session. This informs the person of what to expect during deliverance and helps to relieve any anxiousness regarding what will be an intensely supernatural experience.

The other handout contains guidelines for cleaning the person's place of dwelling from demonic effects (resulting from various objects and articles owned).

PREPARATION FOR YOUR DELIVERANCE SESSION
(Hand-out #1)

I. Practical Issues
   A. **Eating**
   We are often asked if you should fast before deliverance. This is between you and God. Commit this issue to prayer and follow the Holy Spirit's guidance. We obviously appreciate the value of fasting, and have seen positive results, especially concerning taking authority over stubborn strongholds. Some have tried a modified fast with good results (i.e. no sugar, caffeine, T. V., etc. for a period of time before deliverance). Derek Prince's book on fasting is one of the best we have read.

B. Attire

Dress comfortably and casually _jeans and tennis shoes are fine. Wear clothing that allows freedom of movement. Please dress modestly_no shorts, low-cut blouses, etc. If you have long hair, please secure it with clips or pull it back in a ponytail. Women may choose not to wear make-up since deliverance usually brings tears. We suggest that you wear no jewelry other than a watch or wedding ring. Pay attention to images and logos on your clothing. We have had clients come for their deliverance innocently wearing occult symbols on jewelry or clothing.

C. Spiritual Issues

To insure the most thorough, effective deliverance possible, you must engage in spiritual warfare before your session. You must continually set your will against the spiritual strongholds and firmly determine that you will be free. Put the spirits on notice by telling them that their time is short and you choose to be free of their influence. You must resist temptation with all your might and repent immediately if you fall into sin. Be completely honest with your deliverance ministers. Let them know your struggles and failures. The best way to weaken spirits is to deprive them. For example, an addictive spirit will leave easier if it hasn't had a "fix" in a while. We realize that spirits drive people to exhibit certain behaviors, but you still have a free will and the ability to exercise some restraint. Matthew 16:19 says that "whatever you bind on earth will be bound in heaven." As you approach your deliverance, call the spirits by name and bind them away from yourself. This will give you a measure of relief, but must be done frequently.

D. Your Eye Gate and Ear Gate

Take care what you expose your spirit to in the week preceding deliverance (not to mention the rest of your life!) Ungodly music, movies, T. V. shows, books, etc. will feed spirits and weaken you spiritually. Also be careful of the people to whom you expose yourself prior to deliverance. Avoid, if possible, those who are or have been abusive to you in any way. Stay away from ungodly friends, co-workers, or family members who may lure you into sinful behavior. Obviously, you can't avoid everyone who is a bad influence, but where you have choices, make good ones. If your pastor preaches that Christians can't have a demon, it will feed a spirit of doubt and unbelief in you. Religious spirits are the most difficult to deal with. Surround yourself with "faith folks" who believe in deliverance and will pray for you and support you. If you go through deliverance and choose to remain in a church that doesn't believe in deliverance ministry, we cannot be sure of your long-term deliverance success. If no one at your church teaches the authority of believers and can discern spirits, your ability to keep your deliverance is greatly hindered. If your church does not believe in the Baptism in the Holy Spirit or the operation of the gifts of the Holy Spirit, we recommend that you visit a Holy Spirit–filled church several times before deliverance. This will familiarize you with the demonstration of the gifts of the Holy Spirit that will be in operation during your deliverance session.

E. **What to Expect**

Length: it is impossible to predict how long your deliverance will last. Commonly, deliverance sessions are between 2 – 4 hours. Please remove all time restraints from your self. Arrange child-care so that you don't have to pick up children at any certain time the day or evening of your deliverance. Many people take the day off following their deliverance to rest and pray. **No one** may come with you for your ministry time. If a friend or family member wants to pray for you during this time, that's fine _ they just need to do it somewhere else. This is for their spiritual protection as well as your own.

II. Directions/Guidelines for Deliverance
   A. **Order of Deliverance**
      1. Deliverance prayers
      2. Renunciation and forgiveness
      3. Break iniquity
      4. Break soul ties
      5. Command spirits to come out by name
      6. In – filling of the Holy Spirit (with fruit and gifts of the Spirit)
      7. Prophecies

   B. **Laying on of Hands**
      "It shall come to pass in that day that his burden will be taken away from your shoulder, and his yoke from your neck, and the yoke will be destroyed because of the anointing oil" (Isaiah 10:27)

      After anointing you with oil, we will establish a point of contact and reinforce spiritual authority over the demons by the laying on of hands. When dealing with mental spirits, we will place our hands on your head; with emotional spirits, your heart; and so forth. When breaking soul ties, we will ask you to put you hand on your stomach and we will put our hand over yours. For infirmity spirits, we will place our hands on or near the affected area. Rest assured, we will be appropriate and modest as we do this. Just as the healing virtue of Jesus is released through touch, so is the anointing authority for deliverance.

   C. **Iniquity**
      The word "iniquity" means a predisposition or evil "bent" within people. Another common term for iniquity is generational sin or curse. It involves sin patterns that are passed down from generation to generation (Exodus 20:5, Psalm 51:5, Jer. 32:18). God says if we regard iniquity in our heart He will not hear us! The good news is that Jesus was "Bruised for our iniquities" (Isaiah 53:6). He paid the price

for it all. Iniquity must be dealt with by faith. If you don't break iniquity within your self, your children will inherit it, and they will likely repeat the sins you have committed. We must forgive our parents, grandparents, etc. of their iniquity then confess and repent of our participation in the same sins. We then ask God to pass the sword of the Spirit between the generations and yourself and cut the cords of iniquity. You may still feel temptation in the areas where family sin was strong but you will have the power and desire to resist.

D. **Travail**

Travail is a "birthing' process, complete with possible shaking, crying, groaning, straining, and sometimes screaming. It is a physical reaction to God's power within us. Don't allow the physical manifestations of travail to frighten you. Travail will loose the bands of wickedness (iniquity), undo heavy burdens, let the oppressed go free, and break every yoke (Isaiah 58:6). The Holy Spirit's power drives the iniquity out. Often this initiates the demonstration of travail among the deliverance ministry team.

E. **Gifts of the Spirit**

Your deliverance ministers could not take authority over the demonic forces in your life without the power that comes through the presence of the Holy Spirit (Acts 1:8). They have received the Baptism in the Holy Spirit and will operate freely in the gifts of the Holy Spirit (I Cor. 12 & 14). If you have not received the Baptism in the Holy Spirit it is strongly recommended that you do so at the conclusion of your deliverance session.

F. **Manifestations**

After reading *Pigs in the Parlor,* you are aware of possible manifestations as the spirits detach from you and leave. We are not looking for specific manifestations. Some people experience dramatic manifestations, while others feel nothing. We encourage you to not resist manifestations. We will not allow the spirits to harm you or anyone present. Don't cross your legs or fold your arms across your chest. That is a stance of resistance, and can help the spirits hold on.

Tell us if you have any strong mental impressions during the deliverance. The Holy Spirit may reveal something to you that is needful for successful deliverance. By the same token, demons may tell you that "you should leave," "this isn't working," "they can't get rid of me," etc. Speak these thoughts out so we can expose the spirits and defeat them.

If you have the Baptism in the Holy Spirit, please do not speak in tongues during your deliverance. Spirits are air, and a common way of expulsion is through the mouth. Your prayer language can prevent spirits from leaving. Mentally, we need your full agreement as we take authority over spirits. Just make sure you don't pray out loud.

G. Expectations

What can you expect from deliverance? You can expect the power of God to gloriously and dramatically set you free from iniquities and demonic forces. You can expect strongholds of the enemy to be pulled down, and his plans and schemes exposed. It is unrealistic, however, to expect that your life will be problem-free or blissful after deliverance. You will battle temptation, especially in areas where there was a ruler spirit operating. You still have the flesh to contend with. The difference is that you will now have the knowledge necessary to do warfare with Satan and his demons, and the power necessary to keep him from reattaching (which is increased through the baptism in the Holy Spirit).

We see all kinds of reactions to deliverance. Some people feel elated and joyful; others peaceful and calm. A few even claim to feel no different whatsoever. Many report feeling fatigued after deliverance and require extra sleep and rest for a day or two. We often hear people exclaim how "light" they feel_like they've shed 50 lbs. Others say they feel weird and "spacey" after deliverance. In those cases, so many spirits have been cast out that the person feels a temporary loss of identity and personality. Don't be alarmed at this. We always pray for the Holy Spirit to occupy all space vacated.

We know that God will do as much in your deliverance as He deems needful. You will not get all the deliverance and inner healing you need in one fell swoop. If you did, it would likely overwhelm you. Just let God be God, and trust that He's begun a good work in you and will perfect it (Philippians 1:6).

H. Cost

What is it worth to you to be free from the snare of the enemy? We could sell all that we own and still feel that it's not enough. Thankfully, God's marvelous gifts are free and cannot be earned or purchased. Even so, we know God's word says, "A workman is worthy of his hire." The ministry team receives no compensation other than love offerings given by you at the time of your deliverance. These individuals volunteer their time to intercede for you and do spiritual warfare on your behalf. All we ask is that you commit this matter to prayer and be obedient to the Lord as He leads.

I. A Final Word

Your attitude makes a huge difference in whether your deliverance will be successful or not. It is important to approach your deliverance with a believing, optimistic, tenacious attitude. If you feel casual or have a "let's see" approach, you're better off waiting. We have nothing to prove, nor do we intend to convince you of Satan's attachments. Deliverance is an awesome ministry and we feel privileged to be a part of it. We take it very seriously and we have no desire to enter into it with you unless you take it seriously also. Next to seeing new converts born into God's kingdom, seeing the captives set free is our greatest joy (Luke 4:18). Derek

Prince states that candidates for deliverance should have a sense of "desperation." One should approach deliverance as determined as the woman who touched Jesus' hem to receive healing. Are **you** as determined? Are **you** intent on being free or do you simply want temporary relief?

SPIRITUAL HOUSECLEANING (Handout #2)

Just as deliverance to cleanse our fleshly "house" is of vital importance to our spiritual growth, so too, is a spiritual cleansing of the natural home we dwell in. Leviticus 14:33-53 contains specific instructions for purifying a "leprous house" in the days of Moses. While we are not subject to the "Law" in these New Testament days, the principle of keeping our homes free of anything that would cause spiritual defilement is still applicable today.

Matthew Henry's Commentary regarding this scripture passage says: "It is supposed that even in Canaan itself, the land of promise, their houses might be infected with a leprosy. Though it was a Holy Land, this would not secure them from this plague, while the inhabitants were many of them so unholy. Thus a place and a name in the visible church will not secure wicked people from God's judgments.... Leviticus 14:35 says, 'It seemeth to me there is as it were a plague in the house.'

Sin, where that reigns in a house, is a plague there, as it is in a heart. And masters of families should be aware and afraid of the first appearance of gross sin in their families, and put away the iniquity, whatever it is, far from their tabernacles, (Job 22:23). They should be jealous with a Godly jealously concerning those under their charge, lest they be drawn into sin, and take early advise, if it but seem that there is a plague in the house, lest the contagion spread, and many by it be defiled and destroyed.

With a house, if the priest upon search, found that the leprosy had gotten into the house, he must try to cure it, by taking out that part of the house that was infected (Lev. 14:40 & 41). This was like cutting off a gangrened limb for the preservation of the rest of the body. Corruptions should be purged out in time, before it spreads....if yet it remained in the house (following attempts at purging), the whole house must be pulled down, and all the materials carried to the dunghill. The owner would be better off without a dwelling than to live in one that was infected. Note, the leprosy of sin, if it be obstinate under the methods of cure, will at last be the ruin of families and churches. If Babylon will not be healed, she shall be forsaken and abandoned."

From Mathew Henry's discussion we determine several directives regarding "housecleaning."

1) It is very important to our deliverance process to establish and maintain our places of dwelling as spiritually healthy and holy.
2) All that would hinder us from achieving this purpose should be purged from the house. These "spiritual infections" will eventually corrupt the entire spiritual climate of our house if not attended to/eliminated.
3) The process of purging may not be accomplished with a localized, specific "elimination" and the entire dwelling may continue to promulgate/harbor that which is unclean (an unhealthy spiritual climate may persist despite all efforts). In that case a relocation of dwelling place by the inhabitants must be undertaken.
4) To remain in a dwelling that maintains an impure (or mixed) spiritual climate will progressively contaminate the inhabitants themselves.

General Guidelines

The following are some overall directions for conducting a "spiritual house cleaning" of your home. Following this is a list of some suggested items to eliminate.

To begin with, remember that a demon's first choice for a dwelling place is you _a nice warm human body. But he will settle for an animal's body or a house as a second choice. Cats and birds are particularly susceptible to demonic influence. No need to get rid of your pets, just pray over them (they are under your spiritual dominion). How do demons come to reside in a house or other dwelling? There are three ways:

1) A demonized person died there. (murder, suicide, or natural causes), and their spirits now inhabit that physical space. These are called familiar spirits, and are what the secular world refers to as 'ghosts" or "haunted houses"

2) <u>Sinful and/or occult practices went on there</u>. For instance, sexual spirits may remain in a house, a room or even around furniture where a person was molested, or where prostitution took place. Some telltale signs of oppression in a room or house are: coldness, feelings of heaviness or eeriness; foggy or smoky looking; musty or sulpherous smells. Many have reported feeling certain emotions like anger, or lust every time they enter their home or a certain room.

   For these reasons, we strongly suggest that you pray over your home and anoint it with oil, especially if you are not he original owner. Command all spirits that dwell there to flee in Jesus' name, then anoint the doorframes and windows with oil. Plead the blood of Jesus over the house and all the property (we suggest you walk your property line as you do this). Claim the house or apartment, (or even hotel room) for Jesus and His purposes, and let Satan know that he and his demons are no longer welcome. Understand that if a guest or even a family member engages in sinful practices in your home, or has strong demonic influences in their lives, you will need to repeat the process. Your house can become defiled by those who enter there, so be cautious.

3) <u>Objects and Articles</u>: Demons will attach to objects that are accursed or occultic. It does not matter whether you use the object for its intended purpose or not. Spirits are drawn to the object because it is familiar to them. When these items are in your home, you will suffer from the spirits attached to them. They can cause strife, sickness, lust, and various other types of temptation and oppression. We say, "When in doubt, throw it out!" We continually hear wonderful testimonies from those who are obedient in this area. You'll be amazed at the "hold" these objects can have on you and how free you'll feel after they're gone. God's word clearly states that we are to have no gods before Him. Many of the objects listed here have been a substitute for God in our lives (at some time). This list is not comprehensive, but will get you started. Remember that the possession and ownership of an

object is an act of the will. Through ownership, agreement with the spirit(s), which move through them, is reached. God will bless your obedience to His will as you seek to follow His will for your possessions.

IDOLS, ITEMS, PARAPHERNALIA, ARTWORK

Gargoyles	Swastikas/Nazi Paraphernalia
Trolls	Egyptian items: ankh, scarabs, deities
Gremlins	Owls
Dream Catchers	Frogs
Yin Yang symbol (and Jewelry)	Hex signs
Peace symbols (broken Cross)	New Age symbols (sun, moon, and
Buddha	stars)
Tarot cards/Psychic aids	New age crystals
Ouija board	Magic 8 ball
Rosary (Buddhist and Catholic)	Zodiac signs, pictures, etc. Ojo De Dios

- ❑ Mythological figures (Pegasus-winged horses,Centaurs- half horse/half man, unicorns, etc.) wizards, magicians, gods and goddesses.
- ❑ Lucky: penny, coin, rabbit's foot, shirt, hat, etc. (superstitious items)
- ❑ Pictures, medals, statuettes of saints, etc.; Catholic Idolatry (Mary "Queen of Heaven)
- ❑ Pagan artifacts or objects (ceremonial masks, whistles/flutes, painting, costumes)

NEW AGE, SATANIC OR WITCHCRAFT PUBLICATIONS & PRINT MATERIAL: Books, bibles, brochures, and instruction manuals including topics of: Some Alternative medicine healing, mythology, reincarnation, yoga, meditation

CULT AND SECRET SOCIETY MATERI

propaganda, ritual aids (rings, swords, uniforms,

– especially Masonic, Shriner and Eastern Star, Mormon (Latter-Day Saints) and Jehovah Witness.

MUSIC: New Age (Yanni), Country/ Western, Hard Rock, Death Metal, suicide, Alternative, discordant, etc.

PICTURES AND FURNISHINGS of any above-mentioned object or theme. Be especially careful of Middle Eastern, Far Eastern/oriental and Indian items. Gcisha figures, martial arts items, costumes, aids, Muslim materials. Don't wear or display objects in a foreign language you don't understand, or with symbols on them that are questionable. Certain famous personalities such as rock stars, movie stars, etc. can be idolized in posters, prints, T-shirts, etc. Any graphics or artwork related to spiritism/pantheism or mythology.

SEXUAL AND PORNOGRAPHIC: Books, videos, magazines, photographs. Perverse "aids" and erotica. Internet sites may need to be blocked. Pray over computer.

JEWELRY AND CLOTHING: Soul ties are strengthened by objects that we wear on our body. If a former spouse, lover, or friend gave you a piece of jewelry or clothing, you will find it hard to sever ungodly ties with them. Beware of family heirlooms, which may carry a curse with it.

MISCELLANEOUS: pray over objects given to you or obtained in garage sales. Ask the Holy Spirit to reveal objects that grieve Him. Pray over consignment shop items of clothing.

TELEVISION: Shows that glorify paranormal events (reincarnation, E.S.P., etc.), occult (mind reading, witchcraft, vampires, were-wolves, U.F.O., ghosts, poltergeists, etc.), perversion, homosexuality, etc.

VIDEO/ COMPUTER GAMES: Many of the games that are sold re violent, perverse, and/or occultic in nature. Current statistics report that 20% of today's teens are classified as psychologically dependent upon video games. These type video games desensitize the viewer and encourage behavior they might not otherwise consider. Beware!

A Final Word...

(Joshua 6:8) do not give away or sell an object. Destroy the objects by smashing or burning. If you are unsure of any object, pray over it, anoint it with oil, and command all spirits to leave in Jesus' name. After purging your house, pray the following prayer:

"Heavenly Father, I confess as sin my obtaining and my possessing objects that were made or originated by anyone who has been involved in ungodly practices that are forbidden in Your Word. I renounce all involvement, whether knowingly or in ignorance, with Satan and the occult. If any evil spirits have gained access to my mind, my life, or my home, I resist them with the blood of Jesus, and command them to leave right now. I break all evil curses that have been brought on me and my family in Jesus' name. Thank you Jesus for being made a curse for me that I might be free."

Chapter 6

The Deliverance Session

1. The Practical Process

If you research the methodology of various deliverance ministries, you will find that most adhere to a similar basic strategy for an effective deliverance session. A groundwork must be laid that will create a spiritual atmosphere conducive to successful ministry. Some may find the methodology tedious and restrictive, but the fact of the matter is that each component is absolutely necessary. You will see in Section II of this chapter an insight connecting the process of the deliverance session to a progression into the Biblical temple's Holy of Holies. The priests of the temple did not "run" into the Holy of Holies without first engaging in a preparatory process. We hold that deliverance is most effective when it is conducted from a base laid through a process of several preparatory actions/prayers. A common complaint is that using "steps" in a deliverance session restricts the flow of the Holy Spirit. This need not be the case at all. We purposely remain sensitive to the Holy Spirit at all times for His direction. We welcome any interruption or change He might direct in the order of the deliverance session. We have found, however, that the Holy Spirit never changes or interrupts the essential spiritual elements that accompany every successful deliverance session. Sessions conducted in this manner may not be as sensational as other methods but we believe they are more thorough and less stressful on the client. We feel that such methodology, when combined with inner healing, ministers to the whole person and achieves a more complete healing effect.

Every deliverance team feels that their method works the best. With God's grace upon each deliverance session, we are constantly finding new information and insights that improve the deliverance process. Yet the more we learn, the more we find that we don't know. The Lord teaches us through every encounter with the demonic (as we learn and grow in this ministry, we are amazed that anyone was set free from our humble attempts years ago!) Even so, after hundreds and hundreds of successful deliverances, we would never be so arrogant as to say that our methodology is the best, or that other approaches are inferior. We desire to remain open-minded and teachable. Yet, we do believe that God has taught us some amazing things. With each additional piece of knowledge, our ministry gets easier, and the results greater. The Lord always and graciously confirms each new insight gained through another deliverance ministry, the Word, or a teaching. As we add each new weapon to our arsenal, winning each battle is more assured and the outcome more certain. Although we feel strongly about every component of our deliverance process, the basics that we feel every deliverance must contain are as follows.

1) Bind the Strongman

Mark 3:27 (amp.) says, "But no one can go into a strongman's house and ransack his household goods right and left and seize them as plunder unless he first binds the strongman; then indeed he may thoroughly plunder his house."

Isaiah 49:25 (amp.) reads, "Even the captives of the mighty will be taken away, and the prey of the terrible will be delivered; for I will contend with him who contends with you, and I will give safety to your children, and ease them." There are those who believe that the "strongman" referred to in this scripture is a ruler demon resident in the client. It is our belief, however, that the strongman is Satan. Since demonic spirits present in our client must be loosed (not bound), in order to be cast out, it doesn't make sense to bind one of them in prayer at the onset of the deliverance session.

Satan has indeed stolen from each of us since our very conception. It is our great delight to see restored to others all that the thief has taken (i.e. peace, joy, health, etc.). We must exercise our God-given authority and render the Accuser of the Brethren powerless against the deliverance.

We would, however, be in agreement with the opinion that this strongman might be Satan's delegated principality over a given geographic area. Thus, when we bind the strongman we are preventing Satan through this principality from hindering the deliverance session from outside interference. But, we state again, this is not any spirit present within our deliverance client. Therefore, as we bind the strongman we are in effect preventing demonic interference from outside the locale of the deliverance session.

2) Plead the Blood of Jesus

Demons know that the shed of blood of the Lamb is active, living and powerful against them. They hate hearing scriptures, songs or conversation about the blood. We remind them and Satan that the blood of Jesus is on our hands as we lay hands on the deliverance candidate. As we speak it, the results are amazing. We've "painted" the person's head with the blood when there were mind-binding spirits at work. Several individuals have told us that they literally saw red in their mind and felt spirits flee quickly as the last inch of space was covered with the blood.

Another highly successful tactic has been to have the individual "drink" the blood. As we speak this, the person begins gagging and choking, and then expels what we call "demons of the tongue or speech" (lying, accusation, profanity, mocking, deaf and dumb, incoherence, etc.). These demons often try to choke the person, cutting off their airway and closing up their throat. Watching someone turn blue before your eyes will make you desperate enough to try something radical (like having them "swallow the blood"). Finding that it works instantly, will convince you to add it to your arsenal.

We apply the blood to everyone present at the deliverance, their families, possessions, jobs, finances, pets, etc. In short – anything that pertains to them. We do not fear retribution from the enemy after deliverance because we have applied the protective powerful blood of Jesus.

3) Angelic Protection

It has been our experience that most Christians believe in angels and agree that one of their main functions is to protect believers. Hebrews 1:4 (amp.) says, "Are you not the angels sent out in the service of God for the assistance of those who are to inherit salvation?" A familiar scripture is Luke 4:10 (amp.) which reads, "For it is written, He will give His angels charge over you to guard and watch over you closely and carefully." As we look at a similar scripture in

Ps. 91:11, we see a condition attached to this promise (amp.): "For He will give His angels [special] charge over you to accompany and defend and preserve you in all your ways [of obedience and service]." As the Amplified version infers, angelic protection comes as we walk in obedience and service to God.

Remember that we cannot command angels; only God can. We can ask God to send angelic protection or assistance, but we cannot give the orders ourselves.

4) Unity and release of the Gifts of the Holy Spirit (Ps. 133:1, I Cor. 1:10)

It goes without saying that the deliverance team must be in one accord for a successful deliverance to take place. The deliverance candidate must also be united with them in purpose and procedure. Although it is not necessary for the candidate to have the Baptism in the Holy Spirit, we believe all deliverance ministers should be Spirit-filled. We cannot imagine conducting a deliverance without the benefit of the Holy Spirit's gifts of discernment, word of knowledge, and the prophetic. Any or all of the gifts of the Holy Spirit can be utilized in a deliverance session. Without the Holy Spirit's help, we are limited to our own perceptions, observations, and the information given by the deliverance candidate. What inadequate preparation for spiritual warfare! We believe deliverance teams that have not been baptized in the Holy Spirit with the evidence of speaking in tongues will only experience a modicum of success.

As for the individual seeking deliverance, we often find that they have sought the baptism in the Holy Spirit without success prior to deliverance ministry. We have had good results praying for the in-filling after deliverance. Often demons of doubt and unbelief or religiosity and doctrinal errors hinder the flow of the Holy Spirit in a person. After these spirits are removed, the Holy Spirit is free to flow. We describe it as the removal of a spiritual "log-jam," which allows the river of God to flow freely.

Opening Prayer

In summary then, a sample prayer incorporating all these elements would be as follows:

Lord Jesus Christ, we come to you now in agreement and unity on behalf of _____.

We declare by faith that we are one unit, one instrument for the flow of your deliverance power to them. We declare as an act of faith that you have provided for all our needs by your death on the cross and your resurrection from the dead.

And, in the spirit realm, in your provision, _____ is free and delivered. We intend to see now the fruit of that provision manifested to them and operating in their life.

Lord Jesus, we know that it is only through you that we can minister deliverance and it was by your blood that our right to minister was purchased. Through that blood you purchased for us salvation, healing, deliverance and access to the Holy Spirit's power.

We thank you for your blood and we now cover ourselves with it.

We declare to Satan that we operate under the Blood covering of Jesus Christ and it now covers each one of us and anything connected to us. It covers this room and this place where we meet to minister.

Additionally, we declare our families, our possessions, our finances and all else in connection to us is now covered by the Blood of Jesus. That blood prevents any outside demonic interference with this deliverance. It prevents the demonic from exacting any price from _____ for receiving deliverance ministry or their attacking us for ministering deliverance.

All is now under the protective Blood of Jesus Christ and all forces of evil must pass over us.

We declare that we have available to us the protection of God's angels and request that God would send angelic assistance to us for this deliverance session. We ask you Father, for a special assignment of angels to guard us and partner with us for this time of deliverance. We ask that angels be stationed around us, about this room and over and around this place where we meet. We pray that they would cut off any demonic spirit that would attempt to hinder, enter in, or connect with demons present being cast out. We pray that God's angels would turn back such demonic powers. We pray God's angels be stationed beside and about anything connected to us; to guard our families and possessions from any form of demonic retribution against the deliverance.

Lord Jesus, we bind the strongman in keeping with your word "If one would enter the house, one must first bind the strongman." We identify Satan as the strongman and the thief and we bind him away from this session of deliverance.

We declare our intention to enter the house, by the Spirit, and return to _____ all that Satan has stolen. And as we do so, Satan, the strongman is bound away from us and bound from causing any interference, or any resistance. We do this in the name of Jesus and by the Blood of Jesus.

We welcome you now Holy Spirit. Without your specific power, presence, anointing and equipping we could not minister deliverance. Therefore, we issue a special invitation to you to enter into this time of ministry. You have all the control. We ask that you direct us and advise us. Expose and illuminate every scheme and strategy of the enemy that we might identify it, reverse it, and defeat it.

Anoint us with your power – especially the anointing of the forehead of David to set captives free. Make each of your gifts accessible to us now, particularly your word of wisdom, your word of knowledge and your discerning of spirits.

Flow now Holy Spirit and release this captive bound by Satan. Consume the sacrifice and cleanse the house. We pray all of this now in the blessed name of Jesus. As we close this prayer we raise that name up over each of us, this place and all connected to us. We confess Jesus as our highest covering and authority. Jesus Christ, at that name every knee bows, every tongue confesses and every creature submits. The name of Jesus is now over us. All demonic powers will submit to our authority in Jesus Christ; and, we pray all of these things in the name of our Lord Jesus Christ. Amen.

II. Biblical Precept

Our deliverance session thus begins with a prayer that covers the four aforementioned deliverance "musts" (with the addition of the "Name of Jesus" professed at the prayer's close). An interesting insight gained through the conduct of deliverances over the years is the similarity this part of the session bears to entering the Mosaic Tabernacle/temple. As we pray this commencing prayer to start the session, it is as if we are entering into God's presence by way of the stations of the Biblical temple: "the Outer Court" (of sacrifice and purification), "the Holy Place" (of the Spirits of God/lamp stand, table of showbread, and alter of incense/praise), and, finally, "the Holy of Holies" (containing the covenantal Ark of God's Mercy Seat).

As we progress inward to God's presence and covering (specifically for deliverance), there is an anointing that is imparted to us. This makes us keenly effective for each specific deliverance session.

For emphasis, then, let's recap each of these elements again, as well as their significance. As we do so, picture us walking through the tabernacle and experiencing God's spiritual provisions. Keep in mind that these are not in rigid order – there is some overlap. But we do progress deeper into God's presence and under His covering as each element is professed through our opening prayers.

A. The Blood of Jesus

Why is this so essential to us, not just for deliverance, but for all ministry? Put simply, it is the blood of Jesus that has purchased our salvation. In fact, without the blood there is no salvation. An individual must accept the fact of that blood shed by Jesus for their sins and acknowledge Him as Lord to receive salvation. Without this occurrence an individual cannot receive salvation; and, salvation should normally precede deliverance. We do not take individuals through deliverance who are not born again. Frank Hammond has founded his ministry upon the fact that "deliverance is the children's bread." More on bread later, but why must there be a blood sacrifice and why do we receive authority and protection by giving assent to its reality? The answer rests in the foundational manner of God's establishment of justice, and allowance for propitiation (payment) and redemption. Two excellent books on this subject are H.A. Maxwell Whyte's classic, <u>The Power of the Blood</u>, and Joyce Meyer's, <u>The Word, the Name, and the Blood</u>.

Essentially, God established in His process for restoration from the curse of sin (once sin had entered the world) a requirement for a blood sacrifice. Just as in the human body where blood functions as a "cleanser" (collecting impurities from the various parts of the body), so too, in the Spirit realm does the shedding of blood bring an atoning cleansing from sin's effects. In the Old Testament system of sacrifices, the blood of various animals was shed for specific types of spiritual needs. The supreme sacrificial act, under this system, was the pouring out of blood upon the mercy seat on the Ark of God's Covenant with Israel. This was done by the High Priest once a year on the Day of Atonement. Only he alone, carrying the blood of a perfect lamb, could enter the Holy of Holies (behind the veil of the tabernacle) and pour it out upon the mercy seat to atone with God for the sins of the people.

Can you see the parallel with Jesus? This is what the book of Hebrews depicts. <u>Once and for all</u>, Jesus Christ, as the perfect sacrificial Lamb, poured out His own blood upon the mercy seat (represented by the cross of crucifixion) in payment, <u>forever</u>, for all our sins.

By that act, God's eternal judgment on mankind's sin was appeased. The payment for sin unto death was paid by our High Priest with His own life's blood. Now, through belief in this act and subsequent faith in Jesus, we are children of God and heirs with Christ.

Consider these scriptures:

"For the life of the flesh is in the blood. And I have given it to you upon the altar to make an atonement for your souls: for it is the blood that makes an atonement for the soul" (Leviticus 17:11). As described in Exodus and Leviticus, sacrifice for sin had to be made year after year, over and over. It was never a completed work, but was a shadow – a type of what Jesus would do completely.

As described in Hebrews 9:12-14:

"He went once for all into the Holy of Holies, not by virtue of the blood of goats and calves, but His own blood, having found and secured a complete redemption. For if the sprinkling of an unholy and defiled person with the blood of goats and bulls and ashes of a burnt heifer is sufficient for the purification of the body, how much more surely shall the Blood of Christ, who by virtue of His eternal Spirit has offered Himself as an unblemished sacrifice to God, purify our consciences from dead works and lifeless observances."

By His shed blood and by His death and triumphant resurrection, Jesus Christ has purchased for us ALL things. Through Him, we have salvation, healing, deliverance, and a way into fullness of life in the Holy Spirit.

Jesus has forever "mediated" a new covenant for us. Again, Hebrews states, "Therefore brethren, having boldness to enter the holiest by the Blood of Jesus, by a new and living way which He consecrated for us, through the veil, that is, His flesh, and having a High Priest over the House of God, let us draw near with a true heart, in full assurance of faith, having our hearts sprinkled from an evil conscience and our bodies washed with pure water. Let us hold fast the confession of our hope without wavering, for He who promised is faithful" (Heb. 10:19-23).

We may enter the Tabernacle at the Altar of Sacrifice (salvation) in the outer court, and progress through to the very Holy of Holies on the path laid by Jesus, our High Priest. There upon the very mercy seat of God, we receive all Christ bought for us with His blood. Deliverance is included in "all" but we must believe it and by faith appropriate it.

Satan knows, fears, and hates this fact, but he must comply with it. Therefore, we plead the blood on our behalf as we begin each deliverance session. In so doing, we acknowledge for ourselves and remind Satan and his demons, before God, that the blood of Jesus provides: Protection (Exodus 12:7, 12,13), Healing (I Peter 2:23), and <u>Power and Authority</u> (Rev. 12:11; Heb. 4:16), in addition to <u>Redemption</u> (II Cor. 5:21) and <u>Forgiveness</u> (Mat.26: 28)

God's system of justice, laws, and precepts mandated death for sin. <u>God's love for us, His creation, inclined Him toward mercy for us.</u> The blood of Jesus provided the way from one to the other. As <u>the scripture says, if Satan had realized this, he would not have orchestrated Jesus' death on the cross.</u>

"But we speak the wisdom of God in a mystery, the hidden wisdom which God ordained before the ages for our glory, which none of the rulers of this age knew; <u>for had they known, they would not have crucified the Lord of Glory"</u> (I Cor. 2:7-8). Now Satan must contend with the reality of this as we plead the blood in commencement of each deliverance session.

B. The Angels of God

As we follow Jesus into the Tabernacle, approaching God for His covering and anointing (by the Holy Spirit), we (as His children and heirs), have a right to ask for angelic assistance. As Jesus is "Lord Sabaoth," <u>the Captain of all the hosts of angelic armies, we can ask for a dispatch of angels to assist us as we engage in the ministry of a deliverance session.</u> We may ask for and expect to receive an assignment of angels to protect us from demonic resistance and shield us from demonic interference surrounding the deliverance session.

Once again, the book of Hebrews states: "But you have come to Mount Zion and to the city of the living God, the heavenly Jerusalem, **to an innumerable company of angels**, to the general assembly and church of the firstborn who are registered in Heaven, to God, <u>the Judge of all</u>, to the spirits of just men made perfect, to <u>Jesus the Mediator of the New Covenant</u>, and to the blood of sprinkling that speaks better things than that of Abel." Heb. 12:22-24.

Let's remind the devil of these facts as we begin our session. Let's loose a "company of angels" sent by the Lord of Hosts against Satan's hosts of evil that would seek to hinder us in the effective ministry of liberation for those held captive.

C. Binding the Strongman

Though there are other demonic "strongmen" encountered in deliverance (various demonic groups may have a strongman over it), we believe that only Satan, the chief strongman, must be bound from interfering with a deliverance session. It may be debated as to whether we are addressing Satan himself or his territorial demonic prince/ruler representing him over our area. We don't debate this point. We simply apply the principle illustrated in Mark 3:27. In truth, Satan has ultimately been bound by Jesus' victory, but it has been left to us to enforce that "binding."

As we move into the Tabernacle, the very stations themselves prevent Satan's access. Unholiness cannot pass through the temple of God without being exposed. At times, the demons will begin to manifest in deliverance as we pray this opening prayer. They do not desire to enter a place of holiness; and, will desire to leave the area saturated with God's righteous presence.

As we bind the strongman away from our session, we render him powerless to stop the restoration of a person's spiritual blessings (their "goods") to rightful ownership. As we progress into the Tabernacle, binding the strongman as we go, we establish the "state" of Psalm 91 in our deliverance session.

"He who dwells in the secret place of the Most High shall abide under the shadow of the Almighty. I will say of the Lord, 'He is my Refuge and my Fortress; my God, in Him I will trust.' Surely, He shall deliver you from the snare of the fowler, and from the perilous pestilence" (verse 1-3).

Indeed, God will answer us in the "secret place" as in verses 14-16, "because (you) have known My Name. (You) shall call on Me, and I will answer (you); I will be with (you) in trouble; I will **deliver** (you) and honor (you). With long life, I will satisfy (you), and show you My salvation."

Consider this:

And while Satan has been bound (determined) to steal the recipient's goods, he is now bound (certain) to be frustrated because he is bound (divinely prevented) from stopping the process of restoration by deliverance.

D. The Holy Spirit

Making our way deeper into the Tabernacle and into the Holy Place, we encounter the golden lampstand of seven candles. As detailed in Isaiah 11:2, these represent the seven spiritual attributes of God residing in and imparted by the Holy Spirit. These attributes or "ministries" of the Holy Spirit are: exalting the Lord's (Jesus') rule, wisdom, understanding, counsel, might, knowledge, and fear (reverence).

How could we minister deliverance effectively without these qualities of the Holy Spirit's nature? We must depend upon the Holy Spirit's guidance as we enter into the supernatural realm to contend with the demonic over a person's freedom. Without the Holy Spirit present with us behind (and through) the veil, we are blind, deaf, and dumb. In "the Holy Place" within the Tabernacle, the only light is provided by the lampstand of the Holy Spirit. Behind the veil within the "Holy of Holies," the only light is provided by God's Shekinah glory. How then can we see to move without God's Spirit to guide us? Every deliverance session is undertaken by the power of the Holy Spirit working through us as ministers. Without His anointing, His discernment, His supernatural knowledge, His divine strategy, we can have no deep and lasting effect upon the demonic. Thus, we call on the Holy Spirit's assistance/anointing as we begin each deliverance session.

E. The Name of Jesus

As we move through the Holy Place, we pass the last two stations – "the Table of Showbread" and the "Altar of Incense." These both speak of Jesus; and, the Name of Jesus is the last element we include in our opening deliverance prayer. Just as the bread that is laid out on the "Table of Showbread," Jesus is the Bread of Life that has been broken apart (in His very body) for the sake of our healing and deliverance. Deliverance and inner healing are under the "umbrella" of healing ministry. The punishment Jesus received upon His body was to purchase healing (including deliverance) on our behalf. This was combined with the bruising He suffered within His body to break forever the power of iniquity over our lives.

Jesus, in His own body, is the Bread of Life for us. This is why deliverance, as part of that bread represented by Jesus, can be "the children's bread." Just as the priests ate the showbread once each week (after it had soaked up God's power and presence before the Holy of Holies), as we "feed" on Jesus' bread, we receive life, power and freedom.

Consider the following passage from The Tabernacle by David M. Levy: "The term 'Showbread' comes from a Hebrew word that means 'Bread of the Face' or 'Bread of Presence', because the loaves were set before the face or presence of Jehovah (who dwelt in the Holy of Holies) as a meal offering from the children of Israel (Lev. 24:8). God gazed with delight on the pure bread offering that sat continually before His face. Bread is called the staff of life and is emblematic of life itself. The showbread was a foreshadowing of Jesus Christ, who is the true bread of life, giving unfailing sustenance to all who partake of Him. He was born in the city of Bethlehem, which means House of bread.

Jesus emphasized that He alone is the true bread from God who will give eternal life to all who believe (John 6:30-33). Jesus then made a startling statement: 'I am the living bread that came down from Heaven; if any man eat of this bread, he shall live forever; and the bread that I will give is my flesh, which I will give for the life of the world (John 6:51)'. The metaphor 'eat of this bread' did not teach the necessity of literally eating the flesh of Jesus to acquire eternal life. Jesus simply taught that as food becomes part of an individual as it is consumed, so all who believe in Him as the one who gives life are completely assimilating Him.

Today many Christians are spiritually starving. Some attend churches that only feed them the humanistic, philosophic opinions of the world. Others attend churches that feed them the husk of spiritual experience without sound teaching from the word of God."

Guide me, O Thou great Jehovah,
Pilgrim through this barren land;
I am weak, but Thou art mighty;
Hold me with thy powerful hand;
Bread of Heaven, bread of Heaven,
Feed me till I want no more, Feed me till I want no more.

Open now the crystal fountain,
Whence the healing stream doth flow,
Let the fire and cloudy pillar,
Lead me all my journey through,
Strong Deliverer, Strong Deliverer,
Be Thou still my strength and shield,
Be Thou still my strength and shield.

God's intent is that we should feed on the entire loaf represented in the person of Jesus Christ. Within that full loaf of Jesus, as our showbread, is salvation, healing and deliverance.

Deliverance is as normative to the Body of Christ as it was to Jesus' ministry. Jesus is the Way, the Truth, and the Life. Jesus is the Word of God become flesh. Jesus is the Bread of God's Word (active and living) as well as the Bread of Life. He came that we might know Him, the Truth, and be set free. He came that we might have life and abundant life. All this He accomplished through the sacrifice of His very body and the out-pouring of His own blood. Confessing this leads us to the "Altar of Incense." Jesus offered Himself up as a sacrifice – a sweet smelling aroma – pleasing to God the Father. The offering up of His own person as a sacrifice for our redemption leads us through the veil into the Holy of Holies. There, ultimately, the very blood of Jesus is poured out upon the "Mercy Seat" and the purchase of our eternal life is complete. This is what is meant by Galatians 2:20 "I have been crucified with Christ; it is no longer I who live, but Christ lives in me, and the life which I now live in the flesh I live by faith in the Son of God, Who loved me and gave Himself for me." Isaiah 53:5 states: "But He was wounded for our **transgressions** (Pesha: rebellion, trespass, sin), he was bruised for our **iniquities** (Avon: crooked direction, bent toward sinfulness/sinning)"

Upon the cross Jesus Christ paid a price within and upon his own body for our sins and our "draw" toward sinning. In so doing, He purchased our deliverance. Upon that cross, Christ's side and heart were pierced by a spear causing a flow of blood and water (John 19: 31-35). That very blood and water birthed our salvation and deliverance. It purchased our redemption by the blood and our purification by the water. The "placenta" of Christ's heart, pregnant with our souls, burst as His "water broke" and the reconciliation of humanity was birthed. We can now be saved from eternal judgment by that blood and regenerated and cleansed by that water. From the blood and the water of Christ's own heart came our justification and our sanctification. The piercing of Christ's own side and internal organs provided for our own **inner healing**. So, through Christ's sacrifice on the cross our salvation, physical healing, inner healing and deliverance are provided for. Upon the name of Jesus, and no other, rests our salvation and our deliverance.

It is in recognition of this fact that we complete our opening prayer "in the Name of Jesus." We raise that Name up over us as an ultimate covering and sign of our authority in Him. It is the banner of the Name of Jesus that is displayed over us as we engage the demonic in deliverance ministry. As Isaiah 59:19 states, "So shall they fear the Name of the Lord from the west, and His glory from the rising of the sun; when the enemy comes in like a flood, the Spirit of the Lord will lift up a standard against him."

As we complete our prayer, we raise that standard, the Name of Jesus, against the flood of the enemy. We remind Satan and his demons that "He who is in us is greater than he (Satan) that is in the world." We remind them of the power contained in the Name, of Jesus, as described in Isaiah 9:6, "And His Name will be called Wonderful, Counselor, Mighty God, Everlasting Father, Prince of Peace, of the increase of his government, there will be no end, upon the throne of David and over His Kingdom." The Kingdom of Jesus – the Kingdom of God has been provided for and justified universally. The establishment of the operation of God's Kingdom is now being accomplished. Remember Matthew 11:12, "And from the days of John the Baptist until now, the Kingdom of Heaven has endured violent assault, and violent men seize it by force (as a precious prize—a share in the heavenly Kingdom is sought with most ardent zeal and intense exertion)" (Amplified Bible). Deliverance ministry, as we have said, initiates this confrontation with the demonic and releases the manifestation of the Kingdom of God (and its blessing) in the life of the believer. Again, Jesus said, "But if I cast out demons with the finger of God, surely the Kingdom of God has come upon you."

As we open the deliverance session, progressing into the Holy of Holies with this prayer, we state our intent to break the grip of the demonic in a believer's life and thus demonstrate "the Kingdom of God has come upon you."

III. Confession, Renunciation and Forgiveness

With the completion of this prayer offered by the deliverance team, the impetus for the deliverance shifts to the recipient. According to Biblical precedent, the one seeking deliverance, as with all seeking reconciliation with God, must **confess** before God, **renounce** old sin practices and patterns, and **forgive** others. Following the Biblical pattern we've been discussing of "Tabernacle" practices, we as deliverance ministers ("priests") have made intercession on behalf of the counselee/recipient. Now, **they** must take action. God always requires some act of faith to be initiated by those seeking from Him (as a demonstration of their earnest desire as well as their dependence upon and trust in Him).

In following the example of Jesus, who sacrificed Himself for our sake, the deliverance recipient must offer themselves up before God for the reception of His ministry, and, at the time, make sacrifice of all that would hinder the process—as Heb. 12:1 says, "Let us lay aside every weight and the sin which so easily ensnares us." The counselee who will **not** do this will not receive deliverance. A person must be willing, following the example laid by Jesus, to enact the plea of Romans 12:1, "I beseech you therefore, brethren, by the mercies of God, that you present your bodies a living sacrifice, holy, acceptable to God, which is your reasonable service."

The literal Old Testament practice of sacrificing animals is passed away. Jesus has replaced it by His own ultimate act, sacrificing Himself instead. As believers in Him, considering the overall plan of salvation and its inherent "mercies (blessings) of God," recipients of deliverance must lay themselves on the mercy seat by the blood of Jesus and seek God's delivering mercy.

Sacrificial Acts

This sacrifice, as related to a deliverance session, has three essential components (which occur next in the order of the session). **First** is a **deliverance prayer** that the recipient repeats. This is the prayer that we use:

Lord Jesus Christ, I thank you for dying on the cross of Calvary for me. I accept you as my Savior. You redeemed me by Your blood, and I belong to You.

Just as you rose again from the dead, I believe you can resurrect me from bondage and deliver me. As my Lord and my Deliverer, I call on You to deliver me and set me free from every bondage of the enemy. I turn from my sin. I ask You, Father, to forgive me for all known and unknown sin. I claim the promise of Your word, "Behold, I give to you authority over all the power of the enemy, and nothing shall by any means harm you" (Luke 10:19). I renounce you, Satan, and all your works in my life. I resist you as an act of my will and in the strength that Jesus Christ gives me. In Jesus' Name, I separate myself from you with the blood of Jesus and the resurrection power of the Holy Spirit. I command you to leave right now, in Jesus' Name! Amen.

This prayer, based on one by Derek Prince, is structured to lead to a confession and public acceptance of certain key spiritual principles. These parallel Derek Prince's nine steps to deliverance: **Personally affirm faith in Christ; humble yourself; confess known (and unknown) sin; repent; break with the occult/demonic; forgive; be restored to God; release from curses; command Satan/demonic to go.**

Second, following this prayer, the one receiving deliverance is led to renounce all past involvement in ungodly/occult/unscriptural practices. For this, we use our "deliverance checklist" (see the appendix). In an attitude of prayer, the recipient is led to renounce, category by category, all such practices. These categories are based on traditional "entry points" of the demonic: superstitions and the occult; sexual sins; false religions; trauma/shock (not usually renounced, but prayed over); iniquities; addictive/compulsive behaviors; drugs and alcohol use.

Third, the one seeking deliverance is taken through a list of individuals to be forgiven (This list is compiled during the last counseling sessions prior to deliverance). The person is asked, with each individual name, to say, "I choose to forgive __(name)__ for __(what)__." It should be understood that often **feelings** of forgiveness and the <u>act</u> of forgiveness may be separate. Let us clarify. A person may forgive another person in Christ (by the power of the Holy Spirit and an act of the will) without liking, respecting, trusting, **or having relationship with** that person. In some instances, where the one being forgiven has not repented and ceased their destructive behavior, it would be unwise for the one who forgives to maintain a relationship with that person. Old "wrongs" may yet be unreconciled and have little potential for being so. Yet, the one who is seeking deliverance can forgive the other in Christ and release them from any personal judgment, committing them to Christ's direction.

It should be noted that forgiveness may come through Christ by the Holy Spirit. Relationship and trust must be rebuilt over time as a result of a demonstrated change in behavior by the one being forgiven. Lacking this, there can be no restoration of trust or relationship. Some, unwisely and wrongly, profess that until an individual can have relationship again with the one who has wronged them, they have not truly forgiven. This line of reasoning and religious error would send the one molested or the one raped back to the offender. It would return the battered spouse to the physically abusive husband at risk of life. It would resign the abused, damaged person to a lifetime of existence within a spiritually abusive church under an errant, controlling, abusive pastor. To this we say, "NO!" **That** would be wrong to do.

One can forgive another as an act of one's will, thereby **choosing** to do so, without returning to old, destructive relationships with abusive individuals. Before God, those who have thus forgiven are truly viewed as having met all scriptural pre-requisites for acts of forgiveness (even if they do not reestablish former relationships).

IV. General Preparations

Upon completion of these items in the deliverance session (opening prayer, personal prayer, renunciation/repentance, forgiveness prayer) the base is laid to proceed with the "core" of the deliverance session – casting out demons. Before discussing that and strategies for the session, let us review some general guidelines for the session.

ROOM SET-UP

We clear all extra furniture from the room except a table to hold items for the session (worksheets, grouping list, water, Kleenex, writing tablets, pens and anointing oil), chairs for client and team, trashcan with clean liner, tape player and music tapes.

We arrange the chairs/ table as follows: Team leaders facing each other with the client seated between them facing into the center of the room. These 3 chairs are at one end of the room with a table flush against the wall behind the client. This allows a place to lay the "groupings" checklist within view of the co-leaders. Also copies of deliverance prayers are placed there for use as needed.

Other team members are seated about 8 feet away and facing this trio. Normally we only have one other team member who is primarily an intercessor. We don't recommend more than four team members in addition to the client. Over the years we have completed 95% of our deliverances with a team of three.

We do recommend a team of both male and female members. All of one gender (either male or female) makes it inappropriate to minister to the opposite gender (i.e.; all male teams or all female teams should not minister to their opposite gender). With both male and female ministers on the deliverance team, the team is released to minister to either male or female.

SUPPORT ITEMS (and reasons)

We utilize the following items for the deliverance session:

A. Chairs – Folding metal chairs are ideal or the padded type used in many churches but **without arms**. Arms can prove a hindrance to the team in "laying hands" on the client and on occasion the demonic spirits use them to resist ministry.

B. Tables – A long narrow folding table (18" x 6') works ideally behind the deliverance client and co-leaders.

C. Kleenex – A Full box of unscented, non-lubricated work well.

D. A small (8 gallon) trashcan – Make sure the liner is fresh.

E. Legal pads and pens – To record prophesies, strategy, insights, and sometimes team members' communications (when verbal directives would alarm the client or alert the demons).

F. Hi-Liters and a medium point marker – To identify spirit groups (added to list if needed) and to check off those groups as they are dealt with. As we met with the client prior to deliverance we Hi-Lighted all demonic groups we determined to be present needing deliverance. The Holy Spirit may reveal additional groups during the deliverance session. If this occurs they are Hi-Lited.

G. Water for Team and Client – Manifestations for the client and verbal commands for the team can create a dry throat. Non-carbonated Bottled spring water provides relief. Water also helps relieve unpleasant tastes for the client (following some manifestations).

H. Anointing oil – Olive oil is sufficient but there are numerous brands available at Christian bookstores throughout the USA. We produce our own based on Old Testament scriptures listing calamus, myrrh, cassia and cinnamon as ingredients. We make this available on request for a modest donation ($7 per _ oz.). See our ad at the back of the book.

DELIVERANCE TEAM

As stated the team should consist of a maximum of four members with both male and female genders included. We require the team to arrive a minimum of 30 minutes prior to the start in order to pray and receive an overview of the client's background and specific deliverance needs.

This helps to establish the spiritual atmosphere conducive to deliverance. We ask the team to remain sensitive to the Holy Spirit throughout the day of deliverance. The Holy Spirit will often reveal strategies for the session based on the specific deliverance needs of the client. During the day, team members may experience travail or prayer burdens for the deliverance recipient._

Presence of spirits such as Jezebel or witchcraft may cause team members to experience nausea or headaches during the day. Spirits of grief or depression or death may cause team members to "feel" the effects of their presence. The Holy Spirit will use this as team preparation for deliverance.

In addition, the team should be diligent to continually take their own spiritual "pulse." Anything that could create what is called "common ground" with a client's areas of deliverance need should be immediately resolved. Common ground is created when the one ministering has the same area(s) of need as the one receiving ministry.

The demons will use this condition to hinder, or even stop, the progress of the deliverance.

Following completion of a deliverance, the team should also pray over each other to prevent any demonic spirits (trailing spirits) from attempting to follow them from the deliverance location. We call this prayer for "dusting off."

SPIRITUAL ATMOSPHERE

Every effort should be made prior to the commencement of the session to establish an environment that is free of distractions, peace-filled and conducive to the operation of the Holy Spirit. To that end we do the following:

- Allow no one in attendance or in the immediate area that would distract the recipient or hinder the team (spouses, children, relatives, prayer partners, etc.) Often these will have a soul tie with the client that cannot be severed with them present.
- Begin to play (at least 30 minutes prior) praise or spiritual warfare music (or a combination of both).
- Upon the arrival of the recipient, demonstrate confidence, encouragement and certainty. They will usually feel somewhat anxious and uncertain at this unfamiliar spiritual encounter. The team should appear upbeat and attentive to them. Introduce team members and assure the recipient of a victorious deliverance. Take care of their "comfort" requirements: Something to drink, room temperature, bathroom break, etc.
- As a general rule we do not meet at the recipient's home. We ask them to come to our ministry center. This helps to assure the proper spiritual atmosphere for conducting deliverance.

V. Order of Deliverance

Immediately prior to casting out the demonic spirits several actions are taken. If applicable, one of several prayers may be prayed.

- A. Forgiveness prayer: On occasion, if this is an area of particular struggle for an individual (rape victim, abuse victim, etc.) a more specific and detailed confession of forgiveness may be offered.
- B. Renunciation of Masonic effect: If there has been direct involvement or extensive generational involvement in the Masonic Lodge (Freemasonry) a detailed prayer renouncing

Masonic practices may need to be offered.

C. <u>Iniquity Prayer</u>: If generational curses (iniquity) is a particular issue a detailed prayer may be offered to counter this and sever "cords" of iniquity. This will be followed during the progress of the session by breaking cords of iniquity over each applicable demonic grouping.

Following any specific prayers needed the deliverance recipient is anointed with oil, the co-leaders lay on hands and all demonic spirits are loosed that have been bound to effect the commencement of casting them out. We have found that verbally loosing all spirits that have been bound to be vital to the effective flow of the deliverance.

We pray a prayer such as this:

"Lord Jesus, we present _____ before you now. We declare that they are consecrated for your ministry by anointing with oil and laying on hands. Deliver them and set them free from every demonic spirit.

We loose every demonic spirit that has been bound. You will release and go as we call your name. Nothing will remain hidden. Everything is revealed in the Light of the Holy Spirit.

You will not tear or torment or cause pain or discomfort. You will only loose and go as we direct you by the Holy Spirit.

We separate each spirit out from one another. No spirit will connect to another. You are cut off from each other by the Blood of Jesus. You will unhook one from another. Now loose and go as we command you."

At this point, we begin to cast out the demons as the Holy Spirit directs. We call them specifically by name and usually begin with "Mind Binding" (occult/witchcraft) spirits first. We typically, say, "I speak to every spirit in the area of _____. I command you to loose and go. Spirits of ...... (name every spirit noted in that particular group on the "Demon Groupings Worksheet"). Loose now and go."

VI. Strategies

We employ certain strategies as we conduct the "casting out" process (unless the Holy Spirit directs otherwise). As stated, we begin with the witchcraft/occult area identified by the grouping "Mind Binding" on our worksheet. We call out this group for <u>every</u> counselee due to the prevalence of the occult in our word/society today.

Groupings that might typically follow would be ones that have a particular probability of hindering the process: doubt/unbelief; escape; deaf and dumb; religious. However, we seek the Holy Spirit's direction upon each subsequent step.

Other strategies that are employed:

- **No conversing with demons.**
  They typically lie and will use conversation to delay being cast out.
- **Go for the strongest spirits last.**
  The strongest demons present will usually "sacrifice" the weaker ones by allowing their exit. Therefore, we use this fact to cast out all weaker spirits until, at the last, the stronger (ruler) demonic grouping(s) has none to draw support from. Keep in mind this is dependent upon the Holy Spirit's allowance. Sometimes, He will direct the addressing of the strongest first.
- **Stay in communication with your partner(s).**
  Both non-verbally and verbally, acting as a team, agree upon each deliverance step conducted (as to timing, group addressed, pacing etc.).
- When possible, and confirmed by the Holy Spirit, **cast out demons in groups of related groups.** This permits a smooth flow to the overall deliverance session and maintains a steady Holy Ghost "pressure" against the demons present. An example would be the groups of "Bitterness" then "Retaliation" then "Rebellion" then "Control," or, all the **"verbal"** spirit groups or all the "mental" spirit groups.

- **The strongest spirits** present, many times, are those that **entered at the earliest age** of the client. Being aware of this may assist in developing an order for casting out spirits (as you consider those demons entering in adulthood, youth, childhood and even womb). Be open to the Holy Spirit's "words" concerning these stages of a client's life and their application to the deliverance process strategy. Awareness of the client's life experiences at each stage of life gives a general strategy for the deliverance. You may thus cast out spirits beginning with the level of adulthood and continuing back to young adult, youth, childhood and "womb" or you may begin with the womb (in-utero) and progress to adulthood. The Holy Spirit will direct you. Keep in mind that this is only a guideline. Each deliverance is different, as we said. Therefore, submission to the Holy Spirit (rather than pat "formulas") is vital to a successful deliverance. Be ready to conduct inner healing as needed with each life stage addressed (and concurrent hurts identified).

VII. Manifestations/Casting Out

A key aspect of the deliverance session is demonic manifestation. As demons are commanded by name to leave their "host" (the person's body) they may cause certain "effects" upon the person. These effects may be any number of bodily actions and even speaking from the person's mouth.

A general guideline to remember with manifestations is that demonic spirits are "air" (they are of the spirit realm). Therefore they may exit the person in any manner that air might be expelled. This may include coughing, sighing, breathing, flatulence, burping or hiccups. Demons may exit through tears, itching, yawning or screaming.

Most counselees are anxious about "throwing up" as a manifestation. In actuality it is rarely the stomach content that is expelled. Most often, it is more like coughing up congestive matter or phlegm. It is important therefore to have a trash can available in the room (with a liner). In our deliverance experience we have seen less and less of this manifestation as we have learned more spiritual "tools" to employ in the process. These would include: complete counseling prior to deliverance; breaking soul ties; canceling iniquity; and, faithfully praying (the prayers discussed) at the start of each deliverance. We have found that there is no substitute for thorough preparation and adhering to a complete deliverance process. This serves to lessen the intensity of the deliverance session by removing systematically, those means by which demons are able to resist deliverance. We call it "cutting off their power source." John and Mark Sandford, in <u>Deliverance and Inner Healing,</u> confirm this same dynamic. They state that as they learned how to implement certain deliverance "tools" that demons left with a "whimper" instead of a "bang." They say insisting on a "bang" reaction indicates that our focus is on the demons instead of God and our client.

With regards to manifestations remember the authority we have in Jesus Christ. Through Him we have authority over not only the demons but also their manifestations. As a rule we counsel the person to allow demons to manifest in the deliverance as they will. Do not try to direct any certain manifestation. Allow the manifestations to flow freely. However, as the minister, if a certain manifestation causes pain or is too intense or is hindering the continuance of the deliverance, you may direct it to cease (by forbidding the demon to "tear" the individual) or even command the demon to change to another form of manifestation.

In Christ, by the Holy Spirit, you have full authority to direct the deliverance session. Exercise that authority, for the comfort and welfare of the counselee. If, for example, most demons in a given deliverance manifest by causing the person to cough and after several hours this causes the throat to be sore, you may, at the Holy Spirit's allowance, direct the demons to manifest another way. And, if a demon is causing intense pain in manifesting (headache, muscle spasms, stomach cramps, etc.) you can direct the demon to cease causing such pain. Likewise, by our authority in Christ we may exercise that authority to limit the intensity of any particular manifestation. Do not allow demons to "show out." Our goal is to cast them out and not to have a sensational session.

Overall, be prepared for foul sights and odors (Phlegm "nests"), offensive behaviors (threats, attempts at physical aggression, insults, lewd and foul language) and taunting, sarcastic or shocking behavior by the demons. Do not let this catch you off guard. The Holy Spirit through you is in total control no matter how much the demons, through the client, try to take control of the session. For the most part, they can only do what you allow them to do. And remember that no matter what they cause the client to do, it is the demons causing the behavior and not the person. Maintain a balance in your conduct of Godly compassion for the person, and, strict authority over and insistence on compliance from the demons. You must be able to separate the person from the demonic manifestation caused by the demons. Clients often describe feeling as if something inside of them was looking out **through** their eyes or speaking out **through** their mouth. They did not desire this, yet it was taking place. This indicates the demons present, illustrates the "dual" effect of a deliverance session, and forever convinces the person of the reality of the demonic realm and their ability to affect Christians. For the deliverance minister it is a personal observance of a time of "glimpsing" the supernatural realm. It is a point in time where the "fabric" between the realms of the natural and the supernatural realm becomes stretched so thin (so to speak) that we are able to see from one to the other. It is an occasion of personal awareness of Jesus' words, "If I cast out demons by the finger of God, then the Kingdom of God has come upon you."

We usually do not maintain continuous direct eye contact with the client. We have never needed to do so to keep the deliverance flowing and it is less stressful. However, at times, with a more resistant demon, we may ask the client to look at us eye to eye. This really tends to either intimidate or aggravate the demon present to the point of leaving. Remember Matthew 6:22 says, "The light of the body is the eye…" It is like catching a rabbit in a spotlight's glare. The light of God radiating from our eyes immobilizes the demon.

At times a demon will close the person' eyes to resist this eyeball-to-eyeball interaction. If so, you may have to pry the client's eyes open and command the demon to look at you. Usually as it does so it will exit immediately. Keep in mind that this is a more intense action taken to enforce our authority upon a resistant demon. It is only needed in unique situations.

Other "special" tactics that may be used in a deliverance include:

1. Having a person/demon drink (symbolically) the Blood of Jesus.
2. Praying over water to sanctify it and having the client drink it to break the "grip" of demonic resistance.
3. Stopping the session to pray intensely out loud in tongues and/or singing praise songs (particularly ones about the Blood of Jesus).
4. Laying hands on specific areas of the client's body where the demon may have "localized" to resist being cast out: the feet, the neck, the head, the back etc. Keep in mind modesty and avoid any inappropriate touch in "private" areas of the body. As a general principle, we constantly lay hands on the client throughout the deliverance. This imparts the power of God to the person and(against the demonic spirits) and facilitates deliverance. We allow the Holy Spirit to direct the location for laying on hands to maintain maximum spiritual "pressure" against those demons present.
5. Having one team member "walk" the room (pace back and forth) in order to block demonic interference from outside the session. They may pray to maintain a wall of fire as the one that protected Moses from Pharaoh's pursuit.

Throughout this part of the deliverance (casting out spirits) keep in mind, as much as possible, the comfort of the client. It is allowable, as needed, to take a restroom break or stand and stretch and sip some water. This will in no way hinder the deliverance flow, provided it is desired by the person and is not repeated too frequently (as a delaying tactic).

Usually after each concentrated flow of casting out several related demonic groups we ask the client if they need a short break. This helps to maintain a comfortable pace for the overall session and does not wear the client out physically. Think of the deliverance session as a marathon (long distance run) rather than a sprint or 100 yard dash.

This is why we have engaged in multiple pre-deliverance

sessions with the client - to build up strength and spiritual endurance for the "long run" of the final deliverance session. Yet, even in marathon runs, for runners who are in shape, there are "break stations" along the route with water and basic supplies. Approach the deliverance session with the same mindset. We have found that once the proper spiritual atmosphere is established for the conduct of deliverance it will not be disrupted by taking occasional breaks.

Demonic Resistance

As you conduct the deliverance session you may encounter various forms of demonic resistance to the completion of deliverance. These may include:

1. Causing pain in the client. This can be sharp stabbing pains, cramps, or headaches.
2. Causing bodily "distress" such as nausea, diarrhea or radical swings in body temperature (intense heat or cold).
3. Atmosphere of confusion projected over the deliverance team and client: An inability to focus/concentrate.

All of these conditions may be alleviated through exercise of the team's spiritual authority. With the command for these effects to cease, in Jesus' name, the demons will stop their resistance. However, this may have to be repeated periodically throughout the deliverance. Usually the power to resist with these means becomes less as the session progresses and more and more demons are cast out.

VIII. Deliverance Shut-Downs

There are times when a deliverance session seems to run into a wall. The flow of demons exiting seems to be blocked. Other times following deliverance, an individual does not seem to receive complete freedom. The following are a number of contributing factors.

1. **Curses directed at the person from individuals** having knowledge of the deliverance session taking place. These are not usually formal curses from those involved in the occult. Mostly they are statements of skepticism and doubt regarding the deliverance process. These persons may include spouse, friends, fellow church members or pastor, relatives or family members. Anything spoken about the session in a negative and skeptical manner can have the affect of a curse. If discerned during a deliverance, these need to be "broken" for the deliverance to progress effectively.

2. **Doubt and unbelief present in the client.** Demons will not exit compliantly if the person receiving deliverance is not fully confident in the process and the power of Jesus Christ to deliver. It should be noted that a person's faith usually strengthens as the deliverance ensues and they feel the increasing effects of liberation. This is normal. However, if the person begins the session in doubt as to its completion and continues to doubt throughout, the session will not be fully successful.

3. **Unforgiveness present on the part of the recipient of deliverance.** We must forgive others as Christ has forgiven us. Failure to do so can result in failure to receive complete deliverance. We have, at times, had a person remember someone they needed to forgive during the progression of the deliverance session. In such case we stop, pray a forgiveness prayer and continue the deliverance.

4. **Any unconfessed sin on the part of the person receiving deliverance.** Shame or fear of embarrassment may result in this. Remember that Satan is a legalist. Demons will hold to anything they feel gives them the right to stay. Therefore, failing to confess sin will provide them with legal ground to remain. It is due to this that we conduct an in depth renunciation prior to commencing the casting out of demons. This renunciation is based on the information gained during pre-deliverance counseling. Note that failure to see a certain

sinful behavior as sin on the part of the counselee can hinder the receiving of deliverance. Individuals come from various theological backgrounds and must be educated by the deliverance ministers as to the various types of sinful practices that open doorways to the demonic. Disagreement with these on the part of the deliverance recipient will affect the completion of deliverance as well as the ability to remain free.

5. **Lack of determined mindset by the recipient.** Derek Prince defines this as, "lack of desperation." For the most effective deliverance a person's will must be solidly "set" to receive. Demons can sense when their "host" is uncertain or casual about the process. A middle-of-the-road approach will result in a difficult or incomplete deliverance session. Recipients should be determined to receive complete deliverance. Like the woman who touched the hem of Jesus' garment, they must be willing to press through any resistance (the crowd) for maximum freedom.

6. **Failure to sever "soul ties" or "chords of iniquity"** may hinder or stop the deliverance, or, prevent the ability to maintain deliverance. We have discussed both of these in detail but we stress the necessity of doing this in relation to a smoother session and prevention of post deliverance difficulties. Severing soulish connections and "chords" connecting to generational sin patterns greatly limit the effectiveness of demonic resistance during the deliverance session. To accomplish this we do the following. **To sever ungodly soulish connections** (soul ties) we have the deliverance recipient place their hand on their abdomen. We then (one of our team) place our hand on top of theirs. Then, by name and soul tie category (co-dependency, control, manipulation, longing, persecution, victimization, sexual) we sever each "tie" with the sword of the Spirit by the authority we have in Jesus Christ. At times with soul ties we may pray (as the Holy Spirit directs) that the connecting point be seared or cauterized with the fire of God. This seems to help prevent

any future reconnection. **To sever connections to generational patterns of sin (chords of iniquity)** we place our
hands on the small of the person's back (lower spinal area) in
the area of the kidneys. Then we break or sever each "chord"
on the father's and mother's side (if both apply).

As to the prayer over the kidney area for severing chords of
iniquity, we believe this is the location point for the "reins."
Scripture speaks of the "reins of a man" and we believe this
is located in the area (in the spiritual body) of where the
kidneys are located in the natural body. Through our experience, we believe this is the connecting point through which
chords of iniquity attach.

For both chords of iniquity and soul ties, travail among the
deliverance team frequently accompanies the severing of
either/both. We normally sever chords of iniquity category
by category (as needed) as we progress through the deliverance session. For soul ties we usually sever them as a whole
(all categories as a block/unit) at some point in the deliverance when the Holy Spirit directs. However, there are times
we may be directed to deal with a particular category prior to
severing all soul ties as a comprehensive action. Example:
The demonic group "control" may not be effectively cast out
until soul ties with controlling individuals in the recipient's
life have been severed first. The same might be the case in a
particular deliverance with soul ties of victimization and the
spirit of rejection or soul ties of persecution and the spirit of
paranoia and so on.

7. **The wrong motive for seeking deliverance** can greatly
   hinder or prevent an individual from obtaining full and lasting freedom through deliverance. We address this motive
   directly in the initial preparation session by questioning the
   candidate for deliverance, "What brings you to the point of
   seeking deliverance?" Even more simply we may ask, "Why
   do you desire deliverance?" or "Why do you think you need
   deliverance?" Any reply other than, "I personally, for
   myself, desire full freedom to follow Christ" (or words to

that effect) causes us to hesitate in the process for further clarification and discussion. One should not seek deliverance for any other motive than to achieve greater freedom to live an abundant Christian lifestyle; and, to eliminate any demonic hindrances to becoming more Christ like.

A person does not seek deliverance to please a spouse, family or relatives. Neither does one seek it to get attention or out of sensational curiosity. And, although enhancement of operating in one's spiritual gifting most often results, that should not be one's sole motive. Our desire in seeking deliverance, as in seeking salvation and the baptism in the Holy Spirit, should be as Paul states in I Cor. 2:2, "...To know nothing among you except Jesus Christ and Him crucified." These points of passage in our Christian walk should be sought earnestly as a means to gaining an increasingly greater revelation of Jesus Christ and His great love for us. They should serve to enlarge our capacity of faith to believe indeed that nothing "shall be able to separate us from the love of God which is in Christ Jesus our Lord" (Romans 8:39).

8. Finally, one last item to consider with the deliverance session is what Derek Prince terms "**a larger battle**." There are times when the recipient of deliverance may experience more intense spiritual warfare/demonic resistance due to their family, community or spiritual "status." If an individual is the first in a family to receive deliverance they may be the key to God setting their entire family free. As the family witnesses the individual's freedom in Christ they may be inspired to seek the same deliverance. This is particularly true of the father of a family. If an individual holds a prominent community position or leadership in a church or ministry they may experience more intense spiritual warfare over their receiving deliverance due to their potential to inspire others.

In each of these cases the recipient of deliverance is representing a larger "scenario" that could potentially impact a number of others. The deliverance team should keep this in mind throughout the process and be quick to lend support and encouragement as needed. In this case more intercession may be needed throughout the deliverance process and during the deliverance session.

IX. Inner Healing

If deliverance is the exodus from slavery and bondage, then inner healing can be likened to entering the promised land. If we don't possess the land of wholeness that God wants us to inherit, we are doomed to wander in the wilderness of wounds and hurts. Granted, the "wilderness" is preferable to "Egypt," but it's a far cry from the "land of milk and honey."

It is impossible to pass through this world without being stung by injustice and heartache. If we don't allow the Holy Spirit to heal us, a single wounding of our soul can poison our whole being. The manifestation of the pain may range from sarcasm and cynicism to rage. It may cause us to withdraw emotionally in order to avoid further pain or it may manifest in a defiant, domineering manner that seeks to control rather than be vulnerable. The possibilities are as varied as the wounds.

In order to obtain the inner healing we need, we may have to confront and overcome the "giants" in the land—fear, hurt, anger, grief, trauma, pain, loss, etc. We can't say *hello* to the promised land until we say *goodbye* to the wilderness.

The subject of inner healing has gotten a lot of attention in the past few years. Some of the press has been negative and rightfully so. As with any spiritual truth, Satan sends a counterfeit, meant to deceive, harm and scare us away from the genuine article. There is a decidedly New Age element in some of the "healing of the memories" and visualization techniques used today. Altered states such as transcendental meditation and hypnosis are open doors to demonic oppression. We must not, however, let these abuses deter us from the much-needed valid ministry of inner healing. Scripture is clear about renewing our mind, putting away former things and becoming a new creation. Salvation is just the starting point. Sanctification is a process. We will not reach perfection this side of heaven yet we are told in the Word of God to seek to be transformed into His image.

There are many good books available on the subject of inner healing. We recommend <u>Healing for Damaged Emotions,</u> by David Seamonds, <u>Deep Wounds, Deep Healing,</u> by Charles Kraft, <u>Beauty for Ashes,</u> by Joyce Meyer, and anything written on the subject by John and Paula Sandford. These resources can be a valued help as you seek inner healing. Nothing can substitute, however, for a trained, capable counselor/minister to walk you through the process. Just as we don't recommend self-deliverance, we warn the novice not to undertake this emotional journey unassisted. More often than not, there is more involved in complete inner healing than we anticipate. What we see is usually just the tip of the iceberg. There is much more beneath the surface and it often involves the demonic, soul ties, and iniquity. To competently handle one area you must be ready and able to handle the others as well. We are convinced that thorough deliverance cannot occur without inner healing. We liken it to having a cancerous tumor removed but leaving a gaping, open wound. If the patient is not sewn up, given antibiotics and a post-operative plan for recovery, they will likely wind up more afflicted than before the surgery.

One thing that you must be aware of and able to discern well before you can be effective with inner healing ministry, is the *spirit of affectation.* We discovered early in our deliverance ministry that not all those who cry and exhibit signs of heartbreak and pain need to be comforted. Demons love to distract the deliverance minister with a *spirit of affectation* which can put on quite a theatrical performance. It pulls on the gift of mercy and compassion within the deliverance minister and can actually cause him to unknowingly comfort a demon! We refer to it as "petting a devil." If a demon can distract you by getting you to feel pity and sympathy, he has succeeded in detouring the deliverance. We must operate in keen discernment so that we can differentiate between true inner healing needs and a demonic ploy for sympathy. We must also remember that when demons know their time is up and they must vacate their "host," they will sometimes cry and beg pitifully. They will make you think that the deliverance candidate is suffering greatly and that you should back off for a while. If you do so, it gives the spirit the opportunity to regroup and tighten its grip, making the deliverance longer and more strenuous for all.

We dealt with a teenage girl once who regularly exhibited affectation in church to gain attention and sympathy. She would go to the altar for prayer after each service then collapse on the floor with profuse, heart-wrenching sobs. Once as she was observed in her display of emotion, it caused us to feel holy anger and revulsion. The Lord instructed that those gathered around her be told to stop comforting her devils. They were quite shocked at this statement and more than a little critical of the assessment. When authority was taken over the *spirit of affectation*, what ensued was a very strong demonic manifestation, complete with immediate cessation of the emotional display. A valuable lesson was learned by all that day.

When dealing with inner healing needs in others we must remember that emotional pain is quite real and must be dealt with tenderly and professionally. We believe clients need to experience some emotional pain before they can be healed and released from soul hurts and wounds. To deny, repress, or even fear the pain serves no purpose. In fact, it is quite dangerous to do so because it is during those very times and seasons that demons can and will attach. Traumatic events give demonic spirits an inroad to our innermost parts. They feed on the negative emotions that result from the wounding. Those who attempt healing of damaged emotions using only the inner healing model will often encounter the demonic without recognizing it. The more we learn about deliverance, the more we find that inner healing and deliverance are inseparable.

To quote Peter Horrobin, Healing Through Deliverance,(p. 251), "When people become experienced in ministry they will interchange freely between deliverance ministry and prayer for inner healing or physical healing and then back to deliverance. Healing is a process involving all the different aspects of personal ministry. Flexibility is important so that we are able to respond quickly to what God is doing and help the person to flow with the leading of the Holy Spirit."

It is fair to say that all deliverance requires inner healing. The opposite, however, is not true (i.e. not all inner healing requires deliverance). As we have previously stated, much of the need for inner healing comes from trauma that the counselee suffered. For the most part, they are innocent victims. No one asks to be molested as a child or to be the victim of rejection or a natural disaster. It is hardly our fault if we witness a violent crime, contract a debilitating disease, or lose a loved one due to a drunk driver or drive-by shooting. Even so, the shock, fear, anger, bitterness, etc., that results from the trauma often opens an emotional door that Satan is only too happy to access. His best chance to attach to us comes when we allow doubt and unbelief in God to torment our minds. If we question God's goodness, His protection or His justice for an extended period of time, we can give place to a *spirit of rebellion.*

We must take care to assure the counselee that he/she is in no way to blame for the trauma. There are exceptions of course, such as poor choices, recklessness, etc., that set us up to be victimized. But in most instances, the individual was truly innocent and blameless. Their greatest need is to forgive God (i.e. release Him from their judgment) and any other individuals concerned (e.g. rapist, burglar, other driver, etc.). Sometimes they need to forgive themselves for "being in the wrong place at the wrong time."

Our reaction to traumatic events is the determining factor in the need for inner healing. What we tell ourselves about the occurrence will affect how much emotional damage is done and how long-lasting it will be. Our ability to handle stress is determined by several factors. One such factor is our temperament. A phlegmatic person is naturally more easy-going and rock steady when the storms of life come. A more melancholy individual will be prone to worry, internalize, and operate in "worst-case scenario" thinking. This negativity results in negative mindsets and "self-talk" and makes them a prime candidate for self-pity as well. For more information on temperament we recommend books on the subject by Florence Littauer or Tim LaHaye.

Another factor in determining ability to handle stress is family patterns. We are prone to imitate and perpetuate the coping skills of our family members, especially our parents. If our parents responded to crisis with a cool head and an ability to problem solve and seek solutions, you may handle stress well. On the other hand, if your family falls apart at the seams when a crisis situation develops, you may tend to panic and "awfulize" just as they did.

In addition to temperament, self-talk, and family coping skills, if the individual facing traumatic events is either young or elderly, in poor health, part of a dysfunctional family or a bad marriage, they will be less likely to weather the storm well. Obviously, the best way to survive trauma and thrive afterwards is to remember that God is "a very present help in times of trouble." The sooner a person receives ministry after the trauma the better their recovery will go. Unfortunately, most candidates for inner healing suffered the trauma years ago and their memories are unreliable and skewed. In such instances we marvel to see how the Holy Spirit transcends time and brings balm to the soul and strength to mind and body.

It is important to understand that *spirits of trauma* come in clusters. For example, a *spirit of rejection* may impact an individual by having them be put up for adoption as an infant, fired repeatedly from jobs, divorced by their spouse, and betrayed by their best friend. The end result is a deeply entrenched *spirit of rejection.* This person would likely be convinced that rejection is inevitable in their life and even come to expect it. Satan will gladly meet those expectations. In fact, the entrance of rejection lays the groundwork for the addition of *spirits of insecurity, inferiority, people-pleasing, condemnation, shame,* and a host of others.

It cannot be overemphasized that it is the love of God and the wonderful comfort of the Holy Spirit that brings about true inner healing. God will custom design a person's inner healing if He is allowed to. Remember that "God's ways are not our ways." He uses "the simple things to confound the wise." Obedience, availability, and humility are what God requires of his ministers. He may allow you to use a tried and true technique/method or He may do something unique and unconventional to bring His healing balm to a wounded soul. We must follow the leading of the Holy Spirit and be ready to operate in whatever gift of the Spirit is required in the situation. We are the least effective when we overanalyze or rely too heavily on psychology. Be ever mindful that God created this individual, was fully present during their trauma, and has the road map laid out for their recovery. Our job is to "get with the program" and stay out of God's way.

God has often instructed us to apply the blood of Jesus to painful images in the mind/memory. As we repeatedly cover a person's mind with the blood, we speak out that the power of the image to torment them is decreasing. Many times we see a dramatic change of facial expression, such as a smile or look of relief, which confirms that the work has been done.

Sometimes, the Lord has us utilize the *water of the word* to cleanse areas where there has been oppression and bring *life* where Satan has tried to bring death and destruction. Likewise, we have spoken the *light* of God to bring insight and illumination to darkened minds. As God's *truth* is applied, spiritual darkness is dispelled and the Father of lies is exposed. In similar fashion, God may have us apply the *breath of God, His resurrection power, His river, or the armor.* He will utilize whatever will best serve His purposes to bring about the healing. We must stay sensitive to the Holy Spirit and follow His leading. We can also look to others in the ministry team for confirmation of a particular strategy.

We have found that God will use travail when we begin to deal with spirits that have attached themselves to trauma. He will also send waves of His perfect love to cast out fear. Many of the individuals we have ministered to say that they can finally believe that God loves them and receive that love. To see that marvelous love water their thirsty souls is truly a blessing.

Victim Spirit

We cannot touch on the subject of inner healing without discussing what is known as a *victim spirit.* We all know someone who seems to attract calamity or is extremely accident-prone. Some people call themselves a "jinx" or say that "Murphy's Law" was written just for them. All of the above can be easily explained —— a spirit of victimization has attached itself to them. *Predator spirits* are drawn to those who have a *spirit of victimization.* For instance, all your friends may rave about a doctor who has greatly improved their health and prolonged their life. If you have a victim spirit the surgery this doctor performs on you will be a disaster and border on malpractice. Or it may be a car mechanic who repaired everyone else's car for a reasonable fee but overcharged you and did a poor job to boot.

We identify this spirit by looking for arenas in people's lives where things constantly turn out poorly for them. From this perspective, we have not found anyone who **doesn't** suffer from a victim spirit in one area or another! Some examples are banking (they lose the checks you ordered or bounce your mortgage payment even though you have overdraft protection), postal service (your mail gets returned to sender or delivered to your neighbor), financial (your investments suffer great losses due to poor management by the firm you use), etc. This spirit can affect relationships as well. You may feel invisible (i.e. no one listens when you speak and they ignore you when you make suggestions or ask questions), you may be constantly misunderstood which angers and alienates others or you may date or marry seemingly wonderful people who promptly turn into monsters when you commit to them. The list goes on and on but you get the picture. We have found that people have put up with one type of victimization or the other for so long that they don't even recognize that it is a spirit. They explain it away by saying things like, "It doesn't go well with me when I deal with government agencies (or the law, or the school system, etc.). Something always goes wrong."

In addition to taking authority over this spirit in deliverance, we find it very effective to have the individual rebuke predator spirits before they go into a situation where they have been victimized in the past.

The Slumbering Spirit

Although we have been talking primarily about demonic spirits, the term *"slumbering spirit"* does not refer to a demonic spirit. It pertains to our human spirit, which can fail to be alert and functioning. John and Paula Sandford have a revelatory chapter on this subject in their book, <u>Healing the Wounded Spirit.</u> They explain that there are two kinds of slumbering spirits. "There are those who never have been drawn forth to life, who early in infancy have fallen asleep and can no longer function. Secondly, there are those who did receive parental and other nurture and so were awake and functioning spiritually, but turned away from worship services, prayer and affection until their spirits fell asleep. In both, the heart has usually hardened as well." They go on to say that these individuals have little or no ability to empathize with others or commune effectively with God. Even when Spirit-baptized, the personal spirit of these folks lies asleep, encased and non-functioning. If their condition persists they will drift further and further from the Lord.

The Sandfords give an insightful list of the nine functions of a healthy, alert, personal spirit. They include: corporate worship, satisfying personal devotions, the ability to hear from God, inspiration, the ability to transcend time, effective communication with others, the glory of marital sexual union, protection from disease and a good conscience. They state (and we concur) that if one of these areas is lacking in a person's life there is a strong probability that their spirit is slumbering.

To revive a slumbering spirit may involve as little as inner healing prayer ministry or as much as re-parenting the individual. In a prayer session we ask the Lord to minister to the inner child. We ask the person to repent and to choose to forgive parents or others who have wounded their spirit. We ask the Holy Spirit to fill them and woo them to life. We ask the Lord to restore what the enemy has stolen (Joel 2:25). We then ask the Lord to awaken and draw their spirit forth to function in liveliness and enthusiasm. Death wishes and bitter-root judgements often must be dealt with as well.

In more severe cases, the individual cannot fully heal and recover unless they experience life-giving power through the investment of a family who is willing to provide what the person's natural family was not able or willing to give. Only rich personal encounter and involvement in their lives will provide the resurrection they so desperately need. Slumbering spirits are awakened by the sacrificial love and support from the body of Christ. We have seen these type prayers and re-parenting efforts yield amazing results. We pray every day that our own personal spirits stay awake and alert to the Lord on every level . . . "so then let us not sleep as others do, but let us be alert and sober" (I Thess. 5:5-6).

As a final word on inner healing, let us reiterate what a privilege it is to be used by the Lord to bring freedom and peace to those who suffer emotionally. It requires a careful combination of tour' and tenderness. It is not easy to hear the gut-wrenching stories that clients tell nor to stand by as they relive some of the pain and heartache. But the reward is well worth the process for both minister and client. It is an awesome thing to see pain-built strongholds topple. To help free minds and hearts of the torment that has plagued God's kids for so many years is indeed deeply satisfying.

X. Closing The Deliverance Session

As a general practice we end the deliverance with prayer over the area of infirmity (sickness, disease, health). We break any generational chords of iniquity causing patterns of sickness and disease. These have been noted prior to the deliverance session. We then cast out any spirits of infirmity and immediately pray for healing.

We follow this prayer with prayer over anything remaining needing deliverance. We call this a "mop up" prayer. We pray deliverance over anything that may remain in the mental, emotional or physical area. This is a last "sweep through" of anything we may not have specifically named.

Finally, then, we pray for the individual receiving deliverance to be filled with the Holy Spirit in every space that has been vacated by the demonic. As the "house" has been swept clean, we want to fill it immediately with God's presence by the Holy Spirit.

This is a good time for prayer to receive the baptism in the Holy Spirit (if desired) and to prophetically pray over the recipient.

We pray for a greater flow of the gifts of the Holy Spirit; and, spend time in celebration and thanksgiving with the deliverance recipient. This is the time to sing the victory song, having passed through the sea as God parted the waters. Behind, the enemy is defeated and drowned in the flood of God's power. We stand with our deliverance recipient on freedom's shore. It is truly a time to "dance and shout and run about," savor the moment and soak in God's presence. The victory's won so enjoy it and do not rush this special reflective time of "pouring in."

Chapter VII

Maintaining Deliverance

As previously stated, deliverance is a process. In most cases, deliverance is not a one-time "cure all." Just as spiritual growth is a progression subsequent to a salvation experience, so too, the process of deliverance begins with an initial "housecleaning" and continues in stages to build on that base. It is very similar to the way Joshua and Israel conquered the Promised Land. The land was theirs, given by God. Yet they had to take it, subdue it and cultivate it. This was accomplished in a process of conquering one geographic area after another.

Following an initial deliverance experience, as we continue to submit to the ministry of Jesus Christ, through the revelation and illumination of the Holy Spirit, we will become increasingly free of demonic influence. The overall effect will be a growth in Christlikeness and subsequent spiritual maturity. This is God's intention for us as we take our Promised Land, both internally and externally. A key to remember in this process of deliverance is committing to build upon each subsequent base that has been laid. As Isaiah 28:10 says, "For precept must be upon precept, precept upon precept, line upon line...."

It is counter-productive and frustrating to continue to conquer and reconquer the same ground. Yet sadly, too many Christians do just that. They often relinquish what has been gained due to lack of knowledge and spiritual discipline. They forget the realities of Matthew 12: 43-45, which states: "But the unclean spirit, when he is gone out of a man....seeking rest and finding it not says, 'I will return to my house where I came out'; and finding it empty, swept and in order, he goes and takes with him seven other spirits more wicked than himself and they enter and dwell there; and the last state of the man is worse than the first...."

It is wise to remember not only this foundational scripture (mandating that we remain free following deliverance) but also others not as frequently cited. Consider for example the account of Achan in Joshua 7:1-15. Note verse 1 which says: "But the children of Israel committed a trespass regarding the accursed things, for Achan the son of Carmi, took of the accursed things." Joshua had been directed of the Lord in the conquest of Jericho, "and you, by all means abstain from the accursed things, lest you become accursed when you take of the accursed things, and make the camp of Israel a curse, and trouble it." Joshua in turn had directed all of Israel to keep this command during and following the destruction of Jericho. Achan alone, of the entire nation, disobeyed this directive as recounted in verse 21, "when I saw among the spoils a beautiful Babylonian garment, two hundred shekels of silver and a wedge of gold...I coveted them and took them. And there they are, hidden in the earth in the midst of my tent, with the silver under it."

As a result of Achan's disobedience, Joshua and Israel were defeated when they first attempted to conquer the fortified city of Ai.

It is a fact that you cannot win in spiritual warfare, fully receive deliverance, or remain free from demonic effect if there is sin/disobedience in your "camp."

Once the sin was discovered, confessed and corrected, Joshua and Israel successfully conquered Ai. Likewise, we must be diligent (and radically so) to be Christlike and continue to grow spiritually if we desire to keep our house clean. Thereby, we will remain increasingly free throughout the process of deliverance.

This chapter addresses specifically the issue of "remaining free" and contains a composite of information gained from personal experience as well as the teachings of Derek Prince, Peter Horrobin, Frank Hammond, John and Mark Sandford and others. Keep in mind that total deliverance may require several stages to complete (often including a mix of deliverance and emotional/inner healing).

So then, following an initial session of deliverance, how does one remain free? As the passage of scripture in Matthew 12:4 warns, we must not allow our "house" to be found empty. The first priority, following deliverance, is to fill any "space" relinquished (by the exit of the demonic) with the infilling presence of the Holy Spirit. We must be quick to take advantage of any victory over evil in our lives by immediately offering the Holy Spirit access to that area. We make it a point at the close of each deliverance session to pray for the person delivered to be filled with the presence of the Holy Spirit. If they have never been baptized in the Holy Spirit this is an opportune occasion to pray with them. It is one of those times when a person may be particularly receptive to the flow of the Holy

Spirit and thus make themselves accessible for the Baptism in the Holy Spirit.

For those who have received the Baptism in the Holy Spirit, it is a timely occasion to pray for a greater flow of the presence and gifts of the Holy Spirit. Often, during this time of prayer for a fresh infilling of the Holy Spirit, the deliverance team receives prophetic "insight" and guidance for the one receiving deliverance ministry. These times of prayer can be especially meaningful and encouraging for all participating - both the recipient and the ministry team.

So, to emphasize, the primary objective following deliverance is to allow the Holy Spirit access to what "space" has been gained. To parallel Paul's statement, "Rejoice in the Lord always. And again I say rejoice." We would say, regarding maintaining deliverance, " Be filled with the Holy Spirit always. And again we say, be filled." We cannot emphasize enough this primary point. Again we say, be filled." We cannot emphasize enough this primary point. Ephesians 5:18 states ". . .But be filled with the Holy Spirit." The original Greek language of this reads more like "Be continuously being filled with the Holy Spirit." We must allow the Holy Spirit to occupy all within us that has been vacated by the demonic. Then, we must continuously seek to be filled to overflowing with the Holy Spirit's presence.

Scenarios for Deliverance

Before continuing with additional principles for freedom we want to offer several scenarios related to deliverance and freedom. These should provide you with a background against which to practice principles for remaining free. Our hope is that you will implement Godly principles for maintaining deliverance combined with the Spiritual insights contained in these illustrations. In this way they will form a framework upon which you can build a life-long discipline of Christ-centered Holy Spirit empowered living. This, in turn, will ensure continuous freedom and spiritual growth as described by Paul in II Corinthians 3:18, "But we all, with unveiled face, beholding as in a mirror the glory of the Lord, are being transformed into the same image from Glory to Glory, just as by the Spirit of the Lord."

Rebuilding the Wall

Our first scenario is drawn from the account of Nehemiah and the rebuilding of the wall around Jerusalem. Through previous conquests the protective wall around Jerusalem had been destroyed. As a result, there was, no way to keep out invaders from other cities and countries. The temple and city had been restored but there was no protection from future invasions. This is the place to which recipients of deliverance often arrive. Following deliverance the "wall" around them that would prevent further demonic invasion is found to be in disrepair. The Spiritual disciplines that would keep the house filled and the wall strong usually have been neglected or not even known. As a result there is immediate potential for re-invasion if action is not taken. However, as Nehemiah demonstrates, the wall can be repaired (or established) and the enemy kept out. This time the wall can be rebuilt to such strength that demonic invaders can never again breach it.

Expanded from a teaching by Ray Kiertekles, consider these lessons from Nehemiah as you rebuild your own wall. **First, determination** is needed if the wall is to be rebuilt. Nehemiah desired deep within his Spirit to see Jerusalem, its people, and its temple restored and protected from invasion. He knew that the city itself had been rebuilt and that the people lived there again. But there was no defense in place to prevent future enemy invasions. A wall was needed and Nehemiah felt directed of the Lord to see that one was built. He, therefore, was **determined** to see that this task was accomplished – at whatever cost. It became paramount in his life.

To remain free following deliverance one must be **determined** that the enemy will not invade our "land" again. One must begin to work at once and repair the damage to our defenses. Rebuild the gates! Repair the breached walls! Clear out any hindering rubble and debris! The enemy will try the walls and gates another day. He must find them secure and in good order with no points of entry. This is vital to remaining free. We must never forget that the Spiritual war continues though we may have won a present battle. Jesus has ultimately defeated Satan and he has an end-time judgment appointed him. But, until that day, he continues to attempt to breach our walls and pull down our gates to gain entry. We must be **determined** that He will never do so again.

   Second, from Nehemiah we learn that we must have **purpose** in rebuilding our Spiritual walls of protection. Our **purpose** initially would be to take back and hold what has been stolen from us. We identify the thief, the trespasser, the squatter and the poacher and we evict him from our property. Then, our immediate purpose is to put up a fence/wall and hang "No Trespassing" signs on it. In fact let's hang one that says, "Trespassers will be prosecuted!"

   Following this initial **purpose** phase, as we grow in the Lord and maintain our freedom, our purpose expands to correspond to the purpose of Jesus: To destroy the works of the Devil (I John 3:8), to resist the Devil (James 4:7) and to give no place to the Devil (Eph. 4:27).

   Additionally, as we become increasingly free and "strong in the Lord and in the power of his might" (Ephesians 6:10) our purpose would be as Jesus described in Luke 4:18,19, "To preach the Gospel...Heal the broken-hearted...Proclaim liberty to the captives...to set at liberty those who are oppressed."

   Third, we learn from Nehemiah that we will encounter **opposition** as we seek to rebuild the wall. Our enemy Satan, though defeated, has power (for a time) to attack and effect mankind. We must actively resist him with the authority we have through Jesus Christ. We should remember and heed the admonition contained in I Peter 5:8,9 "Be sober, be vigilant; Because your adversary the Devil walks about like a roaring Lion, seeking whom he may devour. Resist him, steadfast in the faith." As we resist him with our **determination** and **purpose** established in the authority of Jesus Christ, he **will** flee from us and his **opposition** will be less effective.

   Resist in Greek is "antihistemi" from which we get the word "antihistamine." It means: To withstand, oppose or set against. Resist or withstand as defined in Webster's dictionary means: "Vigorously opposing, bravely resisting, standing face-to-face against an enemy and standing or holding your ground." Remember Matthew 11:12 – "The Kingdom of Heaven suffers violence and the violent take it by force."

Four Forms of Demonic Attack

As you resist Satan, be aware that there are four primary methods Satan uses to attack. His "bag of tricks" has a multiple of tactics but they usually correspond to four arenas of warfare.

First, are **Lies.** Satan is the "Father of Lies." He often will attack you with doubt and unbelief following deliverance to get you to "unlock the door" to your defensive wall. Thoughts of: "Nothing happened,"; "They didn't get them all,"; "It wasn't real;" will attack your mind. Rebuke these voices, stand in Faith and expose the Liar.

Second, are **accusations**. Remember that Satan is "the accuser of the Brethren." He may try to attack you with guilt over past sins, etc. Satan wants to shift your focus from Jesus and your future to the past and your failures. When he tries, remember who you are in Christ. Remember I Peter 2:9 and tell Satan that you are "a chosen generation, a royal priesthood, a Holy nation, part of a peculiar (special) people" and you intend to proclaim the praises of Jesus who called you "out of Darkness into marvelous Light." Remember Romans 8:33, 34 "who shall bring a charge against God's elect? It is God who justifies. Who is He who condemns? It is Christ who died and furthermore is also risen, who is even at the right hand of God, who also makes intercession for us." And do not forget Romans 8:1, when Satan comes with accusations and guilt to steal from us what deliverance has gained, "There is therefore now no condemnation to those who are in Christ Jesus, who do not walk according to the Flesh, but according to the Sprit."

So walk out your deliverance guided by the Holy Spirit (and not the Flesh) and when Satan approaches to condemn, declare, "There is no condemnation to charge against me! Go from me!"

A **third** category of attack, which Satan uses, is **intimidation**. He wants us to believe he is all-powerful. He does, in truth, have power. But it is not greater than the power of Jesus Christ. Remember, "Greater is He (Jesus) who is in you than He (Satan) who is in the world." (I John 4:4) Satan will try to bully you and to produce circumstances and symptoms that would make it appear that deliverance did not succeed. Stand firm in God's full armor! Remember that Satan wants to appear as a fierce, roaring lion. He will devour you if you let him. Don't let him!

Remember what the wolf said to the three little pigs when they refused to let him in? "Then I'll huff and I'll puff and I'll blow your house in!" And he did, too, to the house made of sticks and straw. But to the one made of bricks – No way! So lay your house on the firm foundation of Jesus Christ and rebuild your wall with the solid bricks of the principles in God's word. Cement them together with God's word of Truth. And then, when the wolf comes and you refuse him entry, he can huff and puff and blow but the walls of your house will hold firm.

Don't forget, as Matthew 7:15 says, the wolf may sometimes come in sheep's clothing. Satan is a devious foe and if he can't blow the wall/house down he may attempt to trick his way inside. Do not fear, though, for if your house if filled with the presence of the Holy Spirit, he will give you the discernment to detect the wolf, even if he's dressed like a sheep!

Be aware, Satan **is** a determined adversary. For a time following deliverance, he may launch an all-out effort to regain the house. Remember that the wolf, having failed to talk his way in and "blow" his way in, tried to come down the chimney of the house. And when he did, the pigs heard him coming over the roof. They built a fire and boiled water in the fireplace and the wolf was boiled to death. Allow the Holy Spirit to guide you in keeping the house full. Then, if the wolf tries to force an entry, he will be defeated. The Holy Spirit's fire will rise up within you as you discern the enemy's attack. The water of God's word within you will boil up and consume the enemy!

A **final** means of satanic attack is to use **temptation**. Satan will try, having failed at other attempts to gain entry, to tempt you with former patterns of sin and old ways of living. He will try to heighten their appeal to you causing you to forget their potential for destruction in your life. He may even try to convince you that you can never be truly free of them. At such times, press into and focus on Jesus "looking unto Jesus, the author and finisher of our Faith…"(Hebrews 12:2). Then you will be able to stay on the course set before you.

Satan will attempt to attack your thoughts with temptations of old desires and sins. John and Loren Sandford say in their book, Renewal of the Mind: " The first lesson to learn in the renewal of the mind is not to believe old, carnal feelings and thoughts when they try to come back. Old, dead feelings and thoughts will try to return. If we believe these feelings and thoughts are what we really feel/think we will have our problems back again – because we have

resurrected what was dead and have given it power in our life again. You have the heart and mind of Christ. When the old returns it is only an echo of the old self – only an old habitual way sound ing off with no real life behind it... The purpose behind it is the desire of the old self to regain its mastery of you." Satan uses these strongholds of thinking and ungodly beliefs to tempt us after deliverance. These must be demolished if one is to remain truly free following deliverance. We must keep the old self "dead" to prevent demonic strongholds from being rebuilt and stealing our victory. We will address the issue of strongholds in depth in another section.

Our Most Vulnerable Areas

Related to these four forms of satanic attack, are what E.M. Bounds describes as our most vulnerable areas. In his classic book, Guide To Spiritual Warfare, he lists the following conditions that leave us vulnerable to demonic attack.

1. Ignorance – "To be ignorant of the existence, character and ways of the Devil is the prelude to fatal results in the fight for Heaven. If this is true, how hopeless is the case of one who not only is ignorant of temptations, but also denies or ignores the existence of the tempter. Nothing advances Satan's work with more skillful hands than to be ignorant of Satan and his ways. To escape his snare, we must have a strong faith in the fact that Satan exists. We must also have an intimate knowledge of Him and His plans."

2. Flippant attitude – "Frivolous views of the Devil, his works, or his character, and light talk or jokes that dishonor him are detrimental to any serious views of life's great works and its serious conflicts. Presumption, self-will, and foolishness are the characteristics of those who deal frivolously with these

important concerns. His tongue is smooth as oil; His words circulate and inflame like poison. For this reason, our position must be one of bristling opposition, fortified for war, with no barriers down, no open gates, no low places."

3. Unforgiving Spirit – "Satan's favorite realm is the spirit. To corrupt our spirits, to provoke us to retaliation, revenge or unmercifulness- that is his chosen work and his most common and successful device. When Satan generates an unforgiving spirit in us, then he has us, and we are on his ground." (John Bevere calls "offense" the "bait of Satan")

4. Oaths and Swearing – "Expletives and appeals added to our words are wrong and expose us to the snare of Satan. Satan tempts us to use assertions and declarations to confirm the truth of what we are saying. When we use additional words as a way of substantiating the truth of those already spoken, they expose us to Satan's power. The Devil lies concealed in many words. Simplicity, brevity and seriousness of words will mightily hinder and thwart his ensnaring plans."

5. Religious Fanaticism – "Satan watches and is always on the alert to try to hold us back from the final goal. Or he works in the opposite way to drive us on with an impetus and obsessed spirit to go beyond the goal. It is Satan's purpose to uncover our strongest positions and turn them into vulnerable areas."

6. Being Unequally Yoked – "Becoming unequally yoked with unbelievers in intimate and confiding friendships creates exposed positions of which the devil takes great advantage. Partnerships in business or the more sacred union of marriage with unbelievers is perilous to the believer in Jesus Christ. Separation, cleansing and perfected Holiness are necessary to secure the vantage ground against Satan. The Bible gives strong, explicit and comprehensive commands against union, communion or intimate association with unbelievers. For those unequally yoked there can be no pulling together, no fellowship, no sharing, no communion, no intimacy, no agreement, no voting together. Paul (states) this rule in his first epistle to the Corinthians (1 Cor. 5:9-11).

Paul is not objecting to casual, courteous, Christian conversation but to more intimate and lasting relationships."

7. <u>Worldly Friendships</u> – "Since 'Friendship with the world is enmity with God' (James 4:4), the only way to Heaven is to avoid all intimacy with worldly people. Whatever the cost, flee spiritual adultery! Have no friendship with the world. No matter how tempted you are by profit or pleasure, do not become intimate with world-minded people. So let your fellowship be with those, and those only, who at least seek the Lord Jesus Christ with sincerity. How Satan surrounds us! How strongly he holds us! How he entangles, chains, and binds us with worldly associations! We lie in the sweet friendship, the embraces, and the counsel of these worldly ones, while they lie in the arms of the Wicked one."

8. <u>Undisciplined Body</u> – "Even natural, innocent appetites and passions have to be held in with bit and bridle (1 Cor. 9:27). The apostle (Paul) says the body is an important factor in the contest from Heaven. He teaches us that if it is unrestrained, without the strong repressing hand of discipline, it becomes an easy prey to the assaults of Satan. A listless, drowsy, sleepy, stupid state can put us under Satan's power without a struggle or even the decency of a surrender."

9. <u>Lack of Spiritual Growth</u> – "Low aims in the spiritual life and satisfaction with present circumstances also create an exposed condition. (Satan) will attack the strongest, most mature Giant of Piety, but he works havoc and gains his spoils where the Christian slumbers in the cradle of spiritual babyhood. Spiritual growth, along with constant and sure spiritual development, are the surest safeguards against Satan's assaults and surprises. Satan never finds growth asleep, drowsy or weak. Israel lost Canaan by not possessing Canaan. Satan has the vantage ground when we do not maintain an aggressive forward march. To stand still in our faith is to lose it. To set up camp at the place of salvation is to forfeit regenerating grace. To stop at any station of progress is to go backward."

10. <u>Spiritual stagnation</u> – "The tendency in religion is to be satisfied with spiritual birth and then to die in infancy. Stopping and standing still in a non-growing, non-fighting condition is a position fully exposed to Satan. Many run well and fight well, but at some point their running and fighting cease. When this happens, spiritual development is arrested, and the devil moves at once to an easy victory. To begin as babes is expected, but to remain babes for forty years (like Israel) is a fearful deformity. However, spiritual stagnation is not confined to the initial steps. Spiritual development's lifeblood may chill and its step halt at the point of highest advance. Many Christians are so enthusiastic over some marked advance, or some higher elevation gained, that they become enchanted with the beautiful and lofty regions. They are lulled to sleep and, like Bunyan's pilgrim, lose their enthusiasm and are unconscious of their loss. It is difficult to make them understand (that)…even after the desert has been crossed, the Jordan has been divided, and their feet have touched the sanctified soil of Canaan, there are many battles to be fought. There are enemies to be destroyed before the good land is all possessed. This is the divine process by which we hold onto what we have by getting more. (Paul) summed it up as fighting, running, watching – ('<u>Fight</u> the good fight'!, Tim. 6:12; '<u>Run</u> the race', Heb. 12:1; 'Be <u>watchful</u> in all things', II Tim. 4:5). There is no position this side of heaven that is free from the dangers of spiritual arrest and secure from the devil's attacks. The conflict and vigilance of advance must mark every step until our feet are within the pearly gates. Arrested spiritual development, either in the initial or the more advanced stages, is always an exposed position. Spiritual immaturity always leaves us vulnerable to Satan's attacks."

Defend the Construction

A final lesson from Nehemiah, related to remaining free, is that the wall had to be defended even as it was being built. The Scriptures state (Nehemiah 4:17) "Those who built on the wall, and those who carried burdens, loaded themselves so that with one hand they worked at construction, and with the other held a weapon."

Satan will not willingly give you time to rebuild the wall if he can prevent it. He will begin immediately to seek to reclaim what he has lost. As a result you will have to drive him away even as you are in the process of rebuilding the wall. Just remember that you do not labor alone. Jesus is with you and the Holy Spirit inhabits the house. They will assist you to fight as you build. Additionally, God will assign guardian and warrior angels to assist if you request them.

As you rebuild, it is understood that you must be keenly watchful for Satan's movements. This should be our continual state during this phase of our Christian life, and ever after. Remember 1 Peter 5:8, "Be sober, Be vigilant; because your adversary the devil, as a roaring lion, walks about, seeking whom he may devour."

Again, from E.M. Bounds' Guide to Spiritual Warfare on "watchfulness" he states: "When the enemy in power is massed in the front, the believer is like a watchman. He stands on the walls of the beleaguered city like a guard over a royal prisoner. This keeping and guarding himself is safety against Satan's inflaming touch. The faithful, vigilant Christian keeps himself pure, and Satan comes and finds nothing in him. Every vantage point is barred and sleeplessly watched. 'Watch' is the keynote of safety. Watchfulness at all times is our only safety. We must not remain wide-awake only when we see his form and fear his presence, but we must also remain wide-awake to see him when he is not to be seen. We must repel him when he comes with any one of his ten thousand disguises (angel of light, wolf in sheep's clothing, etc.) – This is our wisest and safest course. No cry of alarm is so frequent in the New Testament as the call to watch. No call hurts Satan so vitally or defeats him so readily as the call to watch. Being on the watchtower prevents all surprises and is essential to victory at all times. The Son of God made this call the keynote in many of his teachings. It is a call to be sleepless, to be vigilant, to be always ready (Luke 21:36; Matthew 24:42; Rev. 16:15). To watch is to be opposed to all listlessness. It implies a wakeful state as if in the presence of some great danger. It is a cautious state untouched by any slumbering influence. Drowsiness and bewilderment are gone. It quickens us against laziness and spiritual sloth. The herald cry and the trumpet call from (Jesus) to us is to be awake – to be fully awake, to be tremendously awake."

Furthermore, do not neglect to recruit a support group of faithful, mature Christian friends to pray for you and counsel you as you rebuild. Nehemiah had half of the people stand guard with spears, shields, bows and armor over those who worked on the wall. We must, likewise, enlist the support of others to help ward off enemy attack while we labor to build a wall of defense around our house. It is vital following deliverance, in the post deliverance care phase, to enlist a support network to provide encouragement, prayer and spirit-led assistance.

Fill Up the House

As stated previously, take action to fill up the house immediately following deliverance. As walls are being repaired and restored it is essential to seek the Baptism in the Holy Spirit – To be filled with God's Holy Spirit. Again, remember that Matthew 12:43-45 states: "But the unclean spirit, when he is gone out of a man, passes through waterless places, seeking rest, and finds it not. Then he says, I will return into my house whence I came out. And when he is come, he finds it empty, swept, and garnished. Then goes he, and takes with himself seven other spirits more evil than himself, and they enter in and dwell there: and the last state of that man becomes worse than the first. Even so shall it be also unto this evil generation."

It is not enough to simply clean out our house. We must, at once, seek to submit all vacated spaces in the Soul (our mind, emotions and will) to the Holy Spirit and the truth of God's word. With the Baptism of the Holy Spirit comes power for Christian living and spiritual warfare (by means of the gifts of the Holy Spirit). The Holy Spirit will, if allowed, direct and guide all areas of the soul.

There are nine essential gifts of the Holy Spirit made accessible to us via the full presence of the Holy Spirit. Acts 1:8 speaks of this experience, stating "but you shall receive power when the Holy Spirit has come upon you..." This outpouring and infilling of the Holy Spirit to believers was begun on the day of Pentecost (Acts 2:1) and continues today for all who ask to receive it. The specific gifts of the Holy Spirit are: Word of Wisdom, Word of Knowledge, Discerning of Sprits, Tongues, Interpretation of Tongues, Prophecy, Faith, Healing and Miracles. The first three are revelation gifts. The next three are gifts of utterance/verbal. The last three are gifts of power. The first three are vital for effecting deliverance ministry.

There are other gifts bestowed upon the Church but these nine are the ones directly attributed to the ministry of the Holy Spirit. The overall point we are professing here is for all believers, following deliverance particularly, to be completely filled with the power and presence of the Holy Spirit. This, as much as anything, will enable us to remain free from demonic encroachment.

Live above the Snakes

A second scenario related to filling up the house is "Living above the Snakes." Frank Hammond depicts this illustration in his book: <u>Demons and Deliverance in the Ministry of Jesus</u>. He describes the conditions of living that he experienced in Colorado where cities are so high above sea level in elevation that no snakes dwell there. A friend responded to Frank's concern with encountering snakes in the rugged country surrounding their home, "Brother Frank, there are no poisonous snakes in these mountains. You are at ten thousand feet elevation; you live above the snakes as they do not come into this altitude." Frank makes the spiritual comparison that we are to seek to climb to such spiritual heights that we are above the demonic "snakes" sent to attack us. Luke 10:19 says, "Behold, I give you authority to trample on serpents and scorpions and the power of the enemy, and nothing shall by any means hurt you."

Frank Hammond says, further, "If one is being attacked by spiritual serpents (demons), that person needs to climb to the safety of a greater spiritual height." That height is Jesus, our "Strong Tower."

Within His presence is "the secret place of the most High." It is not a coincidence that God is referred to as El Elyon, "the most High." Deuteronomy 33:12 says, "The Beloved of the Lord shall dwell in safety by Him, who shelter him all the day long, and he shall dwell between His shoulders." What a description of safety! What safer place (and Higher place) could there be than between the shoulders of the Lord our God! He **is** EL Elyon, "The Most High God" (Daniel 4:34). That is where we should seek to climb up to; there, riding on God's shoulders – far above all scorpions and snakes. From this vantage point God carries us into any battle we must face. His power forces the enemy to give way or be utterly crushed. We must remain in that position through fellowship with our Father God, through obedience to the Son, Jesus, and, through constant communion and guidance from the Holy Spirit.

Frank Hammond offers the following steps to reaching these spiritual heights:

1. Prompt repentance
2. Walking in God's love
3. Spiritually disciplined living
    a. Winning the battle for the mind
    b. Bringing all emotions under the direction of the Holy Spirit
    c. Submitting our will to God's will
    d. Guarding our tongue/words
    e. Curbing sensual appetites
4. Meeting all trials Scripturally
5. Getting our family in divine order
6. Being a "doer of the Word"

We must develop these Spiritual disciplines in our daily Christian living in order to live "above the Snakes," be filled continuously with God's Spirit, and, remain free following deliverance.

General Principles for Remaining Free

The following are keys to remaining free following deliverance that have been compiled from various sources.

Concerning post deliverance care, John and Mark Sandford

state in their book: <u>Inner Healing and Deliverance,</u>

"Afterward much comfort is needed to restore the wounded spirit. Fellowship and touches of love and acceptance soothe the bruised emotional nature.

When comfort has restored enough strength and stability, inner healing must be administered. People who have been heavily criticized and controlled as children may hate the way they were treated, but that may be the only lifestyle they know. They have unconsciously learned to identify abuse as love.

And when the load of attention they received in the first weeks after deliverance begin to taper off, as supportive Christians become occupied with other pressing duties, they begin to hunger again for touches of love. It is not yet clearly seated in their minds and hearts that affection, respect, and unconditional acceptance are what love really is.

If inner healing has not hauled their false identification of love to the cross, they are vulnerable. If sufficient counseling has not built up decision-making abilities and their strength to stand, they may slip back and seek out some dynamic, controlling leader who not only will tell them what to do but upbraid them, so they can feel loved again. I have seen this happen many times.

Dependent personalities require a good deal of healing and affirmation before they can sustain freedom. Merely casting away spirits of control and doing some mental deprogramming will not get it done.

This means that if we would liberate and heal those who have been deluded or captivated by cults, we must learn what made them vulnerable. Then we must make sure they are grounded in a Christian community that knows how to administer love and healing in close fellowship until the person is strong enough to pick up his pallet and walk! To remain free following deliverance, it is essential to seek the support and care of a Spirit filled group of mature Christian friends."

The following sets of lists of "essentials" or "keys" for remaining free (drawn from the writings of various prominent deliverance ministers) contain some "overlap." We include each in entirety as a means of impressing upon you the consensus throughout on the importance of the same disciplines in remaining free.

Frank Hammond writes in <u>Pigs in the Parlor</u>: Seven steps for retaining deliverance:
1. Put on the whole armor of God
2. Confess positively
3. Stay in the Scripture
4. Crucify the Flesh
5. Develop a life of continuous praise and prayer
6. Maintain a life of fellowship and Spiritual ministry
7. Commit yourself totally to Christ

Roger and Donna Miller of "Trumpet of Gideon ministries" in <u>Curses, Unforgiveness, Evil Spirits and Deliverance</u> offer seven ways to keep free:
1. Fill yourself with the word of God
2. Use the blood of Jesus
3. Resist the Devil and stand firm
4. Maintain a loving Spirit
5. Maintain a forgiving Spirit
6. Maintain a tender Spirit
7. Forsake sin

Derek Prince, in his book, <u>They Shall Expel Demons</u>, states: "We have seen that human personality is like a city, and that demonic invasion can have the effect of breaking down the walls inside us that should protect us. Once our enemy has been driven out, we must begin immediately to rebuild our protective walls. Here are the basic principles to help you rebuild:
1. Live by God's word
2. Put on the garment of praise
3. Come under discipline
4. Cultivate right fellowship
5. Be filled with the Holy Spirit
6. Pass through the waters of Baptism
7. Put on the whole armor of God

Derek Prince states, further, in this same book that deliverance is the first step in the ultimate goal of "possessing our possessions." He says there is a middle step leading from "Deliverance" to our "Inheritance." That step is "Holiness." We agree whole-heartedly with Derek Prince's conviction that "for both Israel and the Church, the first step to restoration is deliverance. The step that must follow is holiness. Holiness is the unique mark of the God of the Bible. It should also be the unique mark of His people….Deliverance is only the first step in a process leading to the recovery of holiness and the restoration of the Church to her original simplicity and purity."

To this we would add the words of Isaiah 35:8-10, "A highway shall be there, and a road, and it shall be called the Highway of Holiness. The unclean shall not pass over it, but it shall be for others. Whoever walks the road, although a fool, shall not go astray. No lion shall be there, nor shall any ravenous beast go up on it, it shall not be found there. But the redeemed shall walk there and the ransomed of the Lord shall return, and come to Zion with singing, with everlasting joy on their heads. They shall obtain joy and gladness, and sorrow and sighing shall flee away."

Peter Horrobin of Ellel Ministries in England offers these instructions for post deliverance:

Post Deliverance After-Care

1. Pray that the Holy Spirit will fill every area vacated by the enemy
2. Give much love and encouragement (to the client) immediately after deliverance.
3. Assure the counselee not to fear "Reinvasion" unless they deliberately invite the enemy
4. Encourage the client to follow these ten steps:
5. The Lordship of Christ must be central in your life
6. Be continuously being filled with the Holy Spirit
7. Read the word of God and allow it to minister to you
8. Wear the armor of God at all times
9. Be on guard against the enemy's counter-attack
10. Be in good fellowship and allow continuing ministry to you

11. Allow the Holy Spirit to produce fruits
12. Walk continuously in forgiveness
13. Praise God in all circumstances
14. Keep the right company

As you can see from these multiple directives on staying free, deliverance does not end with the deliverance session. The days and weeks immediately following are vital and "after care" is essential. The immediate effect of the deliverance session must be shored up and reinforced. Simply casting out a demon (or demons) does not mean the end of spiritual warfare in a person's life. The lock to the door of the Promised Land is now opened and victory and access is assured but the Land remains to be systematically taken.

As the demonic powers witness the newfound confidence, strength and authority in a believer's life, the demons will be discouraged (and hindered) from seeking to regain control. It is essential at this juncture for the one set free to be patient and persistent. It is important to refuse any word not in keeping with God's word and remain in a disposition of prayer. The following are guidelines that we have offered to individuals following their deliv-' erance session.

Disciplines of Deliverance and Foundations for Freedom

1. **Keep** Short Sin Accounts:
Confess sin immediately. Demons are attracted to sin like flies to garbage. Remember Satan is Beelzebub, "Lord of the Flies." Do not allow unconfessed sin to remain in your life. I John 1:9, "If we confess our sins, He is faithful and just to forgive us and to cleanse us from all unrighteousness."

2. **Avoid** past "doors" of demonic entry:
Particularly shun those behaviors, practices, etc. that led to past strongholds of demonic activity. These include addictive patterns of behavior, sexual sins, emotional "outbursts" and imbalances, etc. Avoid individuals/past associates related to these "behaviors." "Do not be deceived: Evil company corrupts

good habits." I Cor. 15:33

3 .**Walk** in the Spirit:

Galatians 5:16 says, "Walk in the Spirit and you shall not fulfill the lust of the flesh." We must learn to be Holy Spirit directed in all we do. Verse 25 states, "If we live in the spirit let us also walk in the spirit." In short, "walk the talk."

4. **Think** "Freedom":

Galatians 5:1 says, "Stand fast therefore in the liberty by which Christ has made us free, and do not be entangled again with a yoke of bondage." Continue to confess the reality of your state of deliverance so that our High Priest, Jesus, can keep it before the Father in fresh reality. Hebrews 7:25 Says, "Therefore He is able to save to the uttermost those who come to God through Him, since He always lives to make intercession for them." Discipline your thoughts and set your mind on "things above," on heavenly things and on things of the Spirit. "For those who live according to the Flesh set their minds on the things of the Flesh, but those who live according to the Spirit, (set their minds on) the things of the Spirit. For to be carnally minded is death, but to be spiritually minded is life and peace" Romans 8:5,6

5. **Confess** Scripture:

As we quote scripture, reasserting our agreement with it, our High Priest, Jesus, validates it at the throne and makes it alive to us by the power of the Holy Spirit (Heb. 4:12; 7:25). God's words of truth in the scriptures are our "Bill of Rights" and we should declare them out loud for all demons, powers and principalities to hear (Ephesians 6:17, 18). Claim the scriptural promise (Isaiah 26:13-15) that demonic powers are dead in your life and shall **not** live there again. Hebrews 10:23 says, "Let us hold fast to the confession of our hope without wavering, for He who promised is faithful." Our Lord Jesus and Father God desire us to be blessed and free. They have promised us this and will be faithful to give as we ask and live according to God's word.

6. **Practice** Prayer:

Prayer is the lifeline of continued freedom. It is our line of defense that guards our position against the enemy, Satan and his demons. Anyone who does not pray often will not remain free and delivered.

I Thessalonians 5:16-18 says, "Rejoice always, pray without ceasing, in everything give thanks; for this is the will of God in Christ Jesus for you." Philippians 4:6,7 says, "Be anxious for nothing but in everything by prayer and supplication, with thanksgiving, let your requests be made known to God; and the peace of God which surpasses all understanding will guard your hearts and minds through Christ Jesus." Taking the concept of peace as a weapon, Romans 16:20 says this "and the God of peace will crush Satan under your feet shortly." Prayer brings us peace as it activates God through the Holy Spirit to take action on our behalf and thereby "crushing" Satan's forces.

7. **Profess** Praise:

This encourages the soul and releases the power of God. The sound of praise invites God's presence and torments and confuses demonic forces (II Chronicles 20:22). Hebrews 13:15 says, "...Let us continually offer the sacrifice of praise to God, that is, the fruit of our lips, giving thanks to His name." Psalm 22:3,4 says, "But you are Holy, enthroned in the praises of Israel. Our fathers trusted in you; they trusted, and you delivered them." The King James Version uses the phrase "that inhabitest the praise of Israel." Notes on this passage in the Spirit-filled Life Bible comment: "The concept here is that praise releases God's glory, thus bringing to the worshippers actualized responses of His Kingly reign...Praise will bring the presence of God...there is a distinct manifestation of His rule which enters the environment of praise. God enters! His presence (through praise) will live and take up residence in our lives. The word inhabit (Hebrew: Yawshab) means to sit down, to remain, to settle, or to marry. God does not merely visit us when we praise Him, but His presence abides with us and we partner with Him in a growing relationship." Notice how this text connects "Praise" in verse 3 with "Trust" and "deliverance" in verse 4. Let this truth increase your faith to praise and trust which leads to deliverance (permanently) from satanic harassments, torment or bondage. As Ruth Ward Heflin said: "Praise until a spirit of worship comes, worship until the glory falls. Then stand in the glory. "God's presence in full is manifest in His glory."

8. **Demonstrate** Discipline and Obedience:
Seek to obey the Lord and the guidance of the Holy Spirit in every area of your life. Hebrews 12:25 says, "Be careful that you do not refuse Him who speaks from Heaven." Practice hearing and obeying God's direction. James urges us to be "doers" of the word and not just "hearers." We must maintain a disciplined Christian life. Romans 12:1 says, "Present your bodies as a living sacrifice, Holy, acceptable to God, which is your reasonable service." I Samuel 15:22-23 says, "Behold, to obey is better than sacrifice... Rebellion is as the sin of witchcraft and stubbornness is as iniquity and idolatry..."

9. **Exercise** Submission and Resistance:
Learn how to crucify the Flesh and resist the devil. Romans 6:11,12 says, "Reckon yourselves to be dead indeed to sin but alive to God in Christ Jesus. Therefore do not let sin reign in your mortal body that you should obey its lusts." Galatians 2:20 says this, "I have been crucified with Christ; it is no longer I who live, but Christ lives in me; and the life which I now live in the flesh I live by faith in the Son of God, who loved me and gave Himself for me." This ongoing process of submission and resistance is a lifelong effort. It is not a one time experience, but a continued stance. It must be based upon **submission** to God so that we may then be able to **resist** the Devil. James 4:7 says, "Therefore submit to God. Resist the Devil and He will flee from you." Submission (to God) is the primary key to resisting (the Devil). Another key to resisting Satan is to fight your enemies while they are small. Begin immediately following deliverance (or any Spiritual victory) to gain power over any areas Satan might have used (and may try to use) to tempt you to sin. Each of us has different points of weakness – of fleshly vulnerability. Satan only tempts us to do what we inwardly might

desire to do. Otherwise, there is no temptation. We must identify these areas and gain dominance over them through the Holy Spirit's power. We must not allow them to grow in power and size until they are irresistible. Determine to confine all areas of temptation to small-scale operation. Satan is drawn to our weakness. He continuously, with his demons, probes our weak areas to gain access and input into our lives. We must therefore submit to God in order to exchange His strength for our weaknesses; and, thereby, resist Satan's temptation through the strength we draw from God (II Cor. 12:9). Finally, remember that the best form of resistance is the one Jesus used when Satan tempted Him – the word of God. Identify specific scriptures that speak to your point of temptation and use them to resist the Tempter and walk in deliverance daily.

10. **Make** Jesus central in your life and **yield** every area of it to his Lordship:

John 15:5-8 says, "I am the vine, you are the branches. He who abides in Me and I in him, bears much fruit; for without Me you can do nothing...If you abide in Me, and My words abide in you, you will ask what you will and it shall be done for you. By this my Father is glorified, that you bear much fruit; so you will be my disciples." You cannot remain victorious over Satan or maintain deliverance without giving Jesus first place in your life. You cannot successfully complete the race He sets before you without remaining centrally focused upon His face (Heb 12:1). I Cor. 2:2 says, "For I determined not to know anything among you except Jesus Christ and Him crucified." This does not mean we only think of him as crucified. It means we acknowledge His Lordship over our lives because he went to the cross for our sake. It means that we make him central in our lives. Then, because of his power, working in us, we can bear much fruit.

11. **Use** your weapons of defense and offense:

These are described in Ephesians 6:13-17 as "the whole armor of God." It is comprised of the helmet of Salvation, the breastplate of Righteousness, the belt of Truth, the shoes of Peace, the shield of Faith, and the sword of the Spirit (God's word). The sword of the Spirit is the sole offensive weapon that we can wield against our enemy – Satan. All other pieces of the armor are for defense against demonic attack. In addition to the full armor of God we have other weapons of war that, if used, will help to maintain deliverance. These are: the blood of Jesus, the name of Jesus and the word of our testimony (Revelation 12:11 "and they overcame Him by the blood of the Lamb and by the word of their testimony.")

12. **Develop** a dynamic faith and **be continuously filled** with the Holy Spirit:

Ephesians 5:18 states, "But be filled with the Spirit." The original Greek tense for "be filled" means "be continuously being filled." Following an initial Baptism in the Holy Spirit we should seek to be filled over and over with the Holy Spirit. Why? Because as human "vessels" we leak! And we must seek to increase our level of faith daily – allowing God to stretch us and grow us. Colossians 1:21-23 exhorts us, "Yet now He has reconciled in the body of His flesh through death, to present you Holy and blameless, and above reproach in His sight – if indeed you continue in the faith, grounded and steadfast, and are not moved away from the hope of the Gospel which you heard." We **must** continue in **the** faith and we **must** grow stronger in **our** faith in Christ Jesus. We must, as Paul exhorts Timothy, "Fight the good fight of faith, lay hold on eternal life, to which you were also called and have confessed the good confession in the presence of many witnesses." A key part in developing your faith is to be part of a fellowship of the body of Christ. It is there that we can receive sound teaching and participate in mutual encouragement (for "iron sharpens iron"). Hebrews 10:24 states, "and let us consider one another in order to stir up love and good works not forsaking the assembling of ourselves together, as is the manner of some, but exhorting one another..." This is what is meant by continue in the faith." Following deliverance we need the support, encouragement and intercession of others as we are "walking out" our deliverance. One point to remember (noted in Breaking Unhealthy Soul Ties by Bill Banks) as you choose a local fellowship to join: "the faith of a congregation apparently cannot exceed that of the one in spiritual authority over them. This is why Paul encourages like-minded fellowship. If you are in a church that doesn't believe in healing and deliverance, you will not be able to muster much faith for those benefits, even though you may mentally believe in them."

Strongholds

Another key to remaining free following deliverance is the pulling down of demonic "strongholds" of activity and power in your life. II Corinthians 10:3-5 is the foundational scripture for understanding and defeating demonic strongholds in your life: "For though we walk in the Flesh we do not war according to the Flesh. For the weapons of our warfare are not carnal but mighty in God for pulling down strongholds, casting down arguments (imaginations, speculations) and every high thing that exalts itself against the knowledge of God; bringing every thought into captivity to the obedience of Christ."

To gain a clearer picture of just what a demonic stronghold is and how it operates, survey the following insights regarding demonic strongholds.

- ❖ "A stronghold is a mindset impregnated with hopelessness that causes one to accept as unchangeable something that we know is contrary to God." Ed Silvoso, Global Harvest Ministries
- ❖ "Strongholds are places from which demons rule. They are part of a veil which prevents unbelievers from being able to receive the revelation of God's love and salvation and believ- ers from receiving total deliverance and inner healing." – Dutch Sheets, Pastor and Author
- ❖ "A demonic stronghold is an intertwining of sins of the fathers (iniquities, generational curses), self-sins, ungodly beliefs, soul-spirit hurts and demonic oppression. It requires a sequence of Holy Spirit-led ministry steps to disassemble and demolish the stronghold."-Chester and Betsy Kylstra, Directors of Healing House, Pensacola, FL
- ❖ "A stronghold is a demonic fortress of thoughts housing evil spirits that 1.) control, dictate and influence behavior 2.)

oppress and discourage us 3.) filter and color how we view or react to situations, circumstances or people." – Mike and Sue Dowgiewics, Authors, Ministers

❖ "Traumatic **facts** from our past can not be changed. They exist. Unresolved trauma creates unhealed hurts, unresolved issues and unmet needs deep within our souls. These hurts, issues and needs become sources of fuel for feelings of pain, fear, distrust, hopelessness, anger and wrong desires, regardless of how many layers our soul puts down to bury them. To survive we all learn behaviors that **temporarily** pacify and take the edge off the pain issuing out of these sources. After becoming a Christian and finding that we cannot break these entrenched coping patterns we begin to justify and defend our inability to overcome them (thereby building strongholds). The key to overcoming every stage of this cycle of defeat and pain is to dismantle the core structure of our soul's power and control that has been blocking out the healing work of the Holy Spirit. Then God's mercy and grace can get to our sources and heal them." – Liberty Savard, Author, Shattering your Strongholds

The topic of "strongholds" is covered in depth in our manual on strongholds. The following information is an abridgement of that information.

In accordance with II Corinthians 10: 3-5 strongholds are fortress centers of demonic activity operating primarily in the mental area of a person and utilizing false mindsets (ungodly beliefs), imaginations, speculations, and pride to remain in place. Thus remaining in place, even following deliverance, they work to hinder and bring defeat to a believer. They offer resistance as that individual seeks to grow and follow the example of Jesus Christ. These strongholds **must** be eliminated ("pulled down") if the individual believer is to experience lasting freedom in Jesus Christ. This castle-like "stronghold" has three main components (Following the description of II Cor. 10:3-5). These are: **an outer wall**, (Vs. 5: "Casting down…every high thing that exalts itself against God,"); **An inner wall** (Vs. 5 "Arguments or reasonings or speculations or imaginations" – Depending on your

Bible translation) and a **Core/inner prison** (the main theme of a given stronghold).

The outer wall is made up of various forms of pride. In our study we have identified what we call "The Seven Heads" of pride. These are pride of appearance, pride of knowledge, pride of position, pride of wealth and riches, pride of immorality, pride of power and pride of entrapment. These are described in Matthew 23: 1-28. The intermingling of various forms of pride forms a high, defensive outer wall for the fortress-like stronghold structure. This serves to protect the next structure (the inner wall) and keep the core/root (inner prison) of the stronghold from being eliminated. This outer wall is eliminated through Humility, Confession and Repentance. We take the concept of "seven heads" of pride from the seven-headed dragon of the book of Revelation. We believe this dragon to be Leviathan, a demonic prince, called (in Job41) "King over all the children of pride."

The next component of a stronghold, the inner wall, is comprised of: arguments, philosophies and earthly wisdoms, ungodly beliefs, and dependence on human intellect. An ungodly belief is any belief or belief system that does not agree with the truth of God's word. This inner wall is dismantled with the truth of God's word applied through Godly love and compassion. God's spirit of love must permeate this phase of dismantling a stronghold or God's truth will not be received. Four possible sources of ungodly beliefs are: The natural unredeemed mind, experiences of hurt, family heritage and parental messages to children.

The last area of a stronghold is the inner core/prison where the primary demonic power is resident that gives the overall theme and nature to a specified stronghold (i.e.; bitterness, fear, anger, lust etc.). Note that each stronghold has a theme that describes its chief area of operation in one's life. Some general characteristics of strongholds are: they are stubborn, irrational, uncontrollable, counter-productive and always fail you. A partial listing of stronghold "types" is: Suspicion, doubt, independence, false-security, confusion, unforgiveness, distrust, control/manipulation, fear and denial.

Three common sources of strongholds are: The World, Our Experiences, and Wrong/False doctrine. Perceptions gained from any of these source areas can develop into ungodly belief systems (not in accordance with Godly truth) and form a stronghold of defeat in a believer's life.

In summary then, a stronghold is what one uses to fortify and defend an ungodly or false/incorrect personal belief, idea or opinion against perceived outside opposition. This makes up the defense of what you believe. In II Cor. 10:3-5, these are the "speculations," "reasonings," "rationalizations" and "arguments." If you have accepted an ungodly belief as truth, you will fight to defend that belief and with time will erect a stronghold to defend your right to believe it. To reverse this process, pull down strongholds and remain free following deliverance, the believer must "actualize" the truth of Romans 12:2-"And do not be conformed to this world, but be transformed by the renewing of your mind.

We transform our minds by:
– A thorough knowledge of God's word
– An intimate, personal relationship with Jesus
– Actively appropriating the mind of Christ
– Binding your mind to Christ's/God's will

Remember this: **Thoughts** become **feelings** and **emotions** which become **actions** and **behaviors** which then develop into **habits** which produce **strongholds** of **belief systems**. These demonic strongholds must be dismantled for a believer to maintain deliverance.

Spiritual Authority

An essential part of remaining free after deliverance is gaining an understanding of Spiritual Authority. When you, as a believer, begin to exercise God-given spiritual authority over Satan and his army of demons you will truly experience the freedom in Christ and abundant life God desires for you.

The first step in understanding and exercising Spiritual Authority is the belief and confession of Scriptural truth regarding your authority in Jesus Christ.

Meditate on the following scriptural confessions regarding essential **keys** for Kingdom Living (as referred to in Matthew

16:19). These "keys," when confessed and applied, will truly bind Satan's activity against you, loose God's power in your life, and give you power to remain free after deliverance. We encourage you to add similar confessions of your own to these.

More than Conquerors – Begin your confessions with this passage (from the amplified Bible) regarding your spiritual position before God through Jesus Christ; and, the relation of God's love to that position:

"What then shall we say to [all] this? If God is for us, who [can be] against us? [Who can be our foe if God is on our side?] [Ps 118:6] Who shall bring any charge against God's elect [when it is] God who justifies [that is, Who puts us in right relationship to Himself]? Who shall come forward and accuse or impeach those whom God has chosen? Will God who acquits us? Who is there to condemn us? Will Christ Jesus (the Messiah) who died, or rather who was raised from the dead, who is at the right hand of God actually pleading as he intercedes for us? Who shall ever separate us from Christ's love? Shall suffering and affliction and tribulation or calamity and distress? Or persecution or hunger or destitution or peril or sword? Yet amid all these things we are more than conquerors and gain a surpassing victory through Him who loved us. For I am persuaded beyond doubt (I am sure) that neither death nor life, nor angels, nor principalities, nor things impending and threatening, nor things to come, nor powers, nor height, nor depth, nor anything else in all creation will be able to separate us from the love of God which is in Christ Jesus our Lord." Romans 8:31,33, 34,35,37-39 Amplified Bible

In the Vine's Expository Dictionary (page 122) and the Strong's Concordance (5245/3228) the phrase "more than conquerors" translates "hyperconquerors" (above conquerors) and "preeminently victorious." In Christ you have a "preeminent" place of victory over Satan to the degree that you acknowledge and are willing to enforce that position. The position has been provided by the sacrifice/victory of Jesus over Satan. As you "lay hold of that for which Christ Jesus has also laid hold of (you)" (Philippians 3:12), you will reside in a position of victory and Spiritual Authority over Satan.

The following are additional confessions regarding your position before God through Jesus Christ and your subsequent Spiritual Authority. Declare them **out loud** for Satan and your own spirit to hear. Let your spirit be strengthened in the power of God (Ephesians 3:16) and let Satan witness and comply with your exercise of Spiritual Authority (to "flee" at your command, James 4:7). Remember how David encouraged himself in the Lord at Ziklag following one of his worst defeats? This led him to pursue the enemy and turn defeat into victory. These confessions may help you to do likewise. Read I Samuel 30:1-28

1. **God's Love:** John 3:16; I John 3:1; Song 2:4; I John 4:9

Therefore, I confess, how great is God's love for us—He sent Jesus, His Son, to die for us that through Him we could become children of God. I will determine to live as a demonstration of God's love to others, for "His banner over me is love."

2 .**Salvation:** Romans 8:14-17; II Cor. 5:17, 20; I John 4:4

I am a new creation—a child of God and an ambassador of Christ. I have received the spirit of adoption crying, "Abba, Father!" I am an heir of God and a joint heir with Jesus Christ Who loves me and died for me that I might have eternal life. I accept Jesus, as my Lord and my Savior, and greater is He, Jesus, Who is in me, than he, Satan, that is in the world.

3. **God's Kingdom:** James 1:17-18; Exodus 6:6-8; Romans 14:17; Colossians 1:13,14

I will declare that God is good. His desire is to bless me, for every good and perfect gift comes down from the Father of lights. With God, there is no shadow of turning, and He has called me forth by His word of truth to be a first fruit in His Kingdom—to be part of the demonstration of His kingdom in the earth. I will receive the Father's blessing, and I will demonstrate His Kingdom, which is "righteousness," "peace," and "joy" in the Holy Ghost!

4. **Who I Am in Christ:** I Peter 2:9,10; Colossians 2:11-15;

Romans 8:37-39

I have been called from Satan's darkness to God's light to be a chosen generation, and I choose to walk as part of a royal priesthood, a holy nation, and a peculiar people. Having been made more than a conqueror, I will shout the praises of Jesus and declare that nothing can separate me from God's love! I am made one with Jesus and I have been circumcised of the heart, buried with Him in baptism, and raised with Him, by faith, from the dead. He has nailed my sins to the cross, and I am made alive with Him. Now together with Him, I disarm principalities and powers, make a public spectacle of them, and triumph over them through Jesus!

5. **Obedience—Submission—Sacrifice:** Galatians 6:20; Romans 12:1-2; James 4:7,8; Colossians 1:27; Ephesians 5:26

I therefore submit to God and draw near to Him that He may draw near to me. Then, when I resist the devil, he must flee from me! For I have been crucified with Christ, and I no longer live for self. Christ now lives in me and is my hope of glory; and, the life I now live, I do so by faith in Jesus, the Son of God! I present my body as a living sacrifice, holy and acceptable to God. I determine not to be conformed to the world, but to be transformed to the image of Jesus Christ through the renewing of my mind!

6. **Satan's Kingdom:** II Cor. 2:11; Eph. 6:12; I Peter 5:8,9; John 10:10; Romans 16:20; Eph. 1:20-22

I am not ignorant of Satan and his devices, for he is the thief who comes to steal, kill, and destroy. I know that he roams about as a roaring lion to see whom he can devour. And he will not devour me! For I know I do not battle against flesh and blood, but against Satan and his forces...his principalities, powers, rulers of darkness, and spiritual hosts of wickedness in the heavenlies. And I do not fear these forces, for the Lord Jesus is seated in heavenly places far above all principalities and power and might and dominion and every name named. All things are under His feet, and through Jesus,

Prince of Peace, the God of Peace will crush Satan under my feet.

7. **Spiritual Warfare:** II Cor. 10:3-5; Matthew 11:12; Psalm 144:1-2

I know that from the days of John the Baptist until now, the Kingdom of God has been advancing forcefully. I am a warrior, and I determine to storm the very gates of Hell and advance God's Kingdom forcefully.

I will do so with the spiritual weapons that God has given me, for I do not war in the flesh, but the Spirit. The weapons of my warfare are not carnal, but mighty in God for pulling down strongholds, and casting down every high thing that exalts itself against the knowledge of God. Therefore, taking every thought captive to the obedience of Christ, I follow, into victorious battle, the Lord of Hosts, the Lord of the Breakthrough, the Lord my Rock, my Fortress, my Tower, my Shield, my Refuge, and my Deliverer, who trains my hands for war and my fingers for battle—

Jehovah Nissi: "the Lord my victorious Banner."

8. **Power and Authority:** Matthew 28:18; Philippians 4:13; Luke 10:19; Mark 16:15-18; I Cor. 2:4-4.

For I can do all things through Jesus Christ Who strengthens me. I can wage victorious spiritual warfare as Jesus Christ has given me authority. I can trample on serpents and scorpions and over all the power of the enemy and nothing will by any means hurt me. I will go and preach the Gospel in Power. And my speech and my preaching will not be with persuasive words of human wisdom, but with the demonstration of the Holy Spirit and of power—with signs following, with casting out demons, speaking in new tongues and laying hands on the sick to see them healed. For as Jesus has authority over all, then as I follow Jesus, in His Name I too have all authority over the works and power of Satan and his hosts of evil.

9. **Baptism in the Holy Spirit:** Matthew 3:11; Luke 14:49; Acts 1:8; Ephesians 5:18; I Cor. 12:1-11.

I know that my source of spiritual gifts and power is the Holy Spirit. I know that when the Holy Spirit has come upon me and when Jesus baptizes me in the Holy Spirit and fire that I receive power.

I call on you now Holy Spirit to immerse me in Your presence. Saturate me with You and equip me for battle and for serving Christ in power. Release the flow of Your gifts through me now: word of wisdom, word of knowledge, discerning of spirits, tongues, interpretation of tongues, prophecy, faith, healing, miracles.

Manifest through me Your fire, Your wind, Your water and Your sweet oil. Come now as a mighty rushing wind—shake my foundations and stand over me as a flaming tongue of fire.

10. **Power Prayers:** Matthew 12:25-29; I Thess. 5:17; Eph. 6:18

I will apply the power of spiritual warfare prayer against the kingdom of Satan. I will use, in prayer, the keys of binding and loosing, and I will pray without ceasing. Being watchful, I will pray always in the Spirit. In prayer, I will release a river of God's power and tip the bowls of Heaven to bring the birthing of God's Kingdom and the destruction of Satan's kingdom. Through my prayer, I will bring forth the fruit of Calvary and release the rain of the Holy Spirit on earth!

11. **Full Armor of God:** Ephesians 6:10-18

As I prepare for battle, I take up the full armor of God. For I determine that in the day of war against Satan, I will withstand his demonic forces and remain standing against them! I will be strong in the Lord and in the power of His might.

I stand now and put on...
- The Belt of Truth about my waist
- The Breastplate of Righteousness
- The Shoes of the preparation of the Gospel of Peace
- The Helmet of Salvation
- lift up the mighty Shield of Faith and I quench, with it, every fiery dart of Satan
- And, I take up in my hand the powerful, two-edged, razor

sharp, flaming Sword of the Spirit; which is the word of God! And I declare with a loud voice, "Look out powers of darkness, I am standing with you under my feet!"

12. **Praise:** Philippians 4:4; Psalm 34:1-3

Therefore, now, having declared all, received all, and demonstrated all that God has for me, I stand in the power and authority of Jesus Christ. In His Name, I loose fear and confusion into the ranks of Satan's forces with the praises of God from my mouth.

"I will bless the Lord at all times; His praise shall continually be in my mouth. My soul shall make its boast in the Lord; the humble shall hear of it and be glad. Oh, magnify the Lord with me, and let us exalt His Name together."

Names of God

In addition to understanding and confessing your place before God through Jesus, an understanding of the character and nature of God will enhance your effectiveness in wielding Spiritual Authority. Meditate, confess, and study the following names of God. They reveal various aspects of His divine nature; and, as your Father He is able and desirous to demonstrate them on your behalf.

1. The Great I am – Exodus 3:14
2. El Elyon – The most High God – Genesis 14:18
3. El Shaddai – The all sufficient one – Genesis 17:1
4. Elohim - The only God; The Trinity – Exodus 20:4-6; Exodus 23:17
5. Adonai – Lord and Master – Deut. 10:17
6. Jehovah Nissi – The Lord is my banner and victory – Exodus 23:17
7. Jehovah Shammah – God who is there – Deut. 31:6
8. Jehovah Tsidkenu – God is my righteousness - Jer. 23:6
9. Jehovah M'Kaddesh – God is my sanctifier – Lev. 1:17
10. Jehovah Rohi – God is my shepherd – Ps. 23
11. Jehovah Shalom – God is my peace – Judges 6:24
12. Jehovah Rapha – God is my healer – Exodus 15:26

13. <u>Jehovah Sabaoth</u> – The Lord God of Hosts – Ps.24: 7-10/Gen.2: 1
14. <u>Jehovah Jireh</u> – God is my provider – Genesis 22:14
15. <u>El Roi</u> – The God who sees everything (and acts on my behalf) –Gen. 16:13

Diet and Fasting

Another consideration in maintaining deliverance and succeeding in Spiritual warfare is the issue of diet and fasting. In addition to the continuous practice of healthy eating habits and balanced diet we have found the eating of protein to be important to the successful conduct of spiritual warfare. This is not to be practiced dogmatically. However, we believe that eating protein (especially meat) is important to maintaining deliverance and conducting Spiritual warfare. Much of the following information is taken from <u>Prepare for War</u> by Rebecca Brown. Please prayerfully consider these guidelines as you seek to remain free from demonic influence.

Spiritual warfare causes a particular drain on the physical body that results in a noticeable loss of protein. We must be careful to replenish that protein or we will become weakened and thus less effective in Spiritual warfare. The scriptures have a good deal to say regarding the eating of meat (which provides protein) and its importance.

God instructed Noah to eat meat after the flood (Genesis 9:1-4). God knew the Spiritual battles Noah and his family would face in order to resist demonic influence. Meat protein would replenish them as needed. In the Old Testament account of God's Law for Israel the Levite Warrior Priests are directed to eat diets high in beef and lamb. Both Noah and Abraham offered sacrifice of burnt meat (bulls, calves, lambs) to God (Genesis 8:20,21). Genesis 18:1-7 contains the account of Abraham offering a meal including meat to the Lord. Throughout the Old Testament are accounts of spiritual warriors eating meat prior to engaging in battle: <u>Gideon</u> – Judges 6:19-27; <u>David</u> – II Samuel 6:17-19; <u>Joshua</u> – Joshua 8:31. <u>Elijah</u>, before his battle with the priests of Baal on Mount Carmel was directed by God to the brook Cherith. There, ravens fed him with bread and meat in the morning and the evening.

In spite of much attention and publicity there are really no conclusive medical studies verifying that **lean** red meat is harmful to the body. Please note that this is not referring to fat meat or meat high in fat content, but lean meat full of protein. There has even been research demonstrating the merits of protein supplements in treating a wide range of illnesses.

A number of popular health food teachings today promote abstinence from meat. If a protein substitute is not provided this may lead to a state of weakness and even illness. Without protein the body loses its ability to fight infections. There are people today who have died because they did not supplement sufficiently their protein intake. During intense times of spiritual battle (especially those against witchcraft) it can be necessary to eat protein or meat at least twice daily. Individuals who insist on a vegetarian diet following deliverance may be unable to keep demons out or at least have difficulty in warding off demonic attacks. It is wise for individuals who have experienced a "strenuous" personal deliverance to eat a diet very high in quality protein for several weeks after deliverance.

Satan is very aware of this need of our bodies for protein and its relation to spiritual warfare. Note that today's Hindus and other Eastern religions (all based in Demon worship) promote the practice of vegetarianism. They believe that an "adept" or medium's success in wielding demonic power depends upon the presence in their bodies of a fluid called akasa. It can only be replenished/regenerated by a vegetarian diet and chastity.

All new age teaching, particularly as professed by Yogis, encourages vegetarianism. They instruct followers that the "vibrations" of meat are harmful and diminish spiritual sensitivity. In response, consider this scripture: "Now the Spirit speaketh expressly, that in the latter times some shall depart from the Faith, giving heed to seducing spirits, and doctrines of devils; speaking lies in hypocrisy; having their conscience seared with a hot iron; forbidding to marry and **commanding to abstain from meats**, which God hath created to be received with thanksgiving of them which believe and know the truth. For every creature of God is good, and nothing to be refused, if it be received with thanksgiving: For it is sanctified by the word of God and prayer" (I Timothy 4:1-5).

Now, regarding fasting: Fasting can prove beneficial in a Christian's life when directed by the Lord. These times can be experiences of revelation and specific instruction of the Lord for future spiritual endeavors. However, prolonged fasting in times of heavy spiritual battle, unless specifically directed by God, can be dangerous and even harmful. Each of us should fast as God directs us to do so. Our experience has been to not engage in prolonged fasting during times of intense spiritual warfare and deliverance. Individuals who undertake a prolonged fast in a season of keen spiritual battle may become excessively weak and a resultant "casualty" of demonic attack. Always be very sure of the Lord's guidance regarding personal fasting. Don't allow guilt or peer pressure or spiritual "fads" and popular trends (based on emotionalism) to prompt you to fast contrary to God's will.

This being said we offer the following guidelines for fasting.

We have found "juice fasting" and what we call a "Daniel fast" to be most beneficial to us. The first is a fast based on fruit and/or vegetable juices only. The second is based on Daniel 1: 12 and consists of vegetables only (fresh or cooked) with water or juice to drink. These should be prepared with no sugar. All sugar should be avoided during this fast (including honey and syrup).

In our experience these fasts seem to work well with an ongoing schedule of work and still provide maximum spiritual and physical impact. Some fasts, particular water only or even no solids or liquids, can be unsafe. Persons with blood-sugar conditions or other health concerns should usually avoid such fasting. These type fasts, even for individuals in good health, should be conducted in times when little other than fasting is done. These types of more extreme fasting normally weaken a person to the degree that full-time work or school attendance may be difficult to undertake - for some, impossible. For a detailed study on fasting see Derek Prince's book, How to fast successfully. Also, Lou Engle's book, Digging the Wells of Revival, has an excellent chapter on fasting.

In fasting keep in mind, the focus should be on a sacrificial act before God, as He directs, rather than a legalistic religious practice. Fasting can, when conducted with wisdom, result in spiritual gain.

This can be in the form of enhanced ability to wage Spiritual warfare or power to maintain deliverance or sharpened spiritual hearing (as distractions are suppressed). However, be sensitive to God's direction as to timing and type of fasting. God is much more concerned with intentions and attitudes of the heart than outward expressions. With God, "to obey is better than sacrifice" I Samuel 15:22.

Insights from naval commands

As a final guideline for maintaining deliverance, the following analogy is offered as an overall summation of the process- particularly in maintaining Godly defensive walls against demonic attack. It provides insight for taking the initiative/offensive in spiritual battle against demonic powers.

Both historically, in the days of wooden sailing ships, and in today's naval warfare operations, certain commands are given by the ship's Captain to direct the crew's action in battle. These commands are applicable to both our defensive and offensive spiritual actions against demonic attacks.

In sailing ship days, there was what amounted to a wooden basket (man-sized) on the top of the main mast. Sailors took turns maintaining a lookout there in what was called "the crow's nest." In modern ships there is a similar structure called the "conning tower" (derived from the words reconnoiter/reconnaissance). The purpose for the watch, primarily, was to maintain a lookout for enemy ships. When sighted, an alarm was shouted out along with the direction for the Captain to look such as, "Sail Ho! Enemy ship off the Starboard bow!." In modern times the message is delivered via radio to the "bridge" where the Captain is stationed to command the ship's operation. This declaration of the sighting of the enemy is followed by a flurry of commands and activities to prepare against enemy attack. Therefore, the job of the "lookout" is vital to the safety of the ship. For us it is equally vital that we be on the lookout and ready for action against demonic attack. We need to be listening to the Holy Spirit's direction at all times, exercising His discernment within us, while manning our "walls" against the enemy (not asleep on watch- a punishable offense militarily). Remember I Peter 5:8 says, "Be sober, be vigilant; because your enemy, the Devil, walks about like a roaring lion, seeking whom he may devour." *Mizpah* in Hebrew means "to watch" or a "watch tower" or "Lookout post." We should continually keep watch from our " mizpah."

Following the sighting of the enemy, an alarm is sounded to begin making readiness for battle. In the days of sailing ships, when commands were sounded by drummers, the Captain ordered, "Beat to Quarters" or "Sound to Quarters." This directed every member of the ship's crew to a pre-assigned battle station where each crewmember had a specific task in the overall plan of battle. In modern times orders such as "Sound the general alarm" and "All hands to battle stations" notify the crew that battle is imminent. This is a most serious condition and handled with the utmost gravity and expediency. In this battle condition, contact or engagement with the enemy is anticipated. We likewise, should man our battle stations, on the alert for commands from our "Captain" whenever we are aware of the presence of the demonic.

Following the stationing of all hands at their predetermined "battle station," when battle with the enemy is certain, the Captain commands, "Clear for action" this directs the crew to load guns, position ammunition and supplies within easy access, and remove any excess baggage/supplies not needed for the conduct of battle. We should continuously be clearing for action (battle) and allowing the Holy Spirit to progressively remove all that would hinder us in resisting the devil (as well as our Christian growth). We should remain in a continual state of readiness and alert, "cleared for action" against demonic schemes, strategies and activities. We should keep in mind as Christians that we **are** engaged in continuous battle. Until the fulfillment of God's end-time plan we **will** face daily an enemy determined to bring about our defeat. Remember, "The kingdom of heaven suffers violence and the violent take it by force." Matthew 11:12

In naval imagery then, you are God's ship. You are equipped to extend the principles of God's kingdom and enforce the freedom of God's abundant life in the face of keen resistance by a determined foe! But, you must remember that you are a "Man O' War," a "Ship of the Line," A "Battleship." As evangelist Reinhard Bonnke says: "We're on a battleship, not a luxury liner or a pleasure ship." You are not out on a vacation cruise. You are part of God's mighty armada – part of God's battle fleet – on patrol against the forces of darkness. Be diligent to faithfully man your specific battle station in the fleet's battle plan for engaging and sinking the enemy's vessels!

Regarding the development of a militant stance toward maintaining your deliverance, reflect on the following quotation and its battle imagery. It was delivered by Prime Minister Winston Churchill to inspire England during the dark days of World War II. With the invasion by Nazi Germany imminent and possible any day, Churchill defined the attitude that England needed in order to survive. It is the mindset you must have today in order to maintain your deliverance and live in the freedom for which Christ has made us free.

"You ask what is our policy? I will say: It is to wage war; by sea, land, and air, with all our might and all the strength that God can give us...
You ask, What is our aim? I can answer in one word: Victory...at all costs, victory in spite of all terror; victory however long and hard the road may be; for without victory there is no survival..
"We shall go on to the end...we shall fight on the seas and oceans, we shall fight with growing confidence and growing strength in the air...whatever the cost may be; we shall fight on the beaches, we shall fight on the landing grounds, we shall fight in the fields and in the streets, we shall fight in the hills; we shall never surrender."

– Winston Churchill

Bibliography

Quoted material, as noted in this book, is taken from the following collection of works by the authors named. Some passages, as stated, have been summarized for clarity and space. Subject material quoted is used by permission.

Scripture references, except where noted; are primarily from:

The Spirit Filled Life Bible, New King James version, copyright 1991; Thomas Nelson, Inc.

The Amplified Bible, copyright 1987, Zondervan Publishing house.

Banks, Bill. **Breaking Unhealthy Soul ties.** Kirkwood, MO.: Impact Christian Books, 1999.

Basham, Don. **Can a Christian have a Demon?** Kirkwood, MO.: Impact Christian Books, 1991.

Bounds, E.M. **Guide to Spiritual Warfare.** New Kensington, Pa.: Whitaker House, 1984.

Brown, Rebecca, M.D. **Prepare for War.** New Kensington, Pa.: Whitaker House, 1992.

Brown, Rebecca, M.D. **Unbroken Curses.** New Kensington, Pa.: Whitaker House, 1995.

Frangipane, Francis.: **The Three Battle Grounds.** Cedar Rapids, IA.: Arrow Publications, 1989.

Gibson, Noel and Phyl. : **Deliver our Children.** Kent England. : Sovereign World Ltd., 1992.

Gibson, Noel and Phyl. : **Freedom in Christ.** Chinchester, England.: New Wine Press, 1996.

Gray, Nancy. **The Angelic Army**. Tulsa, OK.: Harrison House, 1993.

Greenwald, Gary. **Seductions Exposed**. Santa Ana, CA.: Eagle's nest, 1988.

Hammond, Frank and Ida Mae. **Pigs in the Parlor**. Kirkwood, Mo.: Impact Christian books, 1973.

Horrobin, Peter. **Healing through Deliverance**, Vol.1, Kent, England.: Sovereign World, Ltd., 1991.

Horrobin, Peter. **Healing Through Deliverance,** Vol. 2, Kent, England: Sovereign World, Ltd., 1995.

Joyner, Rick. **Epic Battles of the Last Days**. Charlotte, N.C.: Morning Star, 1995.

Joyner, Rick. **The Final Quest**. Charlotte, N.C.: Morning Star, 1995.

Law, Terry. **The Truth about Angels**. Lake Mary, FL.: Creation House, 1994.

Logan, Jim. **Reclaiming Surrendered Ground**. Chicago, IL.: Moody Press, 1995.

MacNutt, Francis. **Deliverance from Evil Spirits**. Grand Rapid, MI.: Chosen Books, 1995.

Miller, Roger. **Curses, Unforgiveness, Evil Spirits, Deliverance**. Germantown, TN.: Trumpet of Gideon, 1994.

Prince, Derek. **Blessing or Curse, You can Choose**. Grand Rapids, MI.: Chosen Books, 1990.

Prince, Derek. **They Shall Expel Demons**. Grand Rapids, MI.: Chosen Books, 1998.

Sandford, John and Mark. **A Comprehensive Guide to Deliverance and Inner Healing**. Grand Rapids, MI.: Chosen Books, 1992.

Sandford, John and Paula. **Healing the Wounded Spirit**. Tulsa, OK.: Victory, House, 1985.

Sandford, John and Paula. **The Transformation of the Inner Man**. Tulsa, OK.: Victory House, 1982.

Seamands, David. **Healing for Damaged Emotions**. Colorado Springs, CO.: Victor Books, 1991.

Sheets, Dutch. **Intercessory Prayer**. Ventura, CA.: Regal Books, 1996.

Smith, James Wesley. **The Mystery of Iniquity Revealed and the Power of Travailing Prayer**. Lagrange, GA.: Restoration Church, 1992.

Subritzky, Bill. **Demons Defeated**. Tom Bridge, England.: Sovereign World,Ltd., 1986.

Sumrall, Lester. **Exorcism: The Reality of Evil**. Green Forest, AR.: New Leaf Press, 1991.

Whyte, H.A. Maxwell. **Demons and Deliverance**. Springdale, PA.: Whitaker House, 1989.

Appendix A

DELIVERANCE CHECK LIST

Have you, your parents, or your grandparents ever practiced or believed the following?

SUPERSTITIONS

___Wished on a star
___Wished on a pulley bone
___Wished on a birthday cake
___Wishing well
___Thrown salt over shoulder
___Afraid of black cats
___Walking under a ladder
___Friday the 13th
___Breaking a mirror (7 years bad luck)
___Bad luck (deaths) comes in threes
___Wedding traditions (something old, something new . . . penny in shoe)
___New Year's meal (black eyed peas, etc.)
___Pendulum (needle dangled from thread to determine sex of baby)
___Jinx (feeling that you are jinxed or that you jinx situations and others)

___Knock on wood
___Step on a crack (break your Mother's back)
___Leave through same door you entered in
___Dog howling at night –bad omen
___Don't sweep under feet (will cause you to be an old maid)
___Bad luck to open umbrella indoors
___Bird flying into a window pane is bad luck

IDOLS

___Statuettes of saints, Mary, etc.
___Rosary (forerunner of Buddhist prayer beads)
___Buddha (rub his tummy for luck)
___Unicorns
___Wizards
___Gargoyles
___Trolls
___Gremlins
___Dragons
___Frogs
___Owls
___Statuettes of foreign gods (Africa, India, Mexico, etc.)

LUCKY CHARMS

___Rabbit's foot
___Four-leaf clover
___Saint Christopher's medal (or other Saints)
___Horse shoe
___Lucky penny or coin ("see a penny, pick it up . .")
___Lucky hat, shirt, etc.

OCCULT

Have you ever been involved with or sought guidance or information from any of the following, even "just for fun?"

___Seances (communication with the dead)
___Psychics
___Magic 8 ball
___Fortune tellers
___Palm readers
___Ouija board
___Handwriting analysis, graphology
___Crystal ball
___Tea leaves read
___Sun, Moon, Stars (especially with face—New Age)
___Tarot Cards
___Horoscope, Zodiac
___Fortune cookies
___Water witching (divining rod)
___Astral traveling (out of body)
___Levitation, table tipping
___Dungeons and Dragons (board game or computer game)
___Numerology (lucky numbers
___Dream catchers (Spiritism)
___Peace symbol (broken cross)
___Geisha (oriental prostitute)
___Chinese astrology
___Indian Spiritism (dances, ceremonies, jewelry, paintings, music)
___Kokopelli (trickster, charmer)
___Cemetaries (other than for burial after a funeral)
___Obeah (West Indian sorcery and magic)
___Mind control/mind over matter
___Extra sensory perception (sixth sense, premonitions)
___Clairvoyance (ability to see into the spirit realm, especially the past)
___"White Magic" (to remove warts, cure ailments)
___Automatic writing (writing, drawing, or painting while in a

trance state)
___Bermuda Triangle (fascination with, read books, seen movies, etc.)
___Pagan religious objects/artifacts (masks, costumes, articles of war, etc.)
___Poltergeist (Telekinesis—imps that move objects, make noise, etc.)
___Transcendental meditation (Yoga—all practice of, including exercises)
___Witch doctors, voodoo
___Curses or hexes (given by you or put on you by others)
___Crystals (New Age—to cleanse, heal, and restore energy)
___Contact with corpses (hospitals, funeral homes, firemen, police, military)
___Haunted houses, looking for ghosts
___Santeria (potions, rituals, and Catholicism mix)
___Mental Telepathy (reading people's minds or sending them a thought)
___Manipulation (ability to control others by tears, anger, guilt, etc.)
___Harassment by psychic means (hearing, seeing, or feeling a spirit)
___U.F.O. (belief in or have seen them)
___Root-working (common in African culture)
___Witchcraft/Satanism (books, spells, ceremonies, etc.)
___Yin/Yang ("some evil in all good, some good in all evil")
___WICCA ("white witches")

Have you ever submitted to or been involved with:

___Hypnosis, self-hypnosis, subliminal tapes (to relax, quit smoking, etc.)
___Martial Arts (combines Yin Yang, Taoism and Buddhism)
___Non-Christian exorcism ("casting out demons" without the name and blood of Jesus)
___Psychic healing
___Psychometry (telling fortune by holding object belonging to another)
___Color Therapy (using "vibration" from colors to "heal")

___I Ching (stones you toss then "read")
___Acupuncture, acupressure (Oriental occult)
___Phrenology (analysis from feeling the shape of the skull)
___Iridology (diagnosis of medical ills using the eye like a crystal ball and Zodiac quadrants)
___Reflexology (ancient Chinese practice to restore "energy flow" to bodyparts)

Roots and Results of Occult Involvement (check those that apply)

___Do you have disturbed sleep? (insomnia, nightmares, fretful sleep)
___Do you hear inner voices?
___Are you accident-prone?
___Do you suffer from illness or pain with undiagnosable symptoms?
___Do you have lapses of memory? (misplace things, lose train of thought)
___Is there constant family turmoil and tragedy? (deaths, terminal illness, divorce, job failure, abuse, violence, incarceration, etc.)
___Do you have unending, usual expenses which drain your finances?
___Do you exhibit anti-social behavior such as isolation?
___Do you suffer from constant confusion?
___Do you suffer from obsessive thoughts?

Have you ever seen any of the following movies or television shows?
Note: Since new movies and T.V. shows are constantly coming out, this list becomes dated almost immediately. This list is to give you an idea of the type movies and shows that glorify violence, terror and the occult.

___The Exorcist
___Ghostbusters
___Beetlejuice
___Rosemary's Baby

___Freddy Krueger movies (Nightmare on Elm Street, etc.)
___Stephen King movies (Cujo, It, Pet Semetary, etc.)
___The Omen
___Amityville Horror
___Friday the 13th
___Poltergeist
___The Twilight Zone
___Indiana Jones and the Temple of Doom
___Halloween
___The Shining
___Child's Play (Chuckie the doll)
___The X Files
___Aliens
___Carrie (high school revenge story)
___Werewolf movies
___Dracula movies (vampires)
___Blair Witch project
___Harry Potter
___Buffy the Vampire Slayer

Have you ever had a Déjà vu experience? _____ (The feeling that you've been here before or experienced the exact scene before. This is a familiar spirit that comes as a spirit of "light." It's motive is to encourage you to believe in reincarnation and/or E.S.P.)

Have you ever read the following:

___Jonathan Livingston Seagull (written while channeling a spirit)
___Unity Daily Word (Unification Church materials)
___Kahlil Gibran writings ("The Prophet," etc.)
___J.R.R. Tolkien (not a Christian writer as many believe)
___Spiritism
___Science Fiction (many have occult elements and are fear-based)
___Books on witchcraft (Aleister Crowley, etc.)
___Deepak Chopra ("Seven Laws of Success," etc.)
___The Satanic Bible
___Horror books (Stephen King, John Carpenter, etc.)

___Books of psychic phenomenon or the paranormal
___Reincarnation
___Fantasy/magic
___Nostradamus (16th Century occult "prophet")

Have you read any of the following books on Metaphysics (the scientific study of supernatural things)?

___Christian Science (believe that Jesus was human and is now dead)
___Swedenborganism
___Scientology (believe there is no sin, evil, or hell)
___Rosicrucianism (Hindu, Judaism and occult mixture)
___Silva Mind Control
___Religious Science (believe man is divine)
___Edgar Cayce (psychic who interprets dreams)

Have you ever been to a pagan temple or shrine in the U.S. or any foreign country? _____ (including Masonic Temples, Mormon Temple, Hindu, Buddhist, etc.)

Have you had any involvement with the following cults: (All deny the Holy Trinity and the Diety of Christ)

___Moonies (Unification Church)
___Mormon (Latter Day Saints)
___Jehovah Witness
___Hinduism (Karma, Krishna, Transcendental Meditation)
___The Way International
___Islam (Allah) or Baha'I
___Zoroastrianism (believe Ahura Mazday is god)
___Buddhism (reincarnation)
___Taoism (nature, herbal meds)
___Shintoism
___Rastafarianism (hatred of Caucasian)

TRAUMA:

1. Have you ever been in a serious car wreck?
2. Have you ever had a life-threatening illness?
3. Have you ever had surgery? (Anesthesia is an altered state and we are vulnerable during that time)
4. Have you ever been raped or sexually molested as a child, teenager, or adult?
5. Have you ever had a miscarriage? (grief issues, soul ties, etc.)
6. Have you ever had an abortion? (guilt, grief, soul ties and murder)
7. Have you ever recommended an abortion to someone or paid for one?
8. Have you ever been present when a family member died? (Their demonic spirits as well as iniquities prefer to inhabit a family member when they die)
9. Have you ever witnessed a violent crime?
10. Have you ever fought in a war?
11. Have you ever been the victim of a natural disaster (fire, tornado, hurricane, flood, blizzard, etc.)?
12. Did you suffer abuse from either parent (physical, verbal, emotional or neglect?
13. Was either parent unfaithful to the other?
14. Did anyone in your family suffer from addictions (drugs, alcohol, spending, eating, gambling, co-dependency, etc.)?
15. Are you aware of any trauma associated with your conception or birth (unplanned pregnancy, product of rape, pre-mature birth, cord wrapped around your neck, etc.)
16. Have you ever been the victim of spiritual abuse (a controlling, manipulative, domineering spiritual leader)?
17. Have you been abused by a boyfriend, girlfriend, or spouse?
18. Has there ever been a murder or suicide in your family?
19. Did anyone in your family of origin die from an illness, accident, criminal act or addiction?

Death Wish

Have you ever had a death wish for yourself?
Have you ever attempted suicide? If so, how old were you and what means did you use?
Have you ever had a death wish for someone else? If so, who?

Have you ever denied any of the following:

* That Jesus is the Son of God?
* The Virgin Birth?
* The resurrection of Jesus from the dead?

Have you ever been on medication for depression, anxiety or psychosis?

If so, when and for how long? Have you or any member of your family ever been admitted to a psychiatric facility? If so, when and for how long?

Have you ever been on tranquilizers or sleeping pills? If so, when and for how long?

Have you ever used/abused the following substances? (check once for use, twice for abuse)

___Caffeine (more than 3 cups coffee per day or 3 colas per day)
___Nicotine
___Pain killers (Lortab, Oxycoton, Morphine, Demerol, etc.)
___Alcohol
___Inhalents (glue, gasoline, aerosols, etc.)
___Marijuana (Pot)
___Cocaine (Crack)
___Amphetamines ("uppers")
___Barbiturates ("downers")
___Hallucinogens (L.S.D., Ecstacy, etc.)
___Angel Dust, PCP

___Heroin
___Food (gluttony, anorexia, bulimia)

Are you currently using drugs?
If not, how long have you been clean?

Have you or your parents or your grandparents ever committed to a Secret Society?

___Fraternity or Sorority
——Demolays
___Rainbow Girls
___Knights of Columbus
___Black Panthers
___Elks
___Boy Scouts (Order of the Arrow)
___Shriners
___Eastern Star
___Masonic Lodge (mixture of Hindu, Kabbala, and Rosicrucian)
___Ku Klux Klan
___Other

Have you ever been involved with any of the following groups which deny the divinity of Jesus, the atonement of sins by the blood of Jesus and the Holy Trinity?

___Spiritual Frontier Fellowship
___Seventh Day Adventist (one branch of)
___New Age
___Oneness Pentecostalism (Jesus Only sect)
___Universalism, Unitarian
___Ultimate Reconciliation
___Unity School of Christianity
___Other

Have you ever been dependent on any of the following?

___Sports programs/games
___Soap operas
___Television
___Gambling, betting
___Internet
___Video games
___Movies/videos
___Co-dependency (the need to be needed by someone else; unhealthy involvement in someone else's life)

Have you ever been arrested? What were the charges?

Have you ever been to prison? What crime did you commit?

Have you ever been subject to any of the following compulsive habits?

___Day dreaming/fantasy
___Lying
___Profanity/cursing
___Overspending/compulsive shopping
___Stealing
___Gossip
___Excessive telephone use
___Compulsive cleaning/organization
___Nervous habits (biting fingernails, picking skin, pulling hair, etc.)
___Obsessive counting

Have you ever looked at pornography in any of the following forms?

___Photographs, magazines
___T.V. pornographic channels
___X-rated movies or videos
___Internet

___Sensual romance novels

Has your overall exposure to pornography been light, moderate, or heavy?

Is pornography a problem for you currently?

Have you ever engaged in any of the following sexual deviations?

___Fornication (sex before marriage)
___Adultery
___Compulsive masturbation
___Homosexual (fantasies or activities)
___Sodomy (anal sex)
___Oral sex
___Voyeurism (peeping Tom)
___Strip bars
___Exposure ("flashing" or dressing provocatively)
___Prostitution
___Wife swapping ("swinging")
___Child molestation
___Adult book stores
___Perversion (sex toys, bondage, sadism, masochism, etc.)
___Beastiality (sexual acts with animals)
___Incest (sexual contact with a family member)
___Rape (or been raped)
___Demonic sex (Incubus/Succubus)
___Lust/sexual fantasy
___Group sex/multiple partners
___Cross-dressing
___Sexual addiction/compulsive drive
___Bi-sexual
___Phone sex
___Frigidity
___Impotence
___Crude sexual language and jokes

List those persons you have unforgiveness and/or bitterness toward (anyone who has hurt you deeply, rejected you, injured you, or angered you). Your list may include parents, children, siblings, in-laws, relatives yourself, God, friends, former spouses, former lovers, bosses, co-workers, teachers, neighbors, pastors, churches, schools, places of employment, etc.

Appendix B

DEMON GROUPINGS

Please note: This list is not offered in its original page composition. It has been adapted to meet the formatting requirements of the printer for this book. While the information is exact, the lay-out differs from our original form. This form may be more difficult to use and not as conducive to the flow of a successful deliverance session. If you desire a copy of our exact form, please contact us at the address listed in the front of the book.

Bitterness
Resentment
Unforgiveness
Violence
Murder
Hatred
Retaliation
Prejudice
Bigotry
Anger
Temper

Retaliation
Destruction
Hatred
Hurt

Revenge
Spite
Sadism
Cruelty
Betrayal
Sabotage
Threats

Impatience
Agitation
Intolerance
Criticism
Frustration
Resentment

Rebellion
Self-willed
Stubbornness
Childishness
Recklessness
Anti-submissive
Disobedience
Defiance

Control
Possessiveness
Manipulation
Verbal domination
Intimidation

Strife
Contention
Arguing
Fighting
Bickering
Quarreling

Criticism
Accusation
Judging
Fault-finding
Envy
Jealousy

Abusive Speech
Blasphemy
Course jesting
Backbiting
Raving and ranting
Gossip
Profanity
Obscenity
Mocking
Belittling

Lying
Deception
Exaggeration
Fear of Rejection
Fear of Punishment

Competition
Argument
Lawyer/debate
Rivalry
Driving
Ego
Pride

Hyper-activity
Restlessness
Pressure
Driving
Fear of failure

Perfectionism
Performance

Perfection
Pride
Vanity
Ego
Performance
Criticism
Frustration
Irritability
Intolerance
Anger
Fear of failure
Man pleasing

Pride
Self-righteousness
Haughtiness
Importance
Vanity
Ego
Arrogance
Self-justification
Excuse-making
Blaming
Stubbornness
Entitlement
False humility

Mind Idolatry
Intellectualism
Rationalization
Analysis
Pride
Ego
Self-deception

Denial
Self-delusion
Pride

Affectation
Theatrics
Playacting
Pretension
Manipulation
Attention-seeking

Confusion
Frustration
Forgetfulness
Incoherence
Indecisiveness

Deaf & Dumb
Confusion
Inattention
Epilepsy
Mental dullness
Poor Retention

Doubt
Unbelief
Skepticism

Escape
Indifference
Passivity
Stoicism
Sleep
Daydreaming/fantasy
Alcohol
Drugs

Movies, T.V.
Books

Indecision
Procrastination
Forgetfulness
Indifference
Perfection
Compromise
Confusion
Fear of failure

Paranoia
Suspicion
Distrust
Fear
Persecution
Defensiveness

Mental Illness
Fear of Insanity
Bi-Polar
Retardation
Schizophrenia
Mania
Paranoia
Dementia

Worry
Anxiety
Apprehension
Fear
Dread

Covetousness
Materialism
Stealing

Greed
Envy
Hoarding (fear)
Stinginess
Possessiveness
Discontent
Robbing God—God of Mammon

Poverty
Need
Lack

Passivity
Apathy
Lethargy
Indifference
Listlessness

Fatigue
Tiredness
Weariness
Laziness

Heaviness
Gloom
Disgust
Burden

Depression
Discouragement
Despondency
Defeatism
Disappointment
Dejection
Insomnia
Hopelessness
Despair

Morbidity

Grief
Sorrow
Heartache
Wounded spirit
Mourning
Sadness
Heartbreak
Crying

Death
Trauma/accidents
Illness/disease

Suicide
Self-pity
Selfishness
Punishment
Manipulation
Self-hatred
Hopelessness
Escape

Infirmity
Sickness
Illness
Disease
Hypochondriasis

Hereditary Family Illnesses:
Illnesses you suffer from:

Addictive & Compulsive
Nicotine
Drugs
Alcohol

Caffeine
Sugar
Gambling
Spending
Entertainment
Gossip
Internet
Telephone
Exercise
Stealing
Music
Pornography

Obesity
Gluttony
Sexual abuse
Obsession with food
Boredom
Self-pity
Resentment/anger
Nervousness
Self-reward
Frustration

Eating Disorders
Bulemia
Anorexia
Self-hatred
Perfectionism
False self-image
Punishment
Control
Death
Rejection

Rejection
Fear of rejection

Fear of failure
Fear of abandonment
Isolation
Fear of change
Defensiveness
Withdrawal/pouting

Self-accusation
Self-rejection
Self-hatred

Guilt
Condemnation
Embarassment
Shame
Unworthiness

Insecurity
Inferiority
Shyness
Comparison
Loneliness
Low self-esteem
Self-pity
Timidity
Inadequacy

Nervousness
Tension
Nervous habits
Restlessness (verbal or physical)
Excitable
Pacing
Headaches
Insomnia
Fear
Panic/hysteria

Death
Storms
Future
Bodily harm
Pain
Doctors/dentists
Betrayal
Tunnels
Insects, snakes
Rodents
Heights
Crowds
Claustrophobia
Water
Dark
Bridges
Intruders

Fear of Authority
Intimidation
Humiliation
Fear of punishment
Lying
Deceit

Sensitivity
Fear of Man
Self-awareness
Self-consciousness
Fear of embarrassment
Fear of rejection
Fear of confrontation
Compromise
Defensiveness

Persecution
Victimization

Injustice/unfairness
Anger

Jealousy
Envy
Covetousness
Fear of displacement
Insecurity

False Burden
False responsibility
False compassion

Sexual Impurity
Adultery
Beastiality
Crudeness
Exposure
Fornication
Frigidity
Harlotry
Homosexuality
Impotence
Incubus/Succubus
Incest
Lust
Masturbation
Molestation
Oral sex
Pedophilia
Perverseness
Rape
Sexual addiction
Sodomy
Voyeurism
Freemasonry
Luciferian Doctrine

Idolatry
Anti-Christ
Deception
Curses
Infirmities
Entrapment
Abaddon
Apollyon

Mind-binding
Confusion
Occult
Satanism
Witchcraft-Jezebel

Spiritism
Spirit Guide
Séance
Necromancy

False Religion
God of Luck/Superstition
New Age
Humanism
Cults

Religious
Doctrinal Obsession
Doctrinal Error
Fear of Hell
Fear of God
Fear of Satan/demons
Jezebel/Ahab
Legalism/rigidity
Spiritual seduction
Fear of losing salvation
Piety/religious pride

Ritualism
Argumentative

Soul Ties
Persons, Places, Things:
Co-dependency
Dependency
Control
Manipulation
Longing
Victimization/abuse
Persecution/martyrdom
Sexual

Generational Curses/Iniquity
Divorce
Premature death
Learning disabilities
Barrenness
Business failure
Sexual sin
Emotional instability
Out of wedlock pregnancy
Suicide

Appendix C

Deliverance and Children

There are several books available on the subject of children and deliverance.

Three of the best we have found are:

- <u>Deliverance For Children and Teens,</u> by Bill Banks
- <u>Deliver Our Children From the Evil One</u>, by Noel and Phil Gibson
- <u>Children's Deliverance,</u> by Frank and Ida Mae Hammond

Ministering deliverance to children involves a little different approach than the methods used with adults. For one thing, our terminology must be adapted to vocabulary understood by children.

Secondly, care must be taken not to alarm the children or cause shock or fear which demons may take advantage of to hinder the deliverance. This can be a test of patience as there may be demonic manifestation to deal with while trying to maintain a non-sensational tone during the deliverance.

Some items to note with children's deliverance that we would recommend are:

1. First and foremost, we do not minister deliverance to a child without the parent's permission, and, unless both parents

have been through deliverance. It is essential to have the covering and authority of the parent(s) at work for us as we enforce our spiritual authority over the demonic. Establishing this base of authority can be difficult in these days of so many divorce situations that create either single parents or blended families. In the case of single parent situations, with a teenager or child living with one or the other, we sill take a child through deliverance if the custodial parent has received deliverance ministry. If the child is residing with an unsaved parent we will not minister deliverance even at the request of a saved non-custodial parent. This is part of the tragedy of these turbulent times.

2. We do recommend in such cases that the saved parent continue to pray for the child and the child's custodial parent. This does help to provide measures of protection around the child and add agreement to the Holy Spirit's work of conviction to the unsaved parent.

3. In ministering deliverance to children and teens, we prefer not to have the parents in the room. We do allow them to be present elsewhere on the premises covering the session in prayer. We do this for several reasons. One is that unless the parent is an experienced deliverance minister their compassion and emotion "stirrings" for the child can operate counter to the effective flow of deliverance. At times they feel that our command over the demonic manifestations is insensitive since they are unable to discern the tactics of the enemy. This causes a demonstration of fleshly protectiveness that hinders the deliverance. Secondly, the operation of unhealthy ties between parent and child may hinder the deliverance. They seem to be more intense when the parent is in close proximity. Again, part of this is that soul ties are often rooted in the emotions. As the parent is stirred emotionally, the soul tie may gain strength and be more difficult to "sever."

4. With infants that are under one year in age we do require that the parent(s) be present. This seems to calm the child and creates receptivity in spirit to deliverance (though the infant

is not naturally aware of what is happening). In terms of age, we have ministered deliverance effectively to infants fewer than 6 months old as well as unborn infants (in utero). This can be particularly effective in adoption situations when the adoptive parents' covering and authority imparts effectiveness to the canceling of iniquity and severing cords of iniquity.

5. Be aware that demonic manifestations with children during deliverance are generally more mild. A loud or stern voice is not usually required. Demons hear and comply even when spoken to in a softer tone than normal. As stated, the opposite with children (loudness and forceful gesturing) can cause insecurity and fear to increase and hinder the effectiveness of the session. Speak to children encouragingly and with comfort, yet with firmness and decisiveness. This may take some experience to do smoothly. Keep the tone of the session particularly upbeat and hopeful. Praise the child as the child complies with directions.

6. Usually, deliverance sessions for children are shorter in duration than those of adults. This is due partly to the fact that most of the time demons exit more quickly. It doesn't take a process of wearing them down to make them leave. We feel this may be a result of the younger age of children. The demonic has not had as much time to become embedded deeply. When at all possible, sessions for children _should_ be kept shorter (both in preparation and the conducting of the deliverance). They tire more quickly and have shorter attention spans than adults. This can work against you if the session is too long.

7. Again, remember particularly with children to keep it simple. Don't "talk down" to them or use vocabulary beyond their comprehension. You must learn to speak in terms that children will understand. For preparation, we usually meet separately with the parent to complete the deliverance worksheets for the child. This is not needed for teenagersas they usually can understand (especially at ages 15-17) the adult terminology used. We will meet once or twice with the child

prior to the deliverance mainly to establish trust and gain a rapport with them. During the deliverance, we keep our prayers shorter and speak in a simpler manner.

As a final comment on children's deliverance, it should be noted that the one with the most authority to effect deliverance is usually the parent. Much can be done with consistent prayer in the home by a knowledgeable and saved/delivered parent. Measures of deliverance may even be effected through parental prayers over a sleeping child.

Normally, 75% of a child's deliverance (sometimes all) may be accomplished through the in-home prayers of parents. The deliverance minister thereby serves as a coach for the parent with the parent executing the actions of deliverance in the home. The deliverance minister is engaged only if any "road blocks" are encountered (the other 25%). We believe this is the best means of achieving deliverance for children (and even teens). It helps to accomplish bonding, family unity and mutual respect between parent(s) and child/teen when performed successfully.

It does, however, necessitate willingness on the part of the parent as well as constant supervision and facilitation by the deliverance minister.

Appendix D

Angels and Deliverance

As noted in the chapter on "the deliverance session," angels may be of great assistance in conducting deliverance ministry. Given the spiritual warfare dynamic of deliverance ministry, angels have been designated by God for our assistance:

> "And Elisha prayed and said, 'Lord I pray, open his eyes that he may see.' Then the Lord opened the eyes of the young man, and he saw, and behold, the mountain was full of horses and chariots of fire all around Elisha" (II Kings 6:17).

> "The angel of the Lord encamps all around those who fear Him, and delivers them" (Psalm 34:7).

Our intent here is not to present a detailed study of the ministry of angels. That would require an entire book and there are numerous books on the topic presently available. Three very good ones are:

- <u>The Truth About Angels,</u> by Terry Law
- <u>Heaven: The Mystery of Angels,</u> by Grant Jeffrey
- <u>Angelic Army,</u> by Nancy Gray

Most prominent ministers within the arena of deliverance ministry as well as others, have written on the subject. For this appendix our intent is to attest briefly to the availability of angels for our assistance in deliverance ministry.

Several items of note regarding angelic assistance:

1. We do not *command* angels. Angels are at the disposal of God and Jesus. We may *request*, however, that they be assigned to assist us or provided for a specific ministry need. As we do this, we must keep in mind their functions and not request their actions outside their role as messengers, guides, guardians, warriors, and encouragers.
2. Angels appear to have stations and ranks that parallel the demonic hierarchy of principalities, powers, rulers and hosts of wickedness. Some of these are: thrones, dominions and virtues, as well as archangels, cherubim, seraphim and living creatures. God assigns an angel of sufficient power and authority to counter the demonic level of evil that needs to be opposed. This happens in answer to our prayer for assistance. A Biblical passage that illustrates this is Daniel 10:12,13:

> "Then he said to me, 'Do not fear, Daniel, for from the first day that you set your heart to understand . . . your words have been heard; and I have come because of your words. But the prince of Persia withstood me twenty-one days; and behold, Michael, one of the chief princes, came to help me, for I had been left alone there with the kings of Persia."

This describes spiritual warfare as Michael is sent to assist an angel sent in answer to Daniel's prayers. Powerful demonic "princes" oppose the messenger as the messenger attempts to reach Daniel with his answer to prayer.

3. Keep in mind that Satan was an archangel in Heaven. His name was Lucifer, but he became perverted by pride and eventually transformed into Satan, the adversary of God's people. Isaiah 14:12-17 describes the account of Lucifer's fall. It contains the five "I will" statements of Lucifer, declaring his intent to be worshipped as a god. Revelation 12:7 details the war that resulted in Lucifer being cast from Heaven with one-third of the angels who followed him in rebellion against God. This war continues today as we carry on the battle, assisted by God's angels as we overcome Satan and his demons with "the blood of the Lamb and the word of our testimony" (Rev. 12:11).

Appendix E

Recommended Reading

The following books are recommended reading for gaining an understanding of deliverance. We require all candidates for deliverance to read Pigs in the Parlor in preparation for deliverance. This list is not comprehensive as there are numerous other books on the topic. However, these are ones we have found most useful to our ministry.

1. Pigs in the Parlor, Frank & Ida Mae Hammond.
   Contains a wealth of information for the person interested in or engaged in the ministry of Deliverance. As a practical handbook it offers valuable guidance on: "How Demons Enter," "How Deliverance is Accomplished," "How to retain Deliverance" and "Demon Groupings." Includes a unique section on Schizophrenia.

2. Healing Through Deliverance, Vol. 1 & 2, Peter Horrobin
   (Vol. 1) A comprehensive assessment of the place of deliverance ministry in the life of the church. Provides a practical and scriptural understanding of the way powers of darkness can affect people's lives. (Vol.2) Provides founda-. tional material on which to build the ministry of deliverance within the local church and in ministry/counseling centers. It contains a comprehensive summary of how people become affected by demonic powers as well as practical

guidelines for the conduct of deliverance ministry.

3. They Shall Expel Demons, Derek Prince
   A practical and comprehensive handbook of deliverance
   drawn from over 30 years of experience. It offers down-to-
   earth advise on how to receive deliverance and remain free.
   Also described are activities of demons, ways demons gain
   access and steps to deliverance. A scholarly, Biblical-based
   work.

4. Deliverance from Evil Spirits, Francis MacNutt
   A practical manual written by one of the foremost practitioners of Christian healing and deliverance. Addresses in a
   balanced, comprehensive fashion traditional issues of deliverance such as: Scriptural basis for deliverance, curses,
   preparation for and ministering deliverance, deliverance of
   places and maintaining deliverance.

5. Demons Defeated, Bill Subritzky
   Describes demons, who they are, manifestations, personality and behavior as well as principle areas of demonic activity. Includes information on Christians and the demonic,
   methods of deliverance and how to keep your deliverance.
   Discusses demonic strong men and demon strongholds.

6. Demons and Deliverance, Maxwell Whyte
   Provides practical answers to the most frequently asked
   questions about demons and deliverance such as: What is a
   demon? Can a Christian have a demon? How can a Christian
   resist Satanic influence? How can we minister deliverance?
   This book is both informational and practical in format.

7. Deliverance and Inner Healing, John and Mark Sandford
   This comprehensive guide stresses the interdependence of
   deliverance and inner healing. Offering balanced Biblical
   based teaching it shows how both are valuable and necessary to the growth of the Christian. Serves as a comprehen-

sive guide to the practice of each.

8. The Three Battlegrounds, Francis Frangipane
   Explores the three areas of spiritual warfare which the maturing Christian will face: The mind, The Church, the Heavenly Places. It provides a foundation of insight, wisdom and discernment on the nature of the battle and the keys to victory.

9. Curses, Unforgiveness, Evil Spirits, Deliverance, Roger Miller
   Contains much practical information drawn from a multiple of sources and authors (in addition to the book's author) on subjects such as: pulling down strongholds, deliverance from demons, breaking curses, demonic hierarchies and maintaining deliverance.

10. Can a Christian have a Demon?, Don Basham
    A classic book by one of the pioneers of present day deliverance ministry. Offers valuable scriptural evidence supporting the fact that Christians can be indwelt by demons. Very balanced and very thorough. Don Basham was a ministry associate of Derek Prince.

11. The Final Quest, Rick Joyner
    A panoramic prophetic revelation of end-time spiritual warfare and victory over the forces of darkness. Contains a powerful message on the importance of humility as an essential ingredient in Christian growth and victorious spiritual warfare.

12. Epic Battles of the Last Days, Rick Joyner
    Written for courageous saints who will retreat no further – Who turn with resolve to stand against and turn back the greatest demonic darkness of our time. Contains valuable information on "The stronghold of witchcraft," "The religious spirit," "The Gate of Hell" and "Door of Heaven." Closes with "Twelve lessons on Spiritual warfare."

13. <u>Freedom in Christ</u>, Noel and Phyl Gibson
    From Australia, this husband and wife team with many years of ministry experience expound in the fashion of Peter Horrobin and Ellel ministries, England. As they say, this book details a whole personality approach to deliverance. They have served as mentors to numerous deliverance ministers including Doris and Peter Wagner. Contains a detailed deliverance questionnaire.

Appendix F

"OIL OF EXODUS"

For use in our ministry, particularly Deliverance Ministry, we have produced an anointing oil. In doing so, we compiled the following information and offer it as a foundational and scriptural basis for the practice of anointing with oil.

To begin, one must understand the meaning of "anoint" or "anointing." There are three primary words used for anoint.

In our day, we use the term *anointing* or *anointed* , in various ways to describe the empowering presence of God, by the Holy Spirit, on a person or in a worship service. That presence is felt, often literally, as a substance poured out over the minister and/or the people. To understand this let's look at the words for *anoint.*

They are: *cuwk* or *suk,* a Hebrew word, which means "to pour out or over"; *mashach,* also Hebrew, means "to smear on or rub on (like painting)"; and, *chrio,* a Greek word, which means "to rub in." From this last word we derive words such as *Chrisma* (Charisma), used for the gifts of the Spirit and Christ, meaning the anointed one. In Hebrew, Jesus was known as Yeshua Ha Mashiyach, which means "Jesus, the anointed One." This was translated in Greek as Jesous Christos (or Christ), meaning also "Jesus the anointed One."

In the literal practice of anointing with oil in the church today, it is most closely linked to "mashach," to run/smear on. Pouring oil over objects or individuals was a common practice in Biblical times but is a less used application in today's church. The scriptural basis for the practice of anointing with oil today is founded primarily on James 5:14, "Is anyone among you sick? Let him call for the elders of the church and let them pray over him, anointing him with oil in the name of the Lord."

Additionally, the church today follows the Biblical pattern of anointing to consecrate individuals, places or objects for God's service. Anointing with oil in Middle Eastern Biblical times was practiced for three purposes: ordinary/hospitality; sacred/consecrational; and healing.

Ordinary anointing with scented oil was practiced as part of bathing and guests were anointed upon arrival as a gesture of respect and welcome (or were offered a massage with oil). Sacred and consecrational anointing with oil was performed to dedicate unto God persons, places, or things. Prophets (I Kings 19:16), priests (Exodus 28:41), and kings (Isaiah 9:16; 16:1) were anointed for office. Furnishings of the tabernacle were anointed for service (Exodus 30:22-29). Jesus was anointed to be prophet, priest and king.

In Exodus 29:2, Leviticus 2:4 and 7:12, and Numbers 6:15, wafers of unleavened bread were anointed and eaten. Medical and healing practice with accompanying anointing was a common practice as evidenced in Isaiah 1:6; Luke 10:34; and Revelation 3:18.

Today Christians anoint buildings, homes, churches, land, etc. for consecration to God. Individuals are anointed for general church service (including deacons and elders), for missions service, and for the five-fold ministry of apostle, prophet, evangelist, pastor, teacher. In regards to the five-fold ministry, God's hand works through apostolic church leadership in the setting-in of apostles, prophets, evangelists, pastors, and teachers for service. As such, God rubs in His anointing and imparts it to these ascension gift (five-fold) ministers to become His hand on earth for the maturing and equipping of the church.

The Apostle becomes His thumb—touching each of the other four. The Prophet becomes the index finger of His hand—pointing out God's corrective guidance and exhortation. The Evangelist becomes His middle finger— extending the most outwardly to touch the lost and draw them to Christ. The Pastor is as the ring finger—married in covenant service to shepherd the church, God's flock. The <u>Teacher </u>is then the little finger that fits into the ear to guide by instruction in God's Word.

With respect then to deliverance ministry and anointing with oil, we anoint for healing by deliverance and for consecration unto God. We do this within the context of the deliverance session. Normally, this act is performed at the start of the deliverance session as part of the opening prayers (just prior to "casting out").

Several years past, we were led by the Holy Spirit to research Exodus 30:23-25 and subsequently develop from this "recipe" an anointing oil. We call it "Oil of Exodus." It is as true to the original composition as we can determine today. One note, with regard to the apparent admonition in Exodus 30:33 against production of such oil, we feel this ban is not applicable to the New Testament Church. Numerous examples attest to this amongst which are:

1. The New Testament church is a fellowship of priests. As such we have the power, in Christ Jesus our high priest, to execute priestly functions.
2. Many Old Testament prohibitions have been withdrawn from today's church: such as dietary laws (see Acts 10:9-16 and I Cor. 10:23-33); such as directions for women during their menstrual cycle to withdraw from contact with others (go outside the camp); and, such as no one except the high priest is allowed into the presence of God (in the Holy of Holies).

The point may be debated but we feel it is a concern based on scriptural misapplication within the context of New Testament Christianity. Various New Testament scriptures would support this promise. One of which is I Peter 2:9, "But you are a chosen generation, a royal priesthood, a holy nation, His own special people, that you may proclaim the praises of Him who called you out of darkness into His marvelous light."

Thus the New Testament church of believers (in Christ, through Christ) carry a three-fold anointing. Just as Jesus was anointed as prophet, priest and king (and so David before Him) the church today carries this three-fold anointing through Jesus Christ. He is our high priest and head of the church.

To elaborate, King David was anointed as "prophet-type" and "defender-king" (I Sam. 16:13). This was the "suk" anointing: poured over. David was anointed as king of praise over Judah in II Sam. 2:4. This was the "mashach" anointing and speaks of his role as "priestly" king and psalmist-leader of worship. David was anointed finally as ruling king over all Israel in II Sam. 5:3. This was a "chrio/chrisma" type anointing.

Jesus was anointed as priest in the house of Simon the Pharisee (Luke 7:36-50) with power to forgive sins. Jesus was anointed as prophet in the house of Simon the leper (John 12:3-8) in fulfillment of His role as prophet of the cross. Jesus was anointed/prepared for burial as the sacrificed lamb-king (John 19:39-40) prior to His resurrection as king over all (even death).

The corporate, New Testament church carries a similar three-fold anointing and the power to anoint in the name of Jesus. Through Him the corporate anointing of the church has been poured out (suk) by God the Father on the doorposts through the blood of Jesus the Paschal lamb; smeared on (mashach) at Pentecost by the power of the Holy Spirit; and, rubbed in (chrio) by Jesus Christ's nail-scarred hand as He established the church as His tabernacle on earth, led by His five-fold ministers.

So then, we come to the exact ingredients of the anointing oil and their significance in application. We have been able to locate them and reproduce a scriptural based composition (Exodus 30:22-25) in Oil of Exodus. First, is **myrrh** (commiphora myrrha). This is a bitter-gum resin from the stem of the Balsam bush. It's fragrance is smoky-musky. When the plant stems are cut or bruised, the liquid gum oozes out and crystallizes in teardrop form. Myrrh represents death and bitter suffering. It could be said to represent the prophetic qualities of a three-fold anointing. Myrrh was used for embalming and as a pain-deadening medicine. It was offered to Jesus by the wise men following His birth, foreshadowing His being born to suffer and die for our sins (Matthew 2:11). It was offered to Him again with wine-vinegar on the cross (Mark 15:23). Following crucifixion, Myrrh was in the spices used to prepare Jesus' body for burial.

Myrrh would be associated with the Gospel of Mark and Christ, the suffering servant. It would also be related to the Ox of the faces of the four living creatures (Ezekiel 1:5-10).

Next is **sweet cinnamon** (cinnamonum zeylanicum or canella zeylanica). To produce it, small branches of the cinnamon tree are cut, and "quills" are produced by stripping, curling and drying the inner bark. Cinnamon has evergreen leaves and its fragrance is sharp, pungent and spicy-sweet. As the plant gives up its branches to breaking and stripping, its essence is preserved as a spice that is "sweet." Thus it goes from death to life. As represented by its evergreen leaves, it depicts the quality of eternal life in the anointing oil. Jesus is our champion and has overcome death to be our Lord of life (Colossians 2:15). He is "alive forevermore" (Revelation 2:18). We in turn receive this gift of life by the "circumcision" of our hearts (Rom. 2:28-29; Colossians 2:11), in covenant with Jesus' sacrificial act.

Cinnamon represents healing and is associated with the Gospel of Luke. It speaks of the humanity of Christ and His power to heal and restore. It is linked to the face of the man in the four living creatures.

Third is **Calamus** (andropogon calamus aromaticus). It is called "reed of fragrance." It is a cane-like plant and the word calamus means *branch*. It is often called *sweet cane* but is more like a marshy reed plant than sugar cane. When crushed or broken Calamus gives off a strong ginger-like aroma. Calamus is a translation of the Hebrew word "qaneh" which means an erect reed or rod. It's root, "qanah" means to erect, to create, to procure, to own. As such, calamus speaks of rule, reign, divine government and order, and kingship. Isaiah 9:7 says, (speaking of Jesus) "of the increase of His government and peace there will be no end, upon the throne of David and over His kingdom, to order it and establish it with judgment and justice from that time forward, even forever. The zeal of the Lord of Hosts will perform this." Isaiah 11:1 says, "There shall come forth a rod from the stem of Jesse, and a branch shall grow out of his roots."

All this relates to the qualities of Calamus in the oil. Jesus was broken for us and as a fragrant aroma, was released unto God (Ephesians 5:2; II Cor. 2:14-16). By His sacrifice and victory, He is established as King of Kings and Lord of Lords. From heaven He came to be humbled and crushed as an aromatic offering on our behalf. Calamus is related to <u>sacrifice and kingliness.</u> It represents a sacrificial king, a compassionate ruler, a monarch who identifies with our suffering and is moved to action on our behalf. Exodus 3:7 says, "I have surely seen the oppression of my people who are in Egypt, and have heard their cry because of their taskmasters, for I know their sorrows." *Know* is the Hebrew word "yada" meaning an intimate knowledge gained from close identification or interaction.

Calamus is related to the <u>Gospel of Matthew</u> and the <u>lion</u> face of the four living creatures. It bespeaks of Jesus as <u>defender and deliverer</u>, commanding kingly authority gained by sacrifice. He is the lionly standard of Isaiah 59:19, ." . . when the enemy comes in like a flood, the Spirit of the Lord will lift up a standard against him."

The final spice ingredient of the oil is **cassia** (cinnamonum cassia blume). In Hebrew, cassia is "qiddah." It means "aromatic wood" and can mean "bow down or stoop, and, to cleave."

Cassia is a fragrant tree similar to cinnamon, with purple flowers and growing at a high altitude. It was used to perfume garments and its leaves are a source of *senna*, which is an intestinal purgative.

Psalm 45:8 prophetically describes Christ, the church's bridegroom, coming out of "ivory palaces" (a high place) with His garments scented with myrrh and cassia (He came to die and to be king). Cassia's purple flowers speak of the color of royal robes and kingship. Again, Jesus paid a great price and sacrificed on our behalf and has therefore been established as king over all.

Through Jesus (like senna) we can be cleansed and purged from the effects of sin. Malachi 3:3 says, "He will sit as a refiner and purifier of silver, He will purify the sons of Levi, and purge them as gold and silver, that they may offer to the Lord an offering in righteousness."

By the cassia in the oil we are exhorted to embrace the purging of the Lord by the Holy Spirit and thereby make righteous offerings of worship to the Lord. Romans 12:1 says, ." . .present your bodies a living sacrifice, holy, acceptable to God, which is your reasonable service."

Cassia is associated with the <u>Gospel of John,</u> the face of the <u>eagle</u> of the four living creatures, the high soaring <u>Holy Spirit and worship.</u> It reminds us that God has "set before us an open door that no man can close." (Rev. 3:8)

Altogether then, these four elements are to be at work in each Christian believer and each Christian ministry/church. The spices demonstrate a blending of individual properties (giftings) into one compounded mixture (corporate church) to produce a unified effect.

Finally, all these ingredients are contained in (compounded into) **olive oil.** This oil is produced by the beating of the olive "berries" to extract (crush out) their oil. Jesus prayed and was arrested in the Garden of Gethsemane which means "olive press." He ascended into heaven from the Mount of Olives. Jesus was beaten and scourged and released His blood on our behalf.

The ingredients of the anointing oil are immersed in the oil just as we are covered by the blood of Jesus. In this compound mixture all spice properties are released and unified for effect.

For a life to be effective for God in ministry it must be anointed by the oil of the Holy Spirit which contains myrrh (bitterness), cinnamon (sweetness), calamus (order and divine government) and, cassia (worship and humility).

These foreshadowing truths were what God had in mind as He instructed Moses to compound a holy anointing oil. Within it would be contained an anointing agent drawn from the very essence of the personality of God. It is truly a link between Old and New Testament that carries the power of the Gospel of Jesus Christ representationally to effect healing and deliverance. Within it is a picture of the effective New Testament Body of Christ.

To order Oil of Exodus anointing oil call (706)896-0886 or mail the order form below to: *Safe Harbor Ministries*
913 Johnson Road
Hiawassee, GA. 30546

The price is $7.00 per _ oz. Bottle.

• •

Name_____

Address_____

Phone_____

Quantity_____

Amount Enclosed_____Add $2.00 shipping

* Make check payable to Safe Harbor Ministries

About Safe Harbor Ministries

Safe Harbor Ministries is a comprehensive center for Christian Counseling, Deliverance and Ministry. Located in the Northeast Georgia Mountains, Safe Harbor offers Christian Counseling services ranging from scheduled weekly one-hour sessions to intensive three-day residential deliverance ministry. Thereby, clients have the option (regarding deliverance) to complete the process over a period of 6-8 weeks (meeting once weekly) or in one 3-day process of ministry.

Additionally, Safe Harbor offers a place of rest and meditation on a scheduled basis; conducts semi-annual conferences on related issues; operates a school of ministry and training ,and exercises pastoral leadership to two home fellowships.

Active in missions, Safe Harbor has extensive experience in service to Latin America and Costa Rica.

For additional information or to schedule ministry, contact:

Safe Harbor Ministries
913 Johnson Road
Hiawassee, Georgia 30546
Tel. : 706-896-0886
E-mail: Safeharbor7@alltel.net

The staff of Safe Harbor Ministries is available by invitation to present these dynamic conferences:

• **"More Than Conquerors"**

This dynamic conference equips you with the Biblical keys to victorious kingdom living. It lays out a course of conquest for the overcoming Christian in the world today. Both challenging and inspiring it will motivate you to win over the enemy.

• **"Destroying Strongholds"**

This conference lays a base for more effective deliverance ministry and/or serves as an effective follow-up to deliverance. Contains crucial insights for maintaining deliverance and winning the battle for the mind. Both revelationary and revolutionary.

• **Principles of Deliverance**

This vital conference covers the Biblical basis and practical process of this much- needed ministry to the body of Christ. Contains essential instruction on how to conduct the ministry of deliverance.

• **Waging Effective Spiritual Warfare**

Boldly takes you where every Christian needs to go— into the realm of supernatural combat. Reveals indispensable tools for taking back what Satan has stolen—shows you how to "take it by force" (Matthew 11:12).

Printed in the United States
19660LVS00003B/46-90